Fear of Security

Australia's Invasion Anxiety

Anthony Burke

Security has rarely been such a dominant and controversial preoccupation of Australian politics. In this authoritative book, Anthony Burke argues that security has dominated and distorted Australia's foreign policy and national life, from Cook's first voyage to the *Tampa* crisis, 9/11 and Iraq. Whether in the Great War, Vietnam or the treatment of asylum seekers, Anthony Burke shows that Australia's security has been bought with the insecurity and suffering of others. Against this corrosive tradition, he offers a new – cosmopolitan and non-coercive – model of national existence and responsibility.

At once a deep historical survey and an argument with its society, *Fear of Security* is a landmark account of how Australia relates to itself, its region and the world. Turning powerful academic and political orthodoxies on their heads, it is essential reading for those concerned with the burning questions that face Australia and the Asia-Pacific.

Anthony Burke is the author of *Beyond Security, Ethics and Violence*, and co-editor of *Critical Security in the Asia-Pacific* and *Introduction to International Relations: Australian Perspectives* (Cambridge University Press 2007). He has previously worked as a researcher in the Australian Senate, and is currently Associate Professor of international politics at the University of New South Wales.

Fear of Security

Australia's Invasion Anxiety

ANTHONY BURKE

CAMBRIDGE UNIVERSITY PRESS
Cambridge, New York, Melbourne, Madrid, Cape Town, Singapore, São Paulo

Cambridge University Press
477 Williamstown Road, Port Melbourne, VIC 3207, Australia

Published in the United States of America by Cambridge University Press, New York

www.cambridge.org
Information on this title: www.cambridge.org/9780521714273

First published by Pluto Press Australia Limited 2001
First published by Cambridge University Press 2008

Cover design by Mason Design
Printed in Australia by Ligare

A catalogue record for this publication is available from the British Library

National Library of Australia Cataloguing in Publication data
    Burke, Anthony.
    Fear of security: Australia's invasion anxiety.
    Bibliography.
    Includes index.
    ISBN 9780521714273 (pbk.).
    1. Security, International.   2. National security – Australia.   3. Internal security –
    Australia.   4. Australia – Foreign relations.   I. Title.
327.94

ISBN-13 978-0-521-71427-3

For Jenny, Sophia and Nikos
and in memory of Kamal and Michele

Contents

Preface and acknowledgements

This book is a substantially revised and updated version of a project first published as *In Fear of Security: Australia's Invasion Anxiety* in 2001, immediately following the events of 9/11 and prior to that year's national election. I am very grateful to the publishers at Cambridge University Press, especially Susan Hanley and Pauline de Laveaux, for giving the book a new life, as I am to the anonymous readers who recommended its publication. My gratitude also goes to Ken Wark and Tony Moore who first put their faith in the project back in 1999.

The changes I have made are intended to bring the book up to date, to improve upon its arguments and respond to the political climate that followed its publication, and to make it more accessible to a wide readership. A new chapter has been added to cover the period after 9/11, with a particular focus on Australia's treatment of asylum seekers and its involvement in Iraq and the war on terror. A new conclusion has also been written and the introduction revised substantially. Two theoretical chapters in the original book – on security in international relations theory, and on the development of the national security state in Western political thought – have been omitted. A more developed version of that latter chapter can be found in my theoretical work focused on the war on terror, *Beyond Security, Ethics and Violence*. Readers with a particular interest in the theoretical ideas of this book are encouraged to consult that work.

For their assistance while I was preparing the book my thanks to Matt McDonald, Savitri Taylor, Patricia Hall-Ingrey, Katrina Harrison, Di Taylor and the Cambridge readers who gave great advice. I thank all those who have asked me to speak publicly since

2001 on the issues dealt with here – your activism, public spiritedness and concern for justice has been inspiring. And for all the great talks, collaboration and exchange: Peter Mares, Klaus Neumann, Bob Burke, Suvendi Perera, Jim George, Katrina Lee Koo, Christine Sylvester, Chris Reus-Smit, Roland Bleiker, Hazel Lang, Richard Devetak, Lorraine Elliott, Graeme Cheeseman, Paul Keal, Minerva Nasser-Eddine, Pal Ahluwalia, Carol Johnson, Chris Beasley, Greg McCarthy, Kath Gelber, Liz Thurbon, Sarah Maddison, Umut Ozguc, Marc Williams, Ruth Balint, Jie Chen, Marianne Hanson, Alex Bellamy, Richard Shapcott, Mark Beeson, Nick Wheeler and Ed Aspinall.

My wife Jenny has been a truly wonderful source of encouragement and support; without her this book would not exist. It is dedicated to her and our children with my love.

This book is also dedicated to the memory of Kamal Bamadhaj and Michele Turner. Kamal was a tireless and inspired advocate of freedom and dignity for those struggling against the Soeharto regime. He was murdered, with hundreds of others, in the first volleys of gunfire at the Santa Cruz massacre in Dili, Timor Leste, in 1991. Michele spent ten years compiling personal testimonies from East Timorese for her moving 1992 book, *Telling*. The despair that overtook her in 1995 was no doubt deepened by her shame at Australia's abandonment of a people who had kept her grandfather alive during the Pacific war. They were both 'mighty spirits' whom we all miss.

Abbreviations

AATTV	Australian Army Training Team (Vietnam)
ABC	Australian Broadcasting Commission (later Corporation)
ABRI	Angakatan Bersenjata Republik Indonesia (Indonesian Armed Forces, to 1998)
ACJ	Allied Council for Japan (four-power Occupation advisory council)
ADF	Australian Defence Force
AFP	Australian Federal Police
AIF	Australian Imperial Force
ALP	Australian Labor Party
AMS	Australia–Indonesia Agreement on Maintaining Security
ANZAC	Australia and New Zealand Army Corps
ANZUS	Security treaty between Australia, New Zealand and the United States
APEC	Asia-Pacific Economic Cooperation (trade forum)
Apodeti	Timorese Popular Democratic Association
ARF	ASEAN Regional Forum (security dialogue)
ARVN	Army of the Republic of Viet Nam
ASDT	Timorese Social Democratic Association (later Fretilin)
ASEAN	Association of South-East Asian Nations
ASIO	Australian Security Intelligence Organisation (internal)
ASIS	Australian Secret Intelligence Service (external)

ATSIC	Aboriginal and Torres Strait Islander Commission (to 2005)
BCOF	British Commonwealth Occupation Force (Japan)
CIA	Central Intelligence Agency, United States
CPA	Communist Party of Australia
CSIS	Centre for Strategic and International Studies, Jakarta
DIAC	Department of Immigration and Citizenship
DIMIA	Department of Immigration and Multicultural and Indigenous Affairs
DRV	Democratic Republic of (North) Vietnam
ERA	Energy Resources of Australia (mining company)
FPDA	Five Power Defence Arrangement (Malaysia, Singapore, New Zealand, Australia and the United Kingdom)
FMCT	Fissile Material Cut-off Treaty
Fretilin	Revolutionary Front for an Independent East Timor
GDP	Gross Domestic Product
HREOC	Human Rights and Equal Opportunity Commission
HRW	Human Rights Watch
IADS	Integrated Air Defence System (part of FPDA)
ICC	International Control Commission (for Indochina)
ICRC	International Committee of the Red Cross
IGGI	Inter-Governmental Group on Indonesia (aid consortium)
ILO	International Labor Organisation
IMF	International Monetary Fund
Interfet	International Force East Timor
IWW	International Workers of the World (socialist organisation)
JI	Jemaah Islamiyah
Kopassus	Komando Pasukan Khusus (Indonesian Special Forces)

Kostrad	Komando Stregis Angakatan Darat (Indonesian Army Strategic Command)
MAAG	US Military Assistance Advisory Group, Vietnam
MACV	US Military Assistance Command, Vietnam
MCP	Malayan Communist Party
MPR	Majelis Permusyawaratan Rakyat (People's Consultative Assembly, Indonesia)
NATO	North Atlantic Treaty Organization
NEI	Netherlands East Indies (Indonesia)
NGO	non-governmental organisation
NIEO	New International Economic Order
NLF	National Liberation Front of (South) Vietnam
NPT	Non-Proliferation Treaty
NSC	National Security Council (US)
OPEC	Organization of the Petroleum Exporting Countries
OPM	Organisasi Papua Merdeka (Free Papua Movement)
PDI	Partai Demokrasi Indonesia (Indonesian Democratic Party)
PKI	Partai Kommunis Indonesia (Indonesian Communist Party)
POW	prisoner of war
PRD	Partai Rakyat Demokrasi (People's Democratic Party, Indonesia)
PTSD	post-traumatic stress disorder
RAAF	Royal Australian Air Force
RAN	Royal Australian Navy
RRT	Refugee Review Tribunal
RVN	Republic of (South) Vietnam
SAS	Special Air Service (Australian special forces)
SCAP	Supreme Commander Allied Powers (denotes both US occupation authority in Japan and General MacArthur himself)
SEATO	South East Asia Treaty Organization
TNI	Tentara Nasional Indonesia (Indonesian Armed Forces, after 1998)
UDT	Timorese Democratic Union

UK	United Kingdom of Great Britain and Northern Ireland
UN	United Nations
UNAMET	United Nations Assistance Mission East Timor
UNCHR	United Nations Commission on Human Rights
UNESCO	United Nations Educational Scientific and Cultural Organisation
UNHCR	United Nations High Commissioner for Refugees
UPM	unregulated people movements
US	United States (of America)
USIS	United States Information Service
USSR	Union of Soviet Socialist Republics
WMD	weapons of mass destruction
WNG	West New Guinea

Introduction

Ever since the spectacular and terrible terrorist attacks on New York and Washington in September 2001, Western societies have been understandably obsessed with security. On that day we became aware of a frightening new threat not from heavily armed states, or enormously destructive weapons, but from small groups of highly motivated and determined men using the routine apparatus of modern life against us. This was true for Australia, a close ally of the United States, which immediately committed troops to a new 'war on terror' beginning in Afghanistan, then lost eighty-eight of its citizens in the double bombing of nightclubs in Bali a year later. As the US and its allies extended their war on terror from Afghanistan to Iraq, the Philippines, Pakistan, Palestine and Lebanon, and Islamist terrorists struck trains in Madrid and London, housing complexes in Saudi Arabia, tourists at Sharm el-Sheikh and Bali, and sacred Shiite mosques in Iraq, it was clear that the new reality facing large parts of the world was permanent insecurity. Yet such raw facts are meaningless if we fail to bring a critical historical perspective to understanding and acting upon them. Such an understanding is the focus of this book, and it sets out from the premise that assuming to know what security is, and how to achieve it, can be the most dangerous thing of all.

The events of 9/11 and the Western response have profoundly altered the world's strategic and normative landscape, but they derived from, and entered into, a pre-existing world in which states have historically been anxious about security – so much so that they have encoded it into their fundamental structure of being. The desire for security lies at the core of Western political philosophy and its concepts of sovereignty, political identity and statehood. For Thomas Hobbes, the 17th-century thinker who gave us the central ideas underpinning the modern nation-state, the desire for security motivated men to establish states and laws, and submit to the dominance of the sovereign with whom they form a single existence and will, the body politic.[1] This tradition was influential in Australia, given that its colonisation was partly motivated by British concerns about security from crime, and which federated to form a new nation in 1901 primarily because of anxieties about security from the strategic and racial threat posed by Asia. In this way security has been much more than a policy issue; it has permeated the entire society as a powerful form of politics and set of fears. It may be surprising to think that throughout Australian history *security* required the shipping of 180 000 convicts from England, the murder and dispossession of Aborigines, a racist immigration policy, the terrible sacrifice of the Great War, the confrontation of communism within Australia and in wars in Korea, Malaysia, Vietnam and Cambodia, the incarceration of asylum seekers, and an amoral embrace of Asian dictators such as Marcos and Soeharto. Security has been central to the construction of powerful images of national identity and otherness, and central to their use in bitter political conflicts that were too often resolved in violent and anti-democratic ways. In short, security has been a potent, driving imperative throughout Australian history.

Even through the 1990s, as the Cold War ended and Australians seemingly embraced their cultural diversity and the obligations owed to the indigenous traditional owners of the country – symbolised in the High Court's *Mabo* decision, the Native Title Act, and an extraordinary speech by the Prime Minister acknowledging past colonial crimes – a darker tradition named by security flowed on beneath the surface. Defence co-operation with the Indonesian military regime of Soeharto was reaching unprecedented heights, and the people of East Timor struggled for independence against a brutal occupation and determined official indifference from Canberra. The conservative opposition led by John Hewson and then John Howard was strongly opposed to the High Court's (very limited) recognition of Aboriginal land rights, and put this opposition into action when they dramatically wound back such rights in legislation once they were elected.

More dark clouds quickly appeared on the horizon. In November 1999 the federal Minister for Immigration, Philip Ruddock, captured news headlines by telling Australians that they faced a 'national emergency' because as many as 10 000 illegal migrants were planning to flood into Australia from the Middle East. 'The information that is available to us', he said, 'suggests that whole villages are packing up and there is a pipeline. If it was a national emergency several weeks ago, it's gone up something like ten points on the Richter scale since then.' While there were grounds for concern – in the preceding two weeks more than 700 people had entered Australia and been detained – such predictions, made as the Howard government was trying to force harsh new refugee laws through the Senate, were outrageously alarmist.[2] The influx posed administrative challenges, but to elevate it to a national emergency made it seem far more threatening. Ruddock's was an anxiety with profound historical echoes, almost a repetition of Alfred Deakin's fears in 1898, as he argued for federation, that 'from the far east and the far west alike we behold menaces and contagion'.[3]

Rather than portraying the asylum seekers fleeing criminal and abusive regimes in Afghanistan, Iraq and Iran as an administrative or human security problem, Ruddock chose to portray them as a threat to the nation's very integrity. The political ramifications of invoking a 'national emergency' were demonstrated by the new regulations he introduced soon after – and meekly accepted by the federal Labor opposition – which restricted the rights of boat people in relation to other refugees, provided for unlimited mandatory detention, and left them vulnerable to automatic deportation after thirty months – whatever the fears for their own safety.[4] Two years later the Norwegian container vessel MV *Tampa* picked up a boatload of asylum seekers and brought them into Australian waters, New York and Washington were attacked, and the Howard government had folded terrorism and illegal immigration into a single image of existential threat and was improbably returned to power in a 'security' election.

Menaces and contagion

Rhetoric about the need for 'border protection', 'territorial integrity' and 'national security' were placed at the centre of the Liberal-National Party coalition's 2001 campaign strategy. The *Tampa* refugees were shipped to Nauru, and legislation was rushed into Parliament to make it even harder for later arrivals to make asylum claims. A naval and air operation (Relex II) was begun, and by the end of October it had pushed two boats back into Indonesian waters. The patriotism of the Australian Labor Party (ALP) was called into question, as Howard stated that the 'duty of an opposition on an occasion like this is to steadfastly support the national interest'.[5] Less than two weeks prior to election day the Prime Minister threw a grenade into the debate by claiming: ' . . . if we throw up our hands and say we're going to stop doing this we'll be saying to the world anybody can come. I promise you that would be a recipe for the shores of this country to be . . . I don't want to use the word invaded . . . but the shores of this nation to be thick with asylum seeker boats.'[6] As a nation, we had moved no distance from the declaration of Prime Minister Joseph Cook in 1913, as the first Australian naval vessels arrived from Britain's shipyards, that 'this fleet will defend White Australia from less advanced but aggressive nations all around us with lower standards'.[7]

In this world view, security is imagined on the basis of a bounded and vulnerable identity in perpetual opposition to an outside – an *Other* – whose character and claims threaten its integrity and safety. This is not a commonsense use of language but a powerful conceptual operation that seeks to shape and control the real. Historical echoes gave these men's statements added force: ever since Henry Parkes and Alfred Deakin began to argue for the formation of an Australian Federation in the face of the threats posed by the populous and threatening civilisations of Asia, such an image of security and identity has been a constant in Australian life. Its contours live on in significant elements of national policy and in basic modern categories such as 'sovereignty' and the 'national interest'. In this sense to be secure is to be Australian. But what *kind* of Australian?

The problem is that the community imagined in such claims is always an exclusive one, bounded by a power that seeks to enforce sameness, repress diversity, and diminish the rights (and claims to being) of those who are thrust outside its protective embrace. This is the clear implication of the former diplomat Richard Woolcott's argument, in 1995, that 'sentimental notions of self-determination for East Timor or Bougainville . . . threaten our national security'.[8] Likewise Labor Prime Minister Paul Keating, after signing a mutual security agreement with Indonesia's President Soeharto the same year, stated: 'We are not going to hock the entire relationship on Timor. A Prime Minister's duty, his first duty, is to the security of his country.'[9] More than 180 000 Timorese had lost their lives during Indonesia's occupation. How many must die, we might ask, so that we should be secure?

This awful moral calculus has long been central to hegemonic images of Australian security and identity. In 1994 Keating stated that the emergence of the Soeharto regime 'was the most beneficial strategic development to affect Australia and its region in thirty years', and he began to argue, as Gough Whitlam had earlier, that the favour of the regime was central to a renewed and modernised Australian identity that could successfully break free of its colonial roots and integrate with the Asian region. Speaking in Jakarta in 1972, Whitlam said Australia's 'destiny is inseparable from Indonesia's', words echoed by Keating twenty years later as he spoke of Australia's need to accept that in an 'Asia-Pacific future' lay the 'full expression of Australian nationhood'.[10] Thus Australia's security was tied to the region's and, in particular, to the fortunes of a corrupt and brutal regime that had overseen the murder of up to a million people in its first four years of power.

Imagined in such terms, security is a practice of exclusion: a practice of identity and being through exclusion. The 1990s had raised once again the question of whether an 'Australian' community would be imagined on the basis of a walled and insecure identity or a generous and outward-looking diversity. Add to that the rise of Pauline Hanson's One Nation party, the Howard government's response to the High Court's *Wik* decision, and its dithering as Indonesian-backed militias wreaked havoc in 1999 in an attempt to destroy any possibility of East Timorese independence. Should we accept that Australia's 'national interest' and 'sovereignty' would have been better preserved by not antagonising

Indonesia as its army and militias perpetrated genocide in East Timor? This was certainly the Howard government's approach until September 1999, when the scale of the killing crossed even its threshold of indifference. Should we likewise accept that our security demands the suspension of the human rights of one class of refugees over another? Are these really the terms upon which Australians wish to form a community, in relationship with the thousands of other communities who share this planet?

If they are not – and the overwhelming popular support for the deployment of peacekeeping forces to East Timor in 1999 suggests that they are not – we have a lot of work to do. This work, at least in a small way, is the task of this book. The great obstacle it encounters is that Australia's political, media and bureaucratic elites consider a need for security axiomatic, as do many of us. After all, what could be more basic, or given, than a desire for security? However, this book refuses to accept either security's meaning or the politics of its realisation at face value. It considers what it means to be secure in two ways: by interrogating the concept of security itself, and by considering the price of its realisation through Australian history and its impact on the possible forms of an 'Australian' culture and community. It asks whether things had to be this way: what other forms of being, identity and interrelationship might be imagined once the suffocating political embrace of security is escaped.

The politics of security

Yet how are we to understand a security that, in the mouths of diplomats and political leaders, appears a perversion of language itself? Because the clear implication of their arguments is that 'our' security – *our very existence* – is to be wagered on the death and suffering of the 10 000 who perished in Bougainville during ten years of war, the more than 180 000 Timorese victims of the twenty-four-year Indonesian occupation, or the millions who died during the West's thirty-year war on Vietnamese communism. What of *their* security? Wouldn't such a contradiction render security meaningless?

This is exactly what we confront. The history this book describes takes us into an Orwellian universe in which truth is often a cynical device, in which concepts appear to mean their opposites, and in

which our civilisation's grand dreams of progress and enlightenment are drawn aside to reveal an underlying structure of baseness
and horror. This is a place where the oxymoronic slogans of Orwell's
1984 – 'Freedom is Slavery', 'Ignorance is Strength', 'War is Peace' –
appear as a new principle of reality. No doubt we have created some
of our own: 'Prosperity is Want', 'Security is Fear'.

Yet the European political theorist R. N. Berki saw no fundamental contradictions. For him, security *was* fear:

> Seeking after security for oneself and being a cause of insecurity for
> others are not just closely related; they are the same thing, with no
> chance of either logical or existential separation . . . when the chips
> are down, and to a certain degree, they are always down . . . it is my
> life, my freedom, my security *versus* the rest of the human race.[11]

As important as it is to struggle against such dilemmas, they will not
be easily escaped, and not by simplistic appeals to truth. Security
has no truth. This is a reality East Timor's heroic Bishop Carlos
Belo knew well. After the murder of a youth by Indonesian security
forces on the eve of the 1991 Dili massacre (committed in the
higher cause of Indonesia's 'security and stability'), he exclaimed:
'The news put out by TVRI was false! False! The truth turned upside
down. We live in a country where bad is good, light is dark, and
there is no justice!'[12] How can we resist such a situation, where truth
seems just another species of lie? As Belo suggested, *justice* is at stake
here. We must first question and unmask our fundamental political
concepts, along with the entire theory of reality that underpins
them.

Security has no truth. What could I possibly mean by this? Security is always spoken about in tones of deep seriousness, as an
apparently universal political category and desire whose meaning
is obvious. But perhaps something else is going on; perhaps security's power lies in the very slipperiness of its significations, its
ironic structure of meaning, its ability to have an almost universal
appeal yet name very different arrangements of order and possibility for different groups of people. I am strongly committed to
an alternative, *holistic* understanding of security, one that is based
on the security and emancipation of human beings rather than
the defence of states. This draws on the idea of 'human security' as

advanced by the United Nations Development Programme in 1994, and it is a paradigm in which – as Ken Booth remarks – the state is a means, not an end, of security.[13] Hence, when throughout this book I make arguments about what a better or genuine approach to security would be, this is what I mean. However, the complex politics involved in assertions about security means that we also need to pair this understanding with a different kind of analysis: one that looks for the interests being served by, and the social and ethical implications of, particular claims about security and insecurity. This analysis focuses on security as a pervasive and complex system of political, social and economic power.

The idea of security put forward by Keating, Woolcott and Berki seems credible only because it is based upon the thinnest pretence of common understanding – a common understanding that does not in fact exist. Across a range of political positions, theoretical discourses and institutional contexts, the object of security, the means of achieving it, and the set of priorities and needs it implies, remain diverse and at times in dramatic contradiction. Within the academic discipline of International Relations these contradictions are slowly being recognised. For example, Simon Dalby has asked whether the desire for 'environmental security' can be reconciled with the desire for 'economic security' based on free-market capitalism, given that industry has been so destructive of the natural environment; or whether 'human security' is not in fact a casualty of the drive for 'national security', given that states have so often posed a threat to their own populations. He suggests that any critical reformulation of security, like mine, argues:

> the political structures of modernity, patriarchy and capitalism are the sources [rather than the vulnerable objects] of insecurity . . . [this reformulation] is so different as to call into question whether the term itself can be stretched to accommodate such reinterpretations. Inescapably, it puts into question the utility of the term in political discourse after the Cold War.[14]

How do we analyse a concept whose basic principle of reality is irony? Which seems to have universal appeal but no common meaning? We need first to accept that security has no single, ultimate truth, and to see in these contradictions an opening for a new political practice and imagination of life. Following Michel Foucault, I use a theory of language that sees security not as a stable category or state of affairs whose truth can be found and fixed for all time, but as a historically specific 'system of truth' with intimate links to modern regimes of political, social and economic power.

Understanding security in this way demands a new way of thinking. It means letting go of the vague positivism (often called 'epistemic realism') with which we have grown up, which sees language as a simple *reflection* of a reality that exists independently of our attempts to observe or understand it, in favour of a theory that links the use of language, metaphor and knowledge with diverse *practices of and interventions into the real*. We must do this, not because such theories may be fashionable, but because our historical circumstances demand a more sophisticated way of thinking the relation between truth, power and the real.

Security's contradictions arise partly from a confusion of the particular and the universal. Security's claim to be a universal need and desire makes its appeal a compelling one. But the very real danger is that imagining security as a universal experience obscures the concrete *practices* it names and mobilises, along with their social and ethical implications. After all, said Woolcott and Keating, our *security* is at stake. The threat such a quarantine poses for democratic openness and debate ought to be obvious. It is no accident that, just as Paul Keating invoked security to stifle debate on the controversial agreement he signed with the Indonesian military in 1995, which was parallelled by an unprecedented expansion in military training and co-operation, for thirty years President Soeharto's regime used the mantra of 'security and stability' to repress democratic forces in Indonesian life.

Hence where universals like security – and powerful related categories, such as 'sovereignty' and the 'national interest' – are invoked, they must be challenged. 'Sovereignty' presupposes a national unity of need and interest that belies the bitter conflicts over land and political and economic power that have occurred throughout Australian history. Claims to national identity and cohesion have too often been weapons in such conflicts rather than a means to resolve them. The 'national interest' also derives from such fictions of unity: linking images of vulnerable collective identity with the machinery of international policy in a way that elevates a selfish *Realpolitik* over moral responsibility to the Other, and common cause between nations and communities. A critical assessment of Australian policy towards Soeharto's New Order regime shows that where security and the national interest were invoked as values and priorities, they referred primarily to the security of the regime and the interests of the investors and elites, both domestic and foreign, who benefited from its repressive control of labour and other social forces. For the East Timorese, West Papuans and many Indonesians, on the other hand, life was dominated by chronic *insecurity*.

Security: A political technology

To cut through the problems posed by the diverse (and highly political) meanings of security, we should see security not as a thing but as a *practice*. As the theorist Michael Dillon argues: 'Security is not a fact of nature but a fact of civilisation. It is not a noun that names something, but a principle of formation that does things.'[15] Security combines a complex deployment of metaphor, knowledge and rhetoric with systems of social, administrative, economic and geopolitical power. Indeed I would go further, to argue that security is a pervasive *political technology* that has had a profound impact on the political, cultural and economic forms of life that have been held to characterise the Australian nation and the modernisation path of the Asia-Pacific region. In short, security needs to be placed alongside a range of other economic, political, technological, philosophic and scientific developments as one of the most crucial events of our modernity.

To see security as a *political technology* is to see it as a network of practices and techniques that produce and manipulate bodies, identities, societies, spaces and flows. These range from our most private thoughts and relationships to the larger apparatuses of economic production, circulation and power of which they are a part. While these techniques and rhetorics are not always cohesive or tightly co-ordinated, they can be described as a general strategy. Foucault first used the term 'political technology of the body' in his *Discipline and Punish*, to describe the human body's immersion 'in a political field'.[16]

Building on his later work, 'Governmentality', I argue that security is a political technology of the body, the economy and the state simultaneously.[17] It thus cuts across the strict analytical divisions between these realms and also across the moral, political and spatial division long maintained in international relations between the domestic and the international. Thus I see security as a technology that is able to construct and influence individual subjectivity, national life and geopolitics – often all at once. In this way security has been crucial to the cultural, political and economic contours of both the 'Australian' nation and the 'Asia-Pacific' region within (and against) which it has pursued its existence. When John Howard invoked fears of invasion in relation to asylum seekers, demanded acquiescence from the Opposition, and was able to conjure such overwhelming public agreement that he could reverse very negative polls to win an election, this political technology was in use – in use on the asylum seekers expelled or imprisoned, *and* on Australian citizens. It is a linked strategy of coercion and persuasion that is the very antithesis of freedom.

Its effectiveness depends upon mobilising what Foucault called 'the political double-bind', the 'tricky combination in the same political structures of individualisation techniques and totalisation procedures'.[18] Here 'totalising' techniques and rhetorics of national identity, macroeconomic management and administrative organisation are combined with what Foucault termed *discipline*: the 'individualising' techniques of regulation and subjectivity aimed at producing productive and pliable individuals who have an ideal relation with larger social and economic formations. This Foucault called 'governmentality', a form of power that, without having to be directed from a single source or institution, could integrate the management of individuals and populations with the larger totalities of the economy or state.[19] When this articulation of individual self-consciousness, social organisation and economic order is working in an ideal way, our leaders tell us we are *secure*; yet if forms of individuality or social organisation emerge that are seen as threats to such an order, our leaders speak of them as threats to security and move against them.

The 'political double-bind' of security is even more powerful when we consider that security has long been thought of as the most fundamental objective of the nation-state, from the earliest political theory of Thomas Hobbes and John Locke onwards. In search of security men create states and submit to the authority of a sovereign, creating a 'social contract' and 'body politic' that enforce internal sameness and order and alienation from those who lie outside its boundaries.[20] Thus individuals are absorbed into the totality of the state so that they are one being. Added to this coercive politics of identity was the idea, evident in the writings of the British political philosopher Jeremy Bentham, of security as a guarantee of the future. This links security with the seductive idea of *progress* that Western culture takes from the European Enlightenment: Zygmunt Bauman, for example, describes how in modernity the realisation of identity was cast as a *project* in which 'there was a tight and irrevocable bond between social order as a project and the individual life as a project'.[21] This idea has underpinned powerful Australian discourses of progress, nation-building, and regional political and economic change.

Security and justice: A cosmopolitan future

From here the book weaves these theoretical considerations through a detailed historical analysis of the processes by which Australians have defined and fought over their national identity and engaged with their region and the world, from the first decisions to colonise the southern continent, through two world wars and many lesser ones, to contemporary fears of terror, Muslims and refugees. I do so because I find this history fascinating and intrinsically important: no citizen, student or policy practitioner can act responsibly without a critical appreciation of Australia's past foreign policy fears and debates. I do so also because only then can we genuinely understand what security has come to mean and why the present offers so much resistance to progressive and rational change: to an idea and practice of security where the complex interrelationship of actions and processes are understood, and no one's security is sacrificed. It is explore security's *conditions of possibility*: how it is possible to *think* security in any particular time and place, and how security in turn makes it possible to think and act within a given political and cultural community. While this approach may seem painstaking, I believe that before existing techniques of security can be superseded or rethought, their stubborn cultural power must first be understood.

This book went to press just as a new Labor government, led by Kevin Rudd, was elected by a landslide. While the detail of its international policy was yet to be seen, Rudd stated he would withdraw Australian troops from Iraq while continuing their deployment to Afghanistan, ratify the Kyoto Protocol on Climate Change, and develop a more independent stance within the US alliance. In the conclusion to Chapter 6, I analyse the most detailed available statement of Rudd's foreign policy, a February 2007 article he published in *The Diplomat*. There I praise his intention to pursue cooperative efforts to reinvigorate the nuclear non-proliferation regime, but also highlight silences about some of the more profound challenges facing the government, such as relations with Indonesia and China, and Labor's approach to asylum seekers. Here Labor all too slowly moved from an endorsement, in 2001, of John Howard's appalling policy of mandatory indefinite detention and the 'Pacific solution', to (with the publication of its national platform late in 2007) a new policy of short-term detention only and that grants to asylum seekers the full range of rights applicable under international law. If implemented properly, this would be a substantial advance for a more inclusive and sustainable vision of security of the kind I am advocating. Labor's platform also stated admirably that 'grave security threats, including from terrorism, regional instability and accelerating climate change . . . must be confronted without resort to the manipulation of fear and political exploitation'.

In the conclusion to this book I argue for Australians to embrace an outward-looking and generous 'cosmopolitan' future, one that is the best guarantee of their own and everyone else's security. In an era where terrorist ideologue Osama bin Laden claims the right to violate the security of Westerners because of the historic insecurity of Palestinians, Iraqis and others, such a holistic approach to security is no longer a luxury. It is in fact essential to winning the normative and political struggle (so terribly misnamed a 'war') against terror, which is being lost with every day we fail to embrace a better way. And, the longer we continue to disregard the suffering of others while speaking of the purity of our own 'values', the more we need to heed the insights of political theorist William Connolly, who dreams of a new kind of political community 'which affirms an indebtedness to the other while reconfiguring dogmatic interpretations of what it is', and which respects the struggle of 'the other to break out of injurious social definitions'.[22] I read this as a call to abandon the selfish visions of security, sovereignty and national interest in favour of an ethical engagement that crosses the lines of nation, culture and experience that currently circumscribe our sympathies. It might be to cultivate what McKenzie Wark has called 'the Virtual Republic': 'that zone of indifference that constitutes the extension of all the people's desires into a common world of conversation . . . that might have something to say about the ordering of things for people, rather than of people as things'.[23]

Security, claimed Berki, is the ultimate guarantee that we are free, but we ought to wonder whether that too is another Orwellian trick, whether security has for too long been a form of slavery we take for our freedom, a political technology that reduces us to things and others to less than things. To question and rethink security – as a politics and as a goal – is then to rethink what we are, and what our obligations are, in a simultaneous act of justice for the other; an act of justice in which the other might finally speak in its own voice and on its own terms, in which it is neither made an enemy nor reduced to the same. This is the challenge posed by demands for genuine self-determination, democratisation, diversity, security or economic justice: to go beyond the existing categories of thought, identity and political practice that would limit and reduce them to little more than refracted images of elite Western desires and interests. It may be that a genuinely just and secure future demands that we change the basic categories of our being – to believe that beyond the taken-for-granted categories of our world there is a better world to be thought.

1

Securing the Australian subject 1788–1918

. . . here is the irony. If Australianness is elusive as a centre, an essence, a destiny, it is everywhere to be found as a refracting perspective, a melange, a quirk. The baffling circumstances that defeat the search for a centre may well prove to be the thing itself . . .

Nicholas Jose[1]

As Lieutenant James Cook, commander of His Majesty's Ship *Endeavour*, began his voyage to Tahiti in 1768, the modern political technology of security – linking sovereignty, societal order, economic prosperity and geopolitics – was rapidly coming into its own. Although the Dutch were already firmly established at Batavia, and the British themselves in India, the *Endeavour*'s voyage would initiate a far-reaching process in which a 'geographic' space incorporating Australasia and the broader South Pacific was transformed and incorporated into the 'geopolitical' space we associate with security.

Although commissioned by the Royal Society for the purpose of observing the sun's transit across the face of Venus on 3 June 1769, the expedition was dispatched with a larger, secret imperial purpose: to sail south from Tahiti to latitude 40°S in search of the southern continent previously encountered by William Dampier and Abel Tasman, and to claim it for the British Crown. The nature of the *Endeavour*'s encounter with New Holland confirms Cook's narrow aim: despite the presence of the botanist Joseph Banks and the naturalist Daniel Solander, they landed only five times, the longest visit forced on them after the ship was holed on the Great Barrier Reef. With the meticulous care for which he had been chosen, Cook mapped the east coast – naming many of its bays, harbours, islands and observable land features – and finally, on 22 August 1770, after reaching the eponymous Possession Island off Cape York, hoisted the Union Jack and formally proclaimed the sovereignty of King George III over the whole of the eastern coast, from Point Hicks north, under the name 'New South Wales'. The many encounters of the ship's crew with Aboriginal tribes, some of whom displayed great hostility, did not discourage this founding act of dispossession, which effectively gave birth to a new geopolitical space in the southern hemisphere and began the process of obliterating the very different space imagined and lived by a much older civilisation. Cook's task thus completed, the *Endeavour* sailed on to Batavia, where the crew were struck with dysentery and malaria.[2]

The ambiguity of Cook's status as a founder – Paul Carter cites accusations of his 'culpable indifference . . . his descriptions of the Australian coast were less than fulsome and, much worse, he never came back' – seems irrelevant given the discrete task he had been set.[3] His aim, as a vehicle for a much greater political technology, was first to establish that such a place existed, then to map and claim it, thus bringing it firmly within a European political horizon. The term 'discovery', with all its imperial overtones, has rightfully been rejected; but its reverse may be more useful. We can argue that, in a very crucial sense, this was a space that had been *invented*, a space where none had existed before: a new space conceived within the cartographic and naval technologies of the time, whose possibilities would now be hostage to England's political and economic vicissitudes. As Cook began the return voyage its contours remained shadowy, its potential uses and dramas as yet unknown.

Before we continue, a word about the conceptual insights and approaches that this chapter develops. This and subsequent chapters analyse the construction of subjectivity (the idea or sense of who we are), space and cultural life through the constitutive interactions between citizens, the Australian state and the larger world – interwoven by a *leitmotif* that might be contained within the question, *Who, or what, is Australia?* But this book does not intend to provide a single, all-encompassing answer. Instead, it aims at a history of the question itself as a powerful genre of political discourse. In particular, it questions the terrible politics that has flowed from such a powerful and coercive construction of identity. The chapter traces a movement from the geopolitical imagination already present as Australia is first colonised, to the gradual creation of an 'Australian' subjectivity (at once individual, collective and juridical) that might conform to the indivisible body politic of Hobbes and Locke. Of course, even as this process appeared to become more entrenched, after Federation or Gallipoli, it remained a political illusion deployed to strengthen the position of dominant societal forces and efface the social conflicts in which they were engaged. Indeed, the drive to imagine a unified Australian identity remains a potent locus of political conflict to this day, an *aporia*, a contradiction that cannot, to the chagrin of some, ever be closed off.

A particularly strong theme is the development and refinement of a 'strategic imagination', which has been central to security's extension from a relation between state and citizen to a principle for the actions of the body politic itself in the world of nations. This imagination is primarily spatial, but not exclusively so, becoming powerfully linked with temporal discourses of racial superiority, political enlightenment, or cultural and economic progress. With the fundamental objectives of security – political sameness, economic prosperity, and societal order – in mind, strategy implies an attitude toward space and people which seeks to make it more flexible, manipulable and productive. As I have suggested with Cook's voyage, the strategic imagination is not so much an entry into a pre-existing space as the *production* of a new one by a detailed political technology that seeks to make it meaningful as it orders and partitions it into the vehicle, effect and arena of an industrial, political and cultural economy.

Through the mapping and traversal of this space by transport, its appropriation through sovereignty, its defence by acts and means of war, and its cultivation and exploitation by industry, agriculture and commerce, the strategic imagination thus seeks to engender economically and politically useful arrangements of bodies, communities and social institutions. The strategic imagination limits and affects the possibilities for people's lives, given that it embodies an assumption that humans are things to be made use of and manipulated, rather than having intrinsic dignity.[4] In this sense its space is never static and unchanging, but itself has a history – changes in technology introduce changes in its extent and permeability, changes in political doctrine change its meaning, and in turn affect not only the economic and social possibilities of individuals but also their psychic interiors. Its sites become written over with events, names, and narratives, assembled into a mythology which eventually becomes a nationalist (or shameful) history. Space becomes not merely an economic and political problem, but the anchor and contested site of our identity. Thus its *representation* is crucial: is this space threatening or safe, familiar or alien, productive or necessary? What are its flows and boundaries? And above all, what is our capacity for action within its geopolitical and psychic contours?

Colonisation, dispossession and imperial paranoia

It would be more than seventeen years before Europeans visited the southern continent again, this time as the advance guard of a thoroughgoing colonisation. The fleet of eleven vessels, led by Captain Arthur Phillip's *Sirius*, entered Botany Bay during the day and night of 19 January 1788, carrying 1030 people, 736 of them convicts. New South Wales was to be a gaol, and remained fundamentally so for over fifty years, within the strategic context of a larger imperial enterprise. The choice of Phillip, a naval officer, as the colony's first governor suggests as much, as do the military origins of his seven successors to 1821. In short, security – in the forms it then took in the British polity – dictated the Pitt government's motives for the settlement, and provided an enabling philosophical rationale. The juridical illusion of sovereignty, seemingly made real by Cook's ceremony on Possession Island in 1770, had made of it a space for the British general will; the assumed backwardness, docility and sparseness of the continent's Aboriginal peoples, along with their juridical invisibility, conjured legitimacy for the colonisation. Similarly, the British government's desire to rid their island of an entire 'criminal class', to cocoon their society behind an apartheid of sea and unfathomable distance, conformed to the liberal ontology of Hobbes, Locke and Bentham, which imagined a healthy 'Commonwealth' against the virulent Other of the criminal, which could, it seemed, be excised from the social body like a cancer.[5] Whether it be in the figure of the non-economic savage or the morally debased, criminal poor, the Other was already a vast, enabling shadow across Australia's future.

In short, Australia's origins lie in the attempts by the British ruling classes to achieve some sense of economic and *existential* security against enemies 'without and within': against both imperial competitors and an internal threat that was primarily a function of their own position and paranoia. As Robert Hughes explains, within a society in which unemployment and poverty were growing – the effect of rapid industrialisation, a soaring birth rate and the growth of towns – 'the belief in a swelling wave of crime was one of the great social facts of Georgian England'. As one writer commented in 1854, this criminal group 'constitutes a new estate, in utter estrangement from all the rest'. Hughes argues, however, that the existence of an organised criminal class was chimerical: 'Crime was still a cottage industry, the jumble of individual acts of desperation. The failure of language – the tyranny of moral generalisation over social inspection – fed the ruling class's belief that it was threatened from below.'[6] It would not be the last time such a 'failure of language' made history in Australia.

More conventionally geopolitical considerations were also significant, and were to influence later decisions to establish settlements and extend British sovereignty to Norfolk Island, Port Phillip Bay, Van Diemen's Land and the western coast of New Holland. The extent to which strategic arguments influenced the original decision to settle Botany Bay is a matter of considerable controversy, with historians such as Geoffrey Blainey and Alan Frost arguing that they were in fact paramount, while others – such as Hughes – argue that 'New South Wales was too far out on the geopolitical periphery'.[7]

Frost and Blainey argue that the decision to colonise Australia came as England – half bankrupted from war with France and seeking to increase its eastern trade after costly setbacks such as the loss of North America – sought to preclude French gains in India and the East while heading off any French alliance with Holland, who held the East Indies and was thus the key to strategic power there and around the Cape. A settlement in New South Wales appealed

because it would deny the coast to any other European power, and
be in reach of the highly strategic materials (pine for masts and flax
for sailcloth) which were believed to exist in abundance on Norfolk
Island. In addition, argued Frost,

> [Pitt and his advisers] had the more general aim of creating a port
> which in wartime would be self-sufficient in food and naval stores, one
> to which the nation's shipping could retire to refresh and refit, and
> from which squadrons might sail to attack French, Dutch and Spanish
> bases and shipping. To these profound motives, that of the removal of
> the convicts from the realm was secondary – an accompaniment, but
> not a cause.[8]

There seems little doubt that strategic arguments were a factor –
and indeed, Das Voltas Bay in south-west Africa had earlier been
preferred for its strategic location astride the sea route to the Far
East. What Hughes takes issue with is Frost and Blainey's view that
such considerations were paramount. Indeed Frost went further,
seeking to make of it a tendentious argument about the meaning of Australia's origins: '[T]he rag and bone shop of Australia's
beginning,' he wrote, 'was perhaps not so foul as we have for so
long supposed.'[9] While tracing these early strategic perspectives is
important for this study, I incline to Hughes' view that they were
of significantly less importance than the evacuation of the disease-
ridden prison hulks moored on the Thames and in the southern
ports of England.[10] The huge numbers sentenced to transportation (more than 160 000 over eighty years) and the vast administrative effort expended in maintaining the system stand against
a bizarre argument that sees the strategic rationale as somehow
making Australia's origins less abject, and would shoe-horn the
events into a teleological narrative which demands the civilisation
must begin with proud and noble ideals.

Nonetheless, strategic imperatives were present, and were a
prophetic echo of later policy frameworks which seized upon
the South Pacific, the East Indies and Asia as spaces essential to
Australia's security. After moving the fleet to Port Jackson, Phillip
wrote to Lord Sydney that 'We . . . had the satisfaction of finding the
finest harbour in the world, in which a thousand sail of the line may
ride with the most perfect security' – imagining perhaps the day

when this harbour might be a strategic outpost for a British lake in the Pacific, and prefiguring a future in which the cove most adjacent to that they chose to settle, Woolloomooloo Bay, would become a key South Pacific port, sheltering the warships of Australia and her allies. A few days earlier the fleet had encountered two vessels commanded by the French explorer La Pérouse, which stung Phillip into dispatching an expedition to colonise Norfolk Island, directing the *Sirius*'s second lieutenant, Philip Gidley King, to begin sowing crops and retting flax as soon as they were established there. However, the strategic promise of Norfolk was a chimera: its pines, short-grained and lacking in resin, were no good for masts, and the production of sailcloth languished for want of trained flax-dressers and sufficient labour. After two decades as a cruel outpost of punishment, which rose to notorious heights of viciousness under King and his successor Joseph Foveaux, it was abandoned in 1813. Yet even then the British strove to prevent claims by other powers: they destroyed all vestiges of settlement and left behind a dozen dogs to turn into a hunting pack that might attack any visitor.[11]

Strategic imperatives also influenced later decisions to colonise other parts of the continent. Bass Strait was discovered in 1797–98, and the decisions to establish settlements at Port Phillip Bay and Van Diemen's Land were motivated by a view of their strategic importance – the use of the passage took weeks off the voyage from Sydney to Portsmouth. In response to Matthew Flinders' encounter with two French ships commanded by Nicolas Baudin near the present site of Adelaide in 1802, New South Wales Governor King sent an appeal to London for a settlement at Port Phillip Bay. He had been alarmed when, after they put into Sydney, he was shown charts of the southern coast bearing French names – with the southern part of the mainland termed 'Terre Napoleon'. Dismayed by the scandalous possibility of having to share the continent with Napoleon's France, King sent an armed schooner to shadow Baudin as he returned south, and immediately moved to put a settlement on the Derwent River in Van Diemen's Land. At the same time the British government responded to King's request by sending a mission – including 308 convicts – to colonise Port Phillip Bay. This mission landed in October 1803, but found the site – chosen more for its strategic importance than its proximity to supplies of fresh water – so inhospitable that the outpost was abandoned after a few months, and moved to Hobart. Their commander, Collins, ignored King's request that they resettle on the north of Van Diemen's Land or King Island. A settlement was eventually placed at the mouth of the Tamar River in 1804, from where it was hoped strategic control of the strait could be asserted.[12]

The distant observer of this period is struck by both the aggressive colonial effort to name, control and utilise this new space, and its instability and intransigence: an 'Australia' swaying unsteadily on the threshold of its realisation. In succession, Norfolk Island, Port Phillip Bay and Melville Island – all coveted for their strategic location and importance – were colonised and abandoned. Yet whatever their emotional significance as sites of ambition, cruelty and abject failure, they would be now forever contained within the spatial and juridical realm of the British Crown. In 1826 the Crown extended claim to the whole of New Holland and Van Diemen's Land, and further settlements were made at Westernport in Victoria and Albany on the west coast, and in 1829 on the Swan River (now Perth). Albany in particular promised control of the southern sea route around Australia to China. By this time New South Wales Governor Macquarie had begun addressing his dispatches to London under the name 'Australia', after it had appeared on Flinders' charts.[13] This and the 1826 claim effectively extinguished the claims of any other European power to the continent, building on the vast dispossession already in train. While political Federation was not to occur for another seventy-five years, a crucial enabling correspondence – between soil, sovereignty and identity – had been achieved.

A now familiar image of the Other was also appearing, raising both physical and psychological challenges to the sense of 'self' the new colonies were attempting to cultivate. In New South Wales, murderous conflict between whites and local tribes broke out soon after the initial settlement in 1788, and in September 1790 Phillip was himself speared through the shoulder during a confrontation. In response to the spearing of his gamekeeper by the famous warrior Pemulwuy in December, Phillip ordered the first punitive expedition – he sent out a detail of forty marines, which was instructed to kill ten adult males and return with their heads to Sydney. The expedition failed, and Pemulwuy survived to conduct another ten years of guerrilla warfare against the colonisers. It was in this context of increasing armed conflict that local tribes were being decimated by smallpox, brought to the colony as a jar of variolous material for inoculations. David Day has argued that there is 'considerable circumstantial evidence to suggest that officers other than Phillip, or perhaps convicts and soldiers angered by Aboriginal attacks on their fellows, deliberately spread smallpox among the Aborigines'.[14]

Conflict with Aborigines lay at the centre of both the swift, sweeping juridical claims to various parts of the continent, and the slower effort to render the land productive (and therefore meaningful) within a European politico-economic ontology. Aborigines were murdered at Port Phillip Bay by Lieutenant John Murray's party, as they claimed the area for the British Crown in 1802, and armed confrontation – whether between organised groups of blacks and soldiers or police, or more haphazardly in countless instances of murder or revenge – would become a constant feature of colonial politics for the next 130 years, with devastating effects on the local cultures and populations.[15] Thus the colony's first serious strategic threats, and its first attempts to assert a strategic control of space and economic resources, were made and encountered within the struggle for the nation's very *interior* – in a simultaneously material, economic and ontological sense. Aboriginal peoples could never be allowed to inhabit (or disrupt) that interior, in the form of the juridical and psychological unity of the state, its hold on the soil, or its economic progress.

The prophetic psychological image of the Other – as sub-human and threatening to *security*, no less – was captured in colonial historian the Reverend John West's account of the colonial attitude to the Aborigines of Van Diemen's Land:

> Passing from censure to hatred, they speak of them as improvident, importunate, and intrusive; as rapacious and mischievous; then as treacherous and blood-thirsty; finally as devils and beasts of prey. Their appearance is offensive, their proximity obstructive: *their presence renders everything insecure*. Thus the muskets of the soldier, and of the bandit, are equally useful; they clear the land of a detested incubus.[16]

As a juridical and physical boundary was established around Britain's Australian possessions, the strategic imagination was also turned outwards, fuelled by religious, economic and ethnocentric imperatives. The Pacific Islands were the first focus of attention. As before, 'Australian' interest was also driven by the (often groundless) fears of competition from other European powers. In 1840 the New South Wales Parliament and press lauded the British decision to formally annex New Zealand, even as they protested at being asked to finance the growing colony there. Also in 1839 there was premonition of both Australia's future involvement in British wars and a strategic involvement in Asia when New South Wales Governor Sir George Gipps urged the dispatch of three British ships, then at anchor in Sydney Harbour, to China to protect the British Trade Superintendent. He argued that Australia's interests lay with Britain as the 'power responsible for . . . Australia's security'.[17]

France was seen as the primary threat to British–Australian interests in the Pacific at this time. The 1844 announcement of a French protectorate over Tahiti and the 1853 annexation of New Caledonia were bitterly resented by New South Wales, which viewed Tahiti, Fiji and the New Hebrides as being of great strategic importance due to the trade in sandalwood, bêche-de-mer, pigs and (later) labour. After the annexation of New Caledonia, the *Sydney Morning Herald* lamented that 'the opportunity of colonising that fine group had been lost'. Imperial rivalry between Russia and Britain flowed into perceptions of insecurity, with an 1862 visit by a Russian naval contingent fuelling fears of a possible invasion. The construction of Fort Denison in Sydney Harbour in 1854 was publicly justified by the fear of Russian attack, although concerns over American and French activities in the South Pacific were probably uppermost. The first detailed analysis of Australia's strategic environment came in 1877 with a report by Sir William Jervois, a British military engineer who later became Governor of South Australia. While he discounted the possibility of major attack, he thought that danger came in the possibility of small-scale naval raids from the French port of Saigon, or from Russian and American Pacific bases. Earlier, however, others had argued that as war could come to the colonies only as a result of the British connection, Australia should seek a neutral status similar to that Hanover had claimed between 1714 and 1857.[18]

During the 1870s colonial concern about British influence in the South Pacific led to the assertion of an 'Australasian Monroe Doctrine' for the South Pacific. It was aimed, like its North American namesake, at the exclusion of other powers from the area. Betraying an early obsession with certitude, a theme which dominates Australia's modern history, colonial leaders would settle for little less than full sovereignty – annexation. According to Neville Meaney, 'by taking possession of the island groups which stretched in an arc from New Guinea in the north through the Solomons to the New Hebrides and, more distantly, Fiji and Samoa in the east, they hoped to erect a natural barrier … against potential enemies'.[19]

In 1874 they succeeded in convincing Britain to annex the Fijian islands, and the next year requested the annexation of New Guinea, with New South Wales also requesting the annexation of the New Hebrides and the Solomon, Marshall, Ellice and Gilbert islands. In 1883 the Queensland Premier, with the support of New South Wales, Victoria and South Australia, announced that his government was taking possession of the eastern half of New Guinea, on the strength of reports that German newspapers were urging its seizure. The British again refused to support the claim. In a settlement in 1886 Germany gained the Bismarck Archipelago and the North Solomons, while Britain claimed the southern Solomons and the Ellice and Gilbert groups further east. In return for contributing to the expense of New Guinea's administration, the colonies were given a shared role, which was exercised by Queensland until Federation. Over the next fifteen years the colonies also urged the British to force the French from New Caledonia and the New Hebrides, and to take over German Samoa and the Philippines. Victorian Premier Sir George Turner asked his agent-general to press upon the British the importance 'on strategical grounds [that] the Philippine Islands should be in possession of friendly power; also, in interest of trade, being on route China and Japan'. The colonies were thus reassured by the US annexation of both the Philippines and Hawaii in 1898, and of Tutuila in Samoa in 1899. The horrific violence the Americans deployed, killing some 20 000 Filipinos, appeared to make no difference to them.[20]

By the end of the 19th century, then, a potent strategic theme in Australian history had been established: the South Pacific would perform the function of a secure passage to the Americas, a protective zone around the Australian north and east coasts, and an area of overwhelming Australasian cultural, economic and political influence. Strategic fears would reappear as the Japanese took control of the Philippines, the Solomon Islands and parts of New Guinea in 1941, and even more bizarrely during the late 1980s with scares about Soviet and Libyan influence in Vanuatu.[21] Presaging a time when Australia would be Papua New Guinea's biggest aid donor and its corporations the largest investors, Australians opened up the Papuan inland, established the first missions and schools and, with the granting of independence in 1975, accelerated the incorporation of the area's myriad tribal peoples into a difficult (and in many ways deeply destructive) modernity.

Federation and security: Fear of the Other

The aggressive assertion of Australian interest in the Pacific Islands, and its first (external) imperial acquisitions, saw Australian elites striving to influence a process in which the Pacific and Asia were being spatially constructed in ever more complex geopolitical terms.

The strategic gaze outwards – at a space at once opportune and alien – crucially involved the emergence of an anxious political self-consciousness, in the terms of a highly complex (and often ironic) play of self and other. This could be seen in a more assertive foreign policy with Britain, the emergence of republicanism and nationalism, and complex debates about national identity in relation to the Empire, the British cultural and racial inheritance, political obligations to London, and the racial homogeneity of the colonial community. At the same time, the growth and industrialisation of the economy, along with the import of radical ideas and the crises of the 1890s, would lead to increasingly bitter class conflict. While the adoption of an Australian Constitution and the establishment of a federal Parliament in 1901 would fix and solidify this process of self-imagination – particularly in juridical terms – many of its other features would remain highly contested. And with Aboriginal populations having fallen from as many as one and a half million in 1788 to 60 000 by 1888,[22] and the violence of colonisation and removal still underway, a corrosive moral *aporia* was opening up in the very foundations of the Australian national identity – which would be framed, in part, to continue and intensify these processes.

An early catalyst was the presence of Chinese immigrants, who had been coming to the New South Wales and Victorian goldfields since the late 1840s, and by the later presence of Japanese immigrants and labourers from the Pacific Islands. The 1854 Eureka rebellion, perceived to have been fuelled by the presence of Americans with seditious republican values, had already alerted the colonial authorities to the threat to law and order from foreigners. Attention then focused on the Chinese, with the 1855 report into the rebellion warning of 'an unpleasant possibility of the future, that a comparative handful of colonists could be buried in a countless throng of Chinamen'. Despite restrictions in Victoria and South Australia, by 1857 their numbers had reached 35 000. Violent conflict in many goldfields (the most notorious being at Lambing Flat in 1860) was matched with increasing press and public hysteria. R. D. Lang's views were particularly revealing: fearful of unlimited migration and miscegenation, he warned that, left unchecked, it 'could swamp the whole European community of these colonies' and 'obliterate every trace of British progress and civilisation'.[23] By 1888, all the colonies had enacted laws to prevent further Chinese immigration. Speaking before the Bill was presented to the New South Wales Parliament in 1888, Premier Henry Parkes justified the action on the 'philosophical' grounds that it was 'our duty to preserve the type of the British nation, and that we ought not, for any consideration whatever, to admit any element that would detract from, or in any appreciable degree lower, that admirable type of nationality'.[24]

Added to their status as immediate threats to the racial and cultural homogeneity of the colonial community, the Chinese were projected as presaging future strategic threats. These fears in turn played into the drive for Federation, for which the search for national security was a fundamental imperative. Parkes, now commemorated on coins as the 'Father of Federation', began his campaign for an Australian government with the 1889 report on Australia's defence by British Major General J. Bevan Edwards, which argued that an effective defence could only be ensured by 'a federation of the military forces of the colonies' and that, in the absence of political union, the colonies should pass a uniform Defence Act which would enable the use of each colony's forces in any other.[25]

In Parkes' speeches it became clear that he sought to found the new Australian political identity upon a symbiotic relation to an inferior, threatening and barbarous Other. In one he spoke of the threat posed by 'the countless millions of inferior members of the human family who are within easy sail of these shores', and at Wagga Wagga in April 1888 he warned of the menace of China, 'a barbarous power, which is so rapidly creating armies and a formidable navy, that it is sufficient at all events to awaken the intelligent attention of reflecting men'. Perhaps there was irony in the logic which argued that although 'in some respects they are a superior set of people, and we know they belong to a nation of old and deep rooted civilisation', it was 'our first duty, the duty of the working man and capitalist, the duty of the illiterate and the most cultivated, the duty, in fact, of all classes to preserve in these colonies the British type against all other nations'.[26]

There was a sinister elegance to Parkes' rhetorical strategy, which sought to forge a unity among his audience through the effacement of class differences, in confrontation with the greater difference founded on race and culture. As a performance, the speech used the simultaneously totalising and individualising strategy Foucault has noted, and which I argue has been central to security as a mode and vector of power. In this case Parkes sought to advance the realisation of a psychological and juridical totality – an 'Australian' state – by appealing to the most interior subjectivities of his listeners as individuals with larger fears, identities and obligations: 'I intend in the few words which I shall address to you this afternoon . . . to direct your attention to your relations as part of this great colony with the rest of the world . . . to assist you to realise the position you occupy as citizens of a rapidly rising Empire.'[27]

If there were any doubts that these were strategic questions, they would be erased by his speech to the 1891 National Convention to lay down the basis of the new federal Constitution:

I think it is more than likely, more than probable, that forms of aggression will appear in these seas which are entirely new . . . We have evidence abundant on all hands that the Chinese nation and other Asiatic nations . . . are awakening to all the powers which their immense population gives them in the art of war, in the art of acquisition, and all the other arts known to European civilisation, and it seems to me . . . that if we suffer in this direction at any time . . . it will be stealthily, so far as movements of this kind can be made stealthily, effecting a lodgement in some thinly-peopled portion of the country, where it would take immense loss of life and immense loss of wealth to dislodge the invader.[28]

This final comment elucidated a prophetic strategic paranoia that would echo through Australian history, almost always with Asian invaders in mind, and voiced an anxiety that the crucial correspondence between soil, sovereignty and identity – still in many ways under question – might be threatened.[29] Moreover, the repetition of such fears – by cultivating a sense of urgency and silencing dissent by equating it with sedition – helped legitimate the achievement of that correspondence through colonisation and dispossession.

The importance of strategic questions to Federation was also underlined when among the four principles adopted by the 1891 Convention was the objective that 'the military and naval defence of Australia shall be entrusted to federal forces under one command'. The draft Constitutions drawn up at the 1891 Convention and amended at the 1897–98 Convention included broad Commonwealth powers over 'external affairs', defence and 'the relation of the Commonwealth with the islands of the Pacific'.[30] Neville Meaney argues that while diplomacy and defence were not at the centre of controversies surrounding the Constitution, it is important not to underestimate their significance: 'The issue of national security, unlike the problems of small versus large states and protection versus free trade, had been determined by a common experience and spoke to an assured consensus. There was thus little to discuss.'[31]

But as true as it may have seemed, and as crucial as it no doubt was, this 'common experience' did not occur naturally, as the expression of some inevitable pre-existing unity. Rather it had to be

imagined, spoken and entrenched, to be made the very vehicle –
rather than the product – of that unity. Alfred Deakin's speech to the
Australian Natives Association in March 1898, when the Victorian
Parliament was wavering, makes this startlingly clear:

> Let us recognise that we live in an unstable era, and that if we fail
> in the hour of crisis we may never be able to recall our lost national
> opportunities. At no period during the first hundred years has the
> situation of the great Empire to which we belong been more serious.
> From the far east and the far west alike we behold menaces and
> contagion … Happily your voice is for immediate and absolute union.[32]

The invocation of an unproblematic 'we' in such texts activated
both a political appeal and effaced a profound anxiety: about the
security of an Australian sense of self, and about how the nation
might develop as a form of political and economic order. Aware
there was no 'assured consensus', it assumes a subject that, in many
crucial ways, had yet to come into being.

At this time visions of white Australian identity were divided
between loyalties to Britain and the more aggressive republican
stances of the *Bulletin* and other radical journals, and complicated
by intensifying class conflict. Rhetorics of national and racial identity were less attempts to resolve such conflicts than exercises in
mastery, not only of whites over Asians, Islanders or Aborigines,
but also of Capital over Labour, and white labour over coloured.
Already in 1885 Henry Parkes, an avowed servant of the Crown,
believed there were limits to patriotism: in a letter to the *Sydney
Morning Herald* he opposed New South Wales Premier William
Dalley's decision to send 750 men to help restore British authority
in the Sudan. The logic Parkes employed revealed both the emerging
complexities in nationalist rhetorics, and their common ground.
He made no quarrel with British motives, which were to 'establish
a government of purity and order out of elements of corruption
and disorder, and then to retire from the soil of Egypt'. Rather, he
argued, white Australians had more urgent tasks:

> I assert that there can be no greater folly than to foster a spurious spirit
> of military ardour in a country like ours, where every man is wanted
> to take his part, in some form or other, *in colonising work* … with the

right hand we are expending our revenues to import able-bodied men to subjugate the soil, while with the left hand we propose to squander our revenues to deport men to subjugate Sir Edward Strickland's 'saracens'.[33]

It seems that in the 'sad task' of subjugation – whether of nature or the other – there were harsh choices to be made. But they were not made, whether in the Sudan, South Africa, or in the even more terrible wars to come; and Parkes' words, however impoverished, would echo through the debates over Australia's role in future conflicts. Later – and predicting the mythology built around the slaughter at Gallipoli – he argued that in the Sudan 'our Australian heroes will have little chance of distinguishing themselves on the field of battle', and he closed the letter by saying that 'if a time should come when England shall be engaged in a great conflict with a Great Power, even then . . . our first duty will be to hold inviolate the part of the Empire where our lot is cast; and, this sacred trust secured, to give life and fortune freely, if we have them to spare, beyond our own shores'.[34]

Already, as Parkes asserted the gathering unity of an Australian subject against Dalley's compliant response to the tug on 'the crimson thread of kinship',[35] there were both the appearance of ambiguity and opening, and a swift move to shut it off. There would be a time, Parkes suggested, when both could be reconciled – when the recalcitrant Aboriginal nature of the continent had been subdued, and the civilisation had more effectively secured its physical basis, its juridical unity and its ontological stability. Edmund Barton, himself a firm proponent of an Australian Federation, certainly believed that that time had come sooner rather than later. As debate raged over the question of committing colonial troops to the war against the Boers in 1899, Barton argued for an expedition on the basis of an irreducible colonial immersion in the imperial body politic:

> We have arrived at a point when British territory has been invaded, when the empire is at war . . . We are part of that empire . . . and for my part, as long as we are a part of that empire, when our empire is at war with any other power whatsoever, it becomes our turn to declare the motto, 'The empire, right or wrong'.[36]

That this language was being deployed as a 'political double-bind' – which sought to dissolve opposition through the blackmail that merged subject with meta-subject – was unmistakable in his reply to Griffith's retort that he could agree if only 'the empire were in danger, certainly!' Barton snapped back: 'Is it for any one citizen to decide? No it is for the empire itself to decide, and the empire having decided that it is sufficiently in danger . . . it is a decision, I think, which we should respect and follow.'[37]

Such tensions were in turn complicated by more radical strands of nationalism, in which opposition to Britain was more uncompromising. The *Bulletin* of the mid-1890s, for instance, favoured a united Australia with a republican government and the abolition of titles, and attacked the brutalities of British rule in Ireland. For a time it also – most alarmingly for liberals – advocated the abolition of private ownership of land and a democracy based on universal suffrage and the direct election of ministers by Parliament.[38] An editorial from April 1895 contained an extraordinary attack on British imperial hubris, an attack which would be integral to imagining a very different nationalism from that of Parkes, Barton or Deakin:

> The British character has many inestimable sides, and many that are odious. The side that has been turned to Australia is an incarnation of calculating selfishness. The modern John Bull regards the world as his oyster . . . he truckles to the strong and bullies the weak; sends Ambassadors to Russia and armies to Egypt; everywhere grasping all and giving nothing in return . . . His idea of an ally is somebody to squeeze; of an enemy, somebody who refuses to be squeezed . . . We owe him convicts, institutions, and some 400 millions sterling – as much as he can squeeze per cent. When Australians began to show resentment at being squeezed, except indirectly, he sheared off, and is now busy squeezing South Africa with the aid of his Christian principles and the MAXIM gun . . .[39]

Yet the 'crimson thread of kinship', while torn now from the political blackmail of imperial Federation, would still remain powerful, and the racist appeal to blood identity a significant area of common ground. The *Bulletin* also wanted an 'Australia for the Australians – the cheap Chinaman, the cheap nigger, and the cheap European pauper to be absolutely excluded', and anti-British attitudes were often motivated by fears that Australia might be forced to accept coloured immigrants from England's 'nigger empire', an idea which was opposed because of both a concern about cheap labour and a deeper revulsion based on physical and cultural difference.[40]

Also emerging, in the *Bulletin* and in the rhetoric of Labor leaders, were self-conscious borrowings from the European Enlightenment and their convergence with an Australian nationalism. As John Docker has demonstrated, the *Bulletin*'s view that the movement of history was bringing a new spirit of rationality and logic to culture both fed and reposed upon an older racism in which the 'Chinaman' was 'a barbarous, medieval sort of person', frozen in his own culture's Middle Ages. In a close paraphrase, Docker suggests 'that is why a forward-looking, liberal society like the Australian promises to be, a society that is progressive, democratic, secular, reasoning, has to exclude other races like the Chinese or Japanese'.[41]

In a similar vein the 1905 federal Labor Conference voted for a resolution that urged 'the cultivation of an Australian sentiment, based upon the maintenance of racial purity and the development in Australia of an enlightened and self-reliant community'. Perhaps one of the clearest notes was sounded by Sir Charles Kingston – a conservative – on the occasion of the adoption of the final draft of the Constitution in March 1898. He declared that it would be 'the most magnificent constitution into which the chosen representatives of a free and enlightened people have ever breathed the life of popular sentiment and national hope'.[42]

The broad agreement between Capital and Labour about the national identity – a vision of future possibility, blood identity and racialised strategic fear – both masked and played into a bitter economic and political struggle that would have far-reaching effects. In this context historians have located the formation of the Australian Labor Party (ALP), the development of an early defence and foreign policy, and the establishment of the institutions of the Commonwealth and the Conciliation and Arbitration Commission. To this, the continuing destruction of Aboriginal tribes and the gathering geopolitical storm in Europe would be a dark backdrop.

The rapid development of the Australian economy in the last two decades of the 19th century, much of it with borrowed British capital, was accompanied by increasing worker unrest. In 1888 Parkes had repressed striking coalminers and wharfies at Newcastle with troops, while in August 1890 huge crowds turned out in Sydney and Melbourne to offer support for maritime workers striking in defence of their right to be represented by trade unions. Strikes had also broken out among shearers, and in the mines at Broken Hill, Illawarra and Kalgoorlie. In Victoria the government swore in thousands of special constables and deployed mounted police to disperse gas workers; in Sydney troops and police were used to clear crowds attempting to prevent the loading of wool on to ships by volunteer labour. At the same time, the credit squeeze of 1890 had brought great hardships: public works ceased and unemployment leapt to unprecedented levels. Shearers again struck across Queensland in 1891 against pastoralists' demands for freedom of contract. Parkes thought these upheavals – which came close to the capitalist nightmare of a general strike – had shaken 'the whole fabric of commercial industry'; as Manning Clark saw it, 'Bourgeois society was like a city feeling the first effects of an earth tremor and fearful that the tremor might erupt into a destructive quake.'[43]

Clark argues that the Constitution, and the series of federal institutions that accompanied it, were specifically designed to thwart social revolution. The nuanced liberal problematic of 'government' was crucial here. While the political allegiance of the middle classes through their ownership of property and their partnership in prosperity was assured, that of workers was not. While some conservatives felt they had no need to make compromises with the labour movement, liberals such as Deakin and Reid saw that acceding to some labour demands could split the moderates from the radicals: 'Liberalism in politics could rob labour of its revolutionary fervour, and rid the bourgeoisie of the charge that they were indifferent to the well-being of the masses. Though a free trader by conviction [Reid] was not opposed to the use of the state to protect the weak, and to effect conciliation in disputes between Capital and Labour.' Likewise, Deakin 'advocated the use of the state to ensure that the base of the social pyramid was not composed of men and women who had no ties to the existing social order'.[44]

These concerns underpinned the desire of the founding fathers for a Constitution that, while allowing for popular election to the lower house, would also ensure a conservative upper house and, by dividing power between the federal government and several colonial parliaments, would 'prevent any radical change in the ownership or distribution of property by constitutional means':

> They were men who were looking for political institutions which could handle strikes, lockouts, industrial anarchy, commercial depression with more facility, indeed agility, than six or seven colonial governments or parliaments. They were looking for political institutions that would solve the dilemma of the bourgeoisie: how to reconcile a colonial political democracy, with its approximation to political equality, with the survival of the institutions of private property and of the profit incentive. They were men who were reaching for what their political teachers, Alexander Hamilton, Alexis de Tocqueville and John Stuart Mill, had fussed over during their lifetime – how to preserve what they understood by the liberty of the individual in a society with what de Tocqueville had harshly labelled as the 'depraved taste' of the masses for equality.[45]

It was in this context that the liberal problematic of 'government' – and thus of *security* – was developing, at a crucial period in the construction of a unified Australian sense of self and the effort to place firm imaginative and juridical limits around it. The drive to imagine an Australian body politic converged with the problem of liberating a political and economic modernity while controlling its social energies – radical forms of dissent which threatened both the existing and the potential social order. In this, the search for less coercive forms of governmental reason by liberals such as Deakin and Barton combined with a strategic imagination of geopolitical space, one which could bear on the most interior fears and desires of individuals and play into a more general management of the socio-economic totality. The strategic fears and imperial ambitions that drove Federation cannot be divorced from the class conflict of the 1890s.

Although some in the labour movement scoffed at invasion fears and could see that the Constitution was weighted against them, others, such as Billy Hughes, were willing to accept it because it promised a defence guarantee and the means to consolidate a white Australia.[46] Factories Acts (passed by all colonies except

Western Australia between 1873 and 1896) and a Conciliation and Arbitration Act (in New South Wales) were other key planks in moderating potentially explosive class conflict. While there was broad agreement between laborites, liberals and conservatives on the establishment of a federal Conciliation and Arbitration Court, the actual passage of the Bill was drawn out and bitter. Radicals understood how the politics of Federation – monopolised by the conservative colonial premiers and barely democratic – had been used to muzzle organised labour.[47] Further, racism and strategic paranoia had been used to buy the acquiescence of some of their leaders. As Clark so acerbically observed, for the ruling classes, the new federal Constitution would act as 'a fortress against both the enemy without and the enemy within'.[48]

The ghost of the long dead Hegel was present at the ceremony in Sydney's Centennial Park to inaugurate an Australian Commonwealth on 1 January 1901. Its slogan, coined by Parkes and displayed on a large banner draped across a car carrying his bust, was 'One People, One Destiny'. An Australian subject, contained within the protective juridical and strategic armature of the British Crown, had now been imagined as a totalising 'governmental' principle. The ceremony, attended by thousands and marked by a festive atmosphere, gave visible semiotic form to the new nation, which might otherwise have remained an abstract legal idea. Perhaps ironically, it also displayed the limits of its new identity. A literal parade of signs through Sydney's streets – bushmen, shearers, miners, imperial troops just returned from South Africa – showed 'Australians' who they now were. At Centennial Park they listened as an official read the Queen's proclamation and swore in the Earl of Hopetoun, an Englishman, as the first governor-general. The Catholic Cardinal Moran was not present; nor were any representatives of the true owners of the land on which this performance took place. As if to underline the intensifying ontological correspondence of soil, sovereignty and identity, many remarked that it was 'the first time in the history of the world . . . that the boundaries of a nation-state had coincided with those of a whole continent'.[49]

A pivotal image of the Other was cemented into the foundations of the Australian identity with the passage of the *Immigration*

Restriction Act 1901 (Cwlth) later that year, and the 'dialectical' movement of overcoming was symbolised in the continuing task of colonisation: the long war to seize the land from its original peoples. Deakin argued that in the securing of a White Australia, 'the national manhood', the 'national character' and the 'national future' were at stake. Addressing another issue close to the labour movement's heart was the Pacific Islands Labourers Act, passed by Barton's government, which banned the entry of black labourers after March 1904 and provided for their deportation after December 1906.[50]

In a premonition of another crucial element of the Australian identity – its blooding through sacrifice in war – the new Commonwealth took over the recruitment and dispatch of Australian troops for South Africa, and in February 1902 Barton farewelled the first federal contingent to sail from Circular Quay to fight the Boers. The significance of the occasion was not lost on him: for the first time it was *Australia* – rather than any one state or colony – that was going to war. Australia did not stand for militarism, he told the troops, but for truth and justice. Once in South Africa, the troops encountered an enemy that fought with guerrilla-style tactics, which the British countered with techniques that would reappear sixty years later in South Vietnam: massacring prisoners of war, burning villages and herding the survivors into concentration camps where they died at eighteen times the rate that people died in New South Wales. 'Civilisation,' lamented Clark famously, 'was perhaps only a thin veneer over savagery.'[51]

The Constitution specifically failed to recognise the continent's Aboriginal people, who by 1900 numbered only 60 000. This was perhaps unsurprising, given the Constitution's origins in a thoroughly racist liberal ontology and, more specifically, in Benthamite utilitarianism,[52] along with the general white belief that the Aborigines were dying away in the face of a more aggressive and superior form of civilisation. Section 127, later repealed, seemed to confirm this, providing for the exclusion of Aborigines from any census of the population. Clarifying Section 41, the *Commonwealth Electoral Act 1902* (Cwlth) excluded Aborigines from voting in federal elections, as they had previously been excluded from voting in elections in the colonies. At the same time, in a precedent for which Australia has been praised, suffrage was granted by the masculine state to white women, though not without some resistance from conservatives such as Sir Edward Braddon. Labor leader Chris Watson argued that he did not want to see the 'savages and slaves' in the north and west of the country able to run the electorates covering their territories, and the American-born Labor member from Tasmania, King O'Malley, declared that there was no scientific evidence to link the Aborigines with humanity.[53]

Hence, under the terms of a profound juridical fiction, the continent's indigenous peoples did not exist, even as the states retained their power to make laws concerning them. Lacking status as citizens – for some even as humans – they bore the mark of *negative subjects*, even as their land, bodies and struggle were utterly bound up with the myriad historical processes that had made an allegedly 'whole' Australian subject possible.

The Great War: Australian identity and the Anzac tradition

Paralleling the bitter parliamentary debates over the terms of the Conciliation and Arbitration Act and the efforts to cement the White Australia policy were debates over an Australian foreign and defence policy, and the evolving geopolitical space in which the new nation would seek its 'security'. While Australian foreign policy (and formal diplomatic representation) was still formally subordinated to London, and its naval defence guaranteed by the Royal Navy, the Barton government took the view that they could press the British on Australian 'interests' in the Pacific and carry out negotiations with foreign powers; in short, the British should 'make the Australasian view the basis of imperial policy in the region'. Australia sought to take over the administration of British New Guinea and the Solomon Islands, and complained to Germany about discrimination in the Marianas and Carolinas against the trading firm Burns Philp. Under pressure from missionaries, settlers and traders in competition with the French New Hebrides Company, Australia also sought – but failed – to persuade Britain to annex the islands.[54]

Early defence debates were strongly polarised. While some saw threats from powers as diverse as Russia, Japan and France, others felt secure in the embrace of the Royal Navy and resisted calls for higher levels of spending. The first defence Bill failed in deadlock over a dispute about imperial service, and in 1902 Parliament forced the government to cut Australian land forces from 29 550 to 25 000. The Defence Act was only passed in 1904, after a clause relating to overseas service had been excised. Henry Bournes Higgins opposed the formation of an expeditionary force, saying : 'We do not want our men to join in an opium war. We do not want our men to be dragged into a war that may be against their conscience.' Earlier he had criticised the dispatch of troops to South Africa, and in 1901 had warned – like the *Tocsin* of a few years earlier – against establishing 'a military system in grotesque imitation of the military system on the continent of Europe . . . We must keep this country from the ghastly bane of militarism.' In 1902 the Australian military commander W. B. Hutton, in a prescient omen of future Australian policy, pressed for a 30 000-strong garrison and a field force (which could be deployed overseas) because the Indian Ocean, the northern Pacific and the China Sea would become 'the probable scene of the future struggle for commercial supremacy'. If so, Australia would have to not only 'defend her own soil' but also 'take steps . . . to defend those vast interests beyond her shores upon the maintenance of which her present existence and her future prosperity must so largely depend'.[55]

Despite the Anglo-Japanese Alliance, signed in 1902, a steadily industrialising Japan quickly became the locus of Australian strategic fears. With Japan in mind, the Labor leader J. C. Watson said in 1903 that 'the feasibility of an invasion is such that we ought to make adequate provision to repel it', that Australian troop numbers were 'preposterously low', and that he was willing to vote £500 000 for the purchase of 100 000 rifles. Another member, T. T. Ewing, who in 1907 became Defence Minister, spoke in 1903 of the possibility that, having taken 'a few more steps up the ladder of civilization', the White Australia policy might provoke Asian peoples to seek 'revenge'. It was inevitable that between 'the white and the yellow man there is racial hatred . . . they are destined to be enemies for all time'. While there was no imminent danger, the next generation would, Ewing said, experience the 'greatest storm which the world has ever seen when the white man eventually in these latitudes faces the yellow man in deadly war'.[56]

Japan's crushing 1905 defeat of the Russian Navy in the Tsushima Strait aroused even greater anxieties. Deakin urged that harbour defences be strengthened and that Australia develop its own navy. Fearing invasion, he argued that it was 'the duty of able bodied men to fit themselves for defence work'. Fear of Japan had widespread parliamentary and public purchase, as shown by the establishment of the National Defence League and the Immigration League in 1905; such fears were not mollified by the renewal of the Anglo-Japanese Alliance in August of that year. Race, strategy and the anxious claim of whites to the continent merged in the thoughts of Joseph Page, who argued that 'Australia is now coveted by the overcrowded races of the east'; Japan was 'equal to any white race on sea or land, and a very few years may make the Chinese the same'.[57]

Others scoffed at invasion fears. Joseph Cook, now a conservative free trader, thought that 'the balance of power is so even among the nations that none of them could afford to send a marauding army', and that even Japan was fully occupied with nations closer to it.[58] King O'Malley brought some sorely needed wit to the issue:

> Really I must confess that for thirty years I heard the same cry in the United States: 'We are going to have an invasion.' When I lived in Mexico, I heard the same cry that I hear now in Australia: 'Somebody is going to invade us. We cannot tell which nation it is, but surely some nation is coming.' Ever since I have been in Australia . . . I have heard the same cry of 'an invasion', but the only invasions that I ever read of are invasions of rabbits.[59]

The anxious linkage between the Australian identity, Aboriginal dispossession and fear of Asia was made clear in March 1913, as the foundation stone of Canberra – the new national capital – was being laid. The problem, once again, was the security of the correspondence between sovereignty, soil and identity. While O'Malley spoke of his belief that 'according to the divine plans and specifications, God commanded the English-speaking people to secure control of, and constitutionally govern, the earth in the interests of civilisation', Hughes added:

We were destined to have our own way from the beginning and America – two nations that have always had their way, for they killed everybody to get it. I declare to you that in no other way shall *we be able to come to our own except by preparing to hold that which we have now* . . . The people are incapable of nourishing abstract ideals. They must have a symbol. Here we have a symbol of nationality . . . The first historic event in the history of the Commonwealth we are engaged in today without the slightest trace of that race we have banished from the face of the earth. We must not be too proud lest we should, too, in time disappear.[60]

Prophetic concerns about maritime security were raised in a 1907 analysis by Director of Naval Forces Captain W. R. Creswell, an analysis which coincided with heightened concern about Japan and the efforts of the Australian government, against Admiralty wishes, to establish a separate Australian Navy. He concluded that 'uninterrupted sea communication is a *sine qua non* . . . Australia, whenever her coast routes are closed, must stop work'. The isolation which may have protected Australia from attack was 'rapidly diminishing' with the development of coaling stations and the growth of foreign navies. He feared future collusion between Japan or China and a European power: 'The very immensity of our lands opens up the chances of co-operation. German, Jap, and Chinese colonies could be carved out of the North and West of Australia.'[61]

Australian resentments about the British refusal to listen to its Pacific and Japanese concerns led to Deakin's invitation for Roosevelt's 'Great White Fleet' to visit Sydney Harbour in 1908 on its Pacific voyage. The next year Deakin proposed a formal extension of the Monroe Doctrine to the Pacific, which was resisted by Britain. Anxieties persisted through the renewal of the Anglo-Japanese Alliance in 1911, and fed considerable friction in the early years of the decade, as the Admiralty sought to meet a German naval build-up in the North Sea by entrusting the Far East to Japan. These ironies came to the fore during the Great War, when Britain asked the Japanese Navy to occupy the German North Pacific territories and patrol the waters of the Netherlands East Indies. As well as having responsibility for Australian sea lane security, the Japanese Navy also provided escort for Anzacs to Gallipoli.[62]

Having always been suspicious of Germany's Pacific presence, the Australian government leapt at the chance to occupy its bases in New Guinea and phosphate-rich Nauru. In August 1914 Australian forces took Rabaul, and by 17 September had obtained a German surrender of all its possessions north and south of the equator. These sweeping claims were bitter fruit for Australia, which was forced to accept the award of a mandate to Japan over the German North Pacific territories at the Versailles peace conference.[63]

The Great War would be a dark milestone in the imagination of a modern Australian identity. Indeed, others have gone further: in 1943, official historian Sir Ernest Scott asserted that it 'is beyond dispute' that 'the war was the pivotal event in the history of Australia'.[64] While it was certainly an enormous tragedy, we should not accept such claims at face value. A sense of proportion could be gained by considering that the number of Australians killed – almost 60 000 – while still a horrifying total, was well below the loss of Aboriginal life since white settlement. Rather, we might suspect that the narration of the war's historical importance bears a politics of its own. As if by some bizarre, terrible magic, potent and far-reaching myths of Australian character, realisation and purpose would be spun from the war's awful destruction.

In an echo of the deployments to the Sudan and South Africa, the decision to commit Australian forces was explained by Australia's ontological fusion with the British general will, and the obligation of men to enlist argued through the potent chain which, in perfect accord with Hobbes' and Hegel's fusion of state and subject, linked the abstract machinery of Empire with the very interior of the individual self. Like Barton – or, twenty-five years later, Sir Robert Menzies – Joseph Cook declared that 'when the Empire is at war, so is Australia at war'; Prime Minister Fisher vowed to help defend the 'mother country' to 'our last man and our last shilling'; and Billy Hughes declared this was 'a time when none shall be for the party, but all be for the state'. Almost alone among the elite, New South Wales Premier William Holman protested that Australians could 'not be plunged into calamities merely at the bidding of some irresponsible ruler' – but as Clark so eloquently remarked, 'he was a voice shouting into a gale'.[65]

For Sir Ernest Scott the expedition drew on a much deeper heritage, in which the juridical form of the state merged completely with its subjects' historical conditions of possibility:

> Their entire endowment of soil, freedom, tradition, language, nurture and protection came to them as a heritage from the empire to which they belonged. *A menace to that imperial integrity threatened their life*; and they took up arms to bear their share, not in refurbishing some antique grudge, or chastising some historic enemy, or acquiring more territory, but in vindicating obligations which were theirs because they were those of the sovereignty under which they had acquired and maintained their national existence.[66]

This was truly the meaning of Hobbes' and Locke's body politic: that we glorify it with our death and nourish it with our blood. To fully be a citizen within this discourse was to enter into a space of pain, fear and sacrifice which traced, at least in its form, a (Hegelian) movement of realisation at whose end both the individual – masculine, disciplined, courageous – and national subjects would reach their full maturity and take their place among the great of history.

Invoking a complex image of birth, spiritual passage and transfiguration, the *Sydney Morning Herald* described the war as 'a baptism', and in 1915, on the first anniversary of the landing at Gallipoli, the Anglican Archbishop of Sydney declared that 'April 25 was the date on which Australia suddenly found herself lifted to a place among the peoples'. At the Hotel Cecil in London, Hughes told Australian soldiers that their deeds had won them 'a place in the Temple of the Immortals', and that they had 'inspired generations yet unborn with 'pride of race, courage, tenacity of purpose, endurance, and that casting out of fear without which men, though boasting themselves free, are but wretched slaves'. They had, he said, taught that through 'sacrifice alone can men or nations be saved'.[67]

The price of such national realisation was high, and as Alistair Thompson has shown, many who survived the trenches found they could not recognise their experience in its public meaning.[68] Between the landing at Gallipoli in April and the end of the Dardanelles Campaign in December, 7818 Australians died,

40 per cent of those who fought, and in the attacks on Lone Pine alone 800 were killed or wounded, four out of five who were involved. Turkish casualties were even greater.[69] During the British offensive on the Somme in 1916, the Australians took 22 826 casualties in six weeks. After watching them trying to survive the German bombardment, C. E. W. Bean wrote in his diary that the men 'are simply turned in there as into some ghastly giant mincing machine'. After the fighting the British poet John Masefield walked the battlefield: 'There was a cat eating a man's brain . . . they were shovelling parts of men into blankets.'[70]

In April 1917 Britain's General Haig sent the Fourth Australian Division against the German line at Bullecourt, where the Australians took more than 10 000 casualties. Despite being brought to tears by the destruction, the Australian commander, General Birdwood, again wrote home for more men. Between July 1917 and the assault on Passchendaele in November, the AIF in France took another 38 093 casualties, 60 per cent of their strength. By the war's end, 215 585 Australians had become victims of the fighting, 59 342 of them killed in action or dying later of their wounds. Australia's proportionate losses, 65 per cent of their total in the field, were the highest of any Allied country.[71]

Even as casualties were reaching horrifying proportions, the British and Australian commands, supported by Prime Minister Hughes, sought to throw more men into the cauldron. Splitting the labour movement and exacerbating deep social divisions over the war, Hughes put two referenda – seeking a mandate to conscript more men – before the people. Both times, in October 1916 and December 1917, he failed.[72] His arguments that Australians 'were only free as long as Australia remained part and parcel of the British empire' failed to convince. Labor, radicals and the Catholic Church consistently opposed conscription, though often for differing and ironic reasons. In 1916 the *Labor Call* argued that while Europeans were butchering each other in Europe, Asia 'was waiting and grinning'. White Australia was being undermined: the future brought a prospect of millions of Asians invading a war-weakened Australia. Earlier, in 1914, the *Freeman's Journal* had worried that the Japanese Navy would seize Australia and New Zealand if war broke out in Europe. More telling were warnings that a pernicious militarism was being woven into the societal fabric: Labor warned that the Universal Service League was an effort to 'Prussionise democracy', and radicals pointed to the convergence of militarism and Capital in the profits being made from increased production of iron and steel for armaments, and from wool for the uniforms so many would wear into the afterlife.[73]

There were many signs that the war could be a threat to Australia's already flawed democracy. As the Trades Hall Council directed all unionists in December 1915 to ignore recruiting cards, the New South Wales police banned the sale of anti-war newspapers in the Sydney domain. Soldiers broke up anti-war meetings, and in response to a short anti-conscription strike in October 1916, Hughes ordered all government servants who struck to be prosecuted. Issues of the *Socialist* containing the Interstate Trade Union Congress's manifesto on conscription were suppressed, and the song 'I didn't raise my son to be a soldier' (sung at Women's Peace Army meetings) was outlawed.[74]

In Perth nine members of International Workers of the World (IWW) were tried and convicted of attempting to 'raise discontent and disaffection among subjects of the King', and in October 1916 twelve IWW members were arrested for a series of Sydney fires, receiving gaol terms of between ten and fifteen years. A 1920 Royal Commission later found six had been wrongfully convicted. Under the War Precautions Act, many German residents – whom Ernest Scott called 'the enemy within the gates' – were interned and some were deported, licences to publish German newspapers were revoked and the use of German in churches was prohibited. Shares owned by Germans were seized by the public trustee and later credited to the reparations account, and many others lost their jobs. Anti-war meetings were closed and their speakers arrested and fined. During the huge New South Wales railways strike of 1917 – which saw the loss of two and a half million working days – the Hughes government applied to the Industrial Commission for the deregistration of over twenty unions.[75] Further evidence of Hughes' culpability emerged in November 1920, when he was presented with a cheque for £25 000 – raised from business interests in Australia and Britain – for his services to the Empire and Australia during the war and at the peace conference in Versailles.[76]

Yet even as the war increased a whole series of dramatic divisions in Australian society, it was also being appropriated for the task of manufacturing a monolithic Australian subject: the 'Anzac tradition' was being born. The slaughter at Gallipoli had shown the mettle of the Australian character, and blooded the young nation into an adulthood fit for the twentieth century. The *Argus* newspaper wrote: 'It was there that our young and untried troops . . . quitted themselves as men', and Banjo Paterson, in his poem 'We're all Australians now', declared:

> The mettle that a race can show
> Is proved with shot and steel,
> And now we know what nations know
> And feel what nations feel.[77]

This view was retrospectively reinforced, in 1948, by official historian and founder of the Australian War Memorial C. E. W. Bean, who at the end of *Anzac to Amiens* argued that the real significance of the Australians' sacrifice:

> was to help materially in winning a prolongation of the security of the Victorian era for at least a part of the free world, including their own. But for Australia in particular they achieved something more. First they won her a recognised place among the nations; her seat on the League was given in direct acknowledgment of the part played by her forces. Second, though less commonly realised, was the bringing of a new confidence into Australia's national undertakings.[78]

His chapter 'The Anzac Legend' linked security, sovereignty and identity into a potent subjective and historical unity: 'If the cause that led Australians to enlist can be reduced to a single principle, it is the principle of protecting their homes and their freedom by sustaining a system of law and order between nations.' These words, activating the exchange between individualising and totalising power, linked the minutiae of domestic security to the immense clashes of geopolitics, sustaining a potent emotional appeal across a vast, abstract space of reason. The blackmail was overwhelming – while Bean admitted that the war failed to achieve a lasting peace, he argued that its prevention of a German victory was crucial to Australia's own security:

> If the struggle . . . had resulted in German victory, the first term in the peace treaty would have been the abolition of the British Navy; and for the Australian nation this meant either subservience to Germany or *extinction* at the hands of the Japanese.[79]

He concluded by asserting a general ontology of human progress and freedom – and of a fully realised Australian subject – which hinged on sacrifice in war: 'only in conditions ensuring freedom of thought and communication can mankind progress . . . such freedom can be maintained only by the qualities [with] which from Grecian times it has been won . . . the readiness at any time to die for freedom, if necessary, and the virility to struggle for it'. In fact, with the vast tragedy of the First World War a memory, eclipsed in scale by the horrors of the Second World War and the atom bomb,

> we have passed through the test which until now, unfortunately, has necessarily been judged by mankind as the supreme one for men fit to be free; and *we have emerged from that test with the Anzac tradition.* In the Second World War that tradition . . . nobly served humanity.[80]

In the dark dreams of such men Australia was now realised, more fully a nation among nations, more fully a subject that could enter into the progress and unity that would drive it onward, yet be somehow always beyond it. Its foundations and being were now more secure; as US President Woodrow Wilson was asserting *self-determination* as a new principle of human affairs, 'Australia' had achieved its own, through an ontology in which murder and pain and death took their piece and would not be denied.

Conclusion: Making an 'Australian' subject

This chapter has sought to trace the course of a momentous event: the establishment – through the deployment of a complex historical technology of *security* – of a Western civilisation and an overarching political, economic and juridical subject on a hitherto unknown continent in the southern ocean. At the same time, this space was constructed by an anxious cultural and strategic imagination marked by the overwhelming presence of the Other: a 'presence' crucial to a political subjectivity in which the individual and collective might be fused into a potent psychological totality. From the colony's very beginnings, as Aborigines were fought, dispossessed and murdered, to the fears of black and Asian immigration that underpinned Federation, to the demonisation of Germany and Japan through the Great War, a backward and threatening Other was essential to the Hegelian path of realisation that the new civilisation sought to tread.

While there was a general ontological consensus running through this history – one that linked security, prosperity, identity and the fear of others into an imagined national whole – I have also sought to show how a series of bitter conflicts were played out over what otherwise appeared to be common ground. Intense class conflict was central to the politics of both Federation and the Great War and, for conservatives and liberals, rhetorics of race and strategies of industrial management were integral to the politics of security that so preoccupied them. Here sovereignty, racism and political sameness combined as the means and desire of a technology which sought to contain, co-opt and weaken the labour movement. If the political limits of the Constitution, the disabling splits in the Labor Party and the deaths of tens of thousands of unionists on the battlefields of Europe were any guide, by 1918 these tactics had been a dramatic success. Worse, with the establishment of Anzac Day on the anniversary of the Gallipoli landing by the newly formed Returned Sailors and Soldiers Imperial League, a retrospective construction of the meaning of their deaths would play into conservative hands. A special day of remembrance was obviously due them, and for Australians ever since it has become a potent symbol of unity and debt in a nation apparently otherwise lacking unequivocal symbols of its own meaning. Yet as controversy has been bled from their memory by the disciplinary rhetoric of respect, the 'governmental' chain linking sacrifice, nationalism and subjectivity has been strengthened. To recall the disputes and bitterness surrounding the diggers' struggle is not to disrespect them, but to rescue their experience from mythmaking and cynicism; to think that they might deserve more than a circular, self-justifying narrative that does little more than laud the necessity of their deaths.

Manning Clark concluded the fifth volume of his history with a reflection on the public meaning of Gallipoli and Anzac, concluding bitterly that 'Australia's day of glory had made her a prisoner of her past, rather than the architect of a new future for humanity.'[81] While echoing the way the carnage of the war would disturb the West's conviction of its own enlightenment, the statement also underlined the significance of the war – and the war's narration – for the future. The grafting of the myth on to a day of remembrance guaranteed its annual repetition, as its significance increased with each successive conflict and the lengthening roll of the dead. As the retrospective constructions of Bean's and Scott's *Official History* show, such repetition ensured that the events of the war – with all their confusion, conflict and abjection – became ossified into a terrible weight of tradition. In turn future policies and representations, when linked with the Anzac tradition, took on a heavy air of inevitability. Who could argue, when it was the nation's very *being* that was at stake?

Yet this obsession with narrating the past as tradition betrays the instability of the whole enterprise, the way the narrative effacement of social conflict can be undermined by that conflict's retelling, and thus allow the re-emergence of modes and moments of subjectivity which don't conform with the monolithic imaginary of the unified body politic. It is this anxiety about control over the past that underpins later political attempts to link this founding period with new manipulations of collective identity. Almost eighty years later, Labor Prime Minister Paul Keating thought 'the spirit of Anzac' could be retained, but not stifle the need for change; he thought that Australia's founding identity, formed at Federation, could be 'reshaped' into a form 'consistent with the multicultural reality' of 1990s Australia and 'the final passing of the vestiges of our colonial past'.[82] His successor, John Howard, in a deliberate rebuke, maintained that Australians did not face a choice between their history and their geography.[83] As Ann Curthoys and John Docker remind us, history is never settled and its meaning is never fixed, but its profound ethical and political importance remains.[84] The past deserves respect, a respect rarely shown by self-interested political actors who attempt to reduce its complexity to simplistic narratives of partisan purpose, and who disregard the *aporia* that separates the future from the past and the past from its meaning. In 1948 Charles Bean thought the Anzac tradition was very much alive, and that its meaning and purpose were clear: it had 'nobly served humanity' in the Second World War. It is to that story that we now turn.

2

Dreams of Pacific security 1919–45

Have those who think Australia remote from the world which hatches dangers and wars ever looked at the map? . . . So far from being removed from the busy hive of men we live almost within hail of its greatest populations. We have nailed 'White Australia' to the top of the mast. Yet we are but a tiny drop in a coloured ocean.

W. M. Hughes, 14 August 1916[1]

At the close of the Great War a powerful myth of Australian character and realisation had been achieved, at the price of tens of thousands of lives and unprecedented upheaval and division. In addition, 'Australia' had new international status – not as a 'great power' but as an internationally recognised subject whose claims on Pacific territory and international norms would demand, and find, a hearing. The Anzac tradition was already at work: when his status was challenged by Woodrow Wilson at Versailles, Hughes replied that he spoke for 60 000 dead.[2] Were they to see this moment, they would learn that they had endured the cold and filth of the trenches, the lice and poison gas, thrown their bodies before machine-gun fire and shrapnel until they were stopped, so that the old things could continue: a white Australia, a defensive buffer of Pacific territory, the 'crimson thread of kinship'. The diggers' sacrifices won Australia independent representation at the peace conference and Hughes much influence within the British delegation. He chaired the British committee on reparations, backing the desire of Britain's Prime Minister Lloyd George and France's Clemenceau for a punishing bill, regardless of Germany's ability to pay; he successfully fought Japan, with quiet support from Britain and the US, to keep a clause entrenching racial equality out of the League of Nations charter. Yet Australia was now saddled with a further £350 million in war-induced debt, 83 per cent of the total national debt in 1920, and would recover just £5 million from the settlement.[3]

With the historic fear of Japan in mind, Hughes had gone to Versailles with direct orders from the Nationalist Cabinet to seek the permanent annexation of New Guinea, New Britain and the other German Pacific colonies. At the conference he unrolled a large map, declaring that the islands 'encompassed Australia like fortresses' and contained potential coaling stations and submarine bases. He repeated the argument he had made in London earlier that year that they were 'necessary for our security, safety and freedom'. In New York in 1918 he had claimed that 'in this we do not desire empire', but a more revealing opinion came from the chairman of Burns Philp – which had long coveted the islands' copra plantations and trade potential – who declared that their 'natural destiny' was 'that they should come under the control of Australia'. Blocked by Wilson's belief in self-determination, Hughes failed to achieve annexation, but accepted the British proposal for a 'C-class mandate', which gave Australia control of the South Pacific territories under weak League of Nations supervision. The economic motives driving Australian policy became clear in the case of Nauru, when Hughes negotiated a compromise in which Australia administered a British mandate and the UK, New Zealand and Australian governments bought out the phosphate mining interests and shared the ensuing bounty among them. Hughes' treasurer, W. A. Watt, told him the phosphates were essential for the development of Australian productivity.[4]

As well as an enhanced geopolitical purchase, the new Australian subjectivity was gathering greater ontological depth. On his return to Australia Hughes was mobbed by crowds of diggers, and by 1919 the membership of the Returned Sailors and Soldiers Imperial League had reached 150 000. A new conservative consensus was being forged around a war-inspired nationalism: Keith Murdoch argued that only an independent 'Australianism' could counter the 'anti-Australian' forces of Bolshevism and Sinn-Feinism, while Hughes opened the 1919 federal election – which the Nationalists won by a landslide – by questioning the loyalty of the ALP. 'Let our watchword be *Australia*,' he intoned, 'as our splendid boys have fought for it and saved it, let us all live and work for it.' On Empire

Day in 1921 a crowd of 150 000 gathered in Sydney to affirm their loyalty to the Union Jack and their abhorrence of all those who would fly the 'red flag' instead. As the historian Stuart Macintyre argues, nationalism had ceased to be a force for change, but 'was increasingly identified with the *status quo*'.[5]

Yet for all its depth and force, the Australian subject was still an illusion, a product of political and cultural imagination. Its claim to unity and culmination papered over bitter religious, industrial and political conflicts that would only worsen as the nation drifted towards the Great Depression and the Second World War. Surveying the two and a half decades to 1945, one is struck by a paradox: a general strengthening of the ontological force of the Australian subject, through a period when its discursive power was shaken by unprecedented industrial upheaval and social animosity. The experience (and later the narration) of war with Japan fulfilled fears that had surged through the Australian identity since the 1890s, elevating a shadowy image of the Other to the status of an ontological truth – an event with far-reaching cultural and strategic consequences. In a similar way, the war-led recovery in the economy, the constant political demands for patriotism in the face of a threatening and alien enemy, and the Labor government's management of industrial conflict may have mitigated social resentments and divisions. The prewar consensus on the 'crimson thread of kinship' would come under stress as early as the 1920s, and be irrevocably torn by the experience of the 1940s, even as the image of White Australia was strengthened by war with an Asian power.

Security and its enemies: Postwar politics and diplomacy

Hughes returned home in 1919, to a terrible influenza epidemic and massive industrial turmoil. In April, 2000 men and women had clashed violently with armed police on the wharves in Perth. Thirty-three were injured, one man was killed and another speared with a bayonet, while West Australia Premier Hal Colbatch – who had assembled and armed the police with rifles and batons – was pelted with road metal and old iron. By the end of the year 6.3 million days had been lost in strikes and lockouts. The miners' strike at

Broken Hill lasted eighteen months, from May 1919 to November 1920, and a seamen's strike forced the introduction of rationing in some areas.[6]

Speaking in the House in September, to a motion proposing that the Australian Parliament accept the Treaty of Versailles, Hughes would interpret the vast sacrifice of Australians in this new industrial context. Just as the diggers had given Australia 'liberty', 'safety' and 'a name that will not die', the path to salvation lay in political sameness and the productive compliance of liberal subjectivity:

> Industrially, socially, politically, we cannot escape the consequences of the war. The whole world lies bleeding and exhausted from the frightful struggle. There is no way of salvation, save by the gospel of work. Those who endeavour to set class against class, or to destroy wealth, are counsellors of destruction.[7]

This appeal to unity, using the language of the 'political double-bind', came as the class war in Australia took on an appearance of unrelenting permanence, and political leaders spoke more and more in terms that would partition reality into stark, irreconcilable polarities. Hughes himself had set a precedent during the conscription campaigns, when he cast an unholy alliance of Bolsheviks, socialists, the IWW, Sinn Fein and Bishop Mannix against White Australia, liberty and the Empire.[8]

Reaction became national policy under the new Nationalist-Country Party coalition of S. M. Bruce and Earle Page. By 1920 the economy was in recession due to its dependence on exports to a war-sapped Britain. While different sectors of capital were divided on the virtues of protection, they were united in their desire to drive down wages and increase the hours of work, placing the system of conciliation and arbitration under tremendous stress. Reaction was also accompanied by grander visions of national development to match the nation's new geopolitical subjectivity. Prior to the 1923 Imperial Conference, Bruce began to outline his vision.

Defence he marked as the State's first priority, to which end he intended to raise an imperial naval defence scheme: '[W]e can only defend this country,' he argued, 'if we are inside the empire.' While the tug of the 'crimson thread' remained strong, it was no longer so binding: '[W]e cannot blindly submit to a policy which may involve us in war.' This change had become visible in September

1922, when the Hughes government refused Lloyd George's request for an Australian contingent to defend Constantinople from attack by the Turks. In addition to defence, Bruce spoke of the need – if Australia were 'to be a progressive country' – to accelerate the application of science to industry, secure uniform rail gauges, develop the Murray River valley, improve transport and communications, and resolve 'the Northern Territory problem'. This last dilemma had haunted Australians for decades: 'We have to hold this gateway into Australia from the north. We must attempt to populate it and try to develop it.'[9] This in turn would require the development of Australia's pastoral and mining industries, highlighting the way in which the dispossession of Aboriginal people – and the need to make the land productive within a liberal economic ontology – was driven by an ongoing security obsession.

The great slogan became 'Men, Money and Markets', which in Bruce's mind drew the nation ever closer to the imperial bosom. While protection was a central plank, Australia must look to England for markets for the vast surplus of agricultural production, and for capital, and for white immigrants to help develop the nation's industry and interior. The umbilical cord of mutual history and the sacrifices of the war gave Australians special claims: he pointed out that 'we expect from the Motherland some additional consideration for what we have done', and in London later that year told a business audience: 'You brought us into existence. You have some responsibility for us and you cannot shirk it.'[10] As the writer William Lines demonstrates, the idea that immigration was essential for Australia's future security and prosperity owed much to the vision of E. J. Brady, whose 1918 book *Australia Unlimited* predicted the possibility of an eventual Australian population of up to 500 million: 'A sufficient population *must* be established in the Northern Territory, in South Australia, and in Western Australia to ensure permanent, effective occupation, and a realisation of the white Australia policy.' Japan, as it was for Hughes at the dedication of Canberra in 1913, was the unspoken shadow giving emotional form to his words.[11]

During 1923, Victoria, New South Wales and Western Australia signed agreements with the British and Commonwealth governments to join the Imperial Land Settlement scheme. It was a vast failure: by June 1924 group settlement in Western Australia was suspended, after 32 per cent of the immigrants and 42 per cent of the white Australians had abandoned their blocks. Forty thousand hectares of forest had been destroyed.[12] Similar heartbreak ensued for many soldiers who took to the land under postwar settlement schemes, their incomes foundering on falling commodity prices through the 1920s, along with their own paucity of skills, capital and experience. By 1930, 10 000 had abandoned the land, with accumulated losses of £23.5 million, and more were to leave in despair during the Depression. In part the immigration schemes worked in favour of British self-interest: they were accompanied by vast new government borrowings from London and increasing levels of British investment in both public and private capital. During the 1920s state and federal governments borrowed enormous sums for settlement schemes and infrastructure, amounts which reached £672 million by 1927 – given these figures, and the dependence on commodity markets, this phase of growth was built on highly unstable foundations.[13]

Yet as British money and Bruce's faith in imperial defence added new strength to the 'crimson thread of kinship', that same thread was being questioned as a material and symbolic locus of Australian security and identity. In his 1921 book *Money Power*, Labor's Frank Anstey claimed that Australia would one day face 'terrible retribution' as its debts to the money men of London piled higher. Bruce's policy of borrowing for development, he warned, was leading the nation into the abyss.[14] In turn federal Labor leader James Scullin made an unprecedented attack on the imperial assumptions of Australian foreign policy. The bipartisan patriotism that existed in 1914 was now a mirage: after chiding Bruce for travelling 12 000 miles 'in search of a foreign policy', Scullin questioned the conduct of the Great War by the Allied governments. He railed against the 'marvellous hypocrisy of secret diplomacy' revealed in a collection of documents, the *British White Book*, and 'the atrocious conspiracy . . . to impose upon Australia Prussian militarism in the form of conscription'.[15]

Citing the 1917 resolution of the federal Labor Conference which called for peace by negotiation, in a formula remarkably similar to Wilson's fourteen points, Scullin pointed out that in the eighteen months between that Conference and the settlement, four million had been added to the dead and fifteen million to 'the maimed, broken and maddened'. They died, he said, because of the secret treaties 'entered into before war was declared – treaties which were not made known even to the British Cabinet':

> Those treaties provided that the war must continue even after overtures came from Germany and Austria, until Italy could be given Trentino, France Alsace–Lorraine, Russia a warm port in the south, and Britain certain influence in Mesopotamia. All that while the men of Australia were being told from recruiting platforms all over the country that they were to go across the seas to defend little bleeding Belgium, and that they were fighting for principles which would make the world safe for democracy . . . the Versailles Treaty which followed will go down in history as one of the worst huckstering, haggling, sordid pieces of bargaining ever made in the history of the world.[16]

It was a devastating critique, and after it few things could remain the same. However slowly it would occur, the first shudderings of a tectonic shift of discursive ground were being felt. Yet Scullin also feared an earthquake: he wanted the 'silken ties of kinship' to endure and grow, but to be free of the blackmail between leaving the Empire or being 'dragged at its heels in every European war . . . I warn the Prime Minister and other swashbuckling Imperialists that the Australian Democracy will stand by the silken ties of kinship which have endured for so long but will not consent to the cast-iron bonds of imperialism which such people attempt to place upon her.'[17]

Speaking a few days before, Bruce shared Scullin's concerns about Empire unity, and had his own anxieties about the lack of consultation which preceded Australia's entry into the conflagration. Yet he accepted the constitutional fact that membership of the Empire meant being at war when Britain was; this dilemma he now sought to manage through the development of mechanisms in which the dominions might be consulted *before* Britain made its policy. To survive, imperial integrity required new machinery: 'We have to try to maintain unity of the whole and complete autonomy of the different parts.' While Bruce now sought more discretion – following the Turkish crisis of 1922 – over the deployment of Australian forces abroad, the crux for him was Australian defence, which was assured by neither the League of Nations nor the Washington arms limitation agreements. Whereas Scullin suggested it would be possible for Australia to prepare for its own defence, and advocated a greater faith in the League, Bruce argued that only a naval force – the promise of a British fleet base at Singapore – would provide security.[18] As ever, Japan was the unspoken fear. In 1920 Australia's most senior military officers argued that Japan remained 'the only potential and probable enemy', and that Japan's naval superiority could 'delay almost vitally the arrival of help in Australia. So advantaged, it is probable she could land troops at almost any place desired on the Australian coast, continue to reinforce them, and supply them with fresh munitions.' Australians should feel particularly vulnerable, because the White Australia policy could 'be made a *casus belli* apart from all other considerations'.[19]

Ensuring the security of White Australia meant that the control of Aborigines remained a priority. Having achieved the general submission of the indigenous population through counter-insurgency in the previous century, this period saw a massive intensification of control through a disciplinary and coercive machinery applied to enforce the separation of 'full bloods' from the white society and genetic pool. Under the guise of 'protection', various provisions of state and Commonwealth law prevented Aborigines from working for wages, or marrying or living with a non-Aborigine without permission of the State. Others enabled the prosecution of non-Aborigines cohabiting with Aborigines and of Aborigines found with firearms.[20]

It was during this period that the enforced removal of children from Aboriginal families began. C. D. Rowley explains how

> Governments with large 'full-blood' populations tried by means of segregation to limit further part-Aboriginal births. At the same time they came to formulate policies which involved the disappearance of part-Aborigines through miscegenation. Conveniently the 'full-bloods' seemed to be dying out; the part-Aborigines were to be placed in such situations that there would eventually be no traces of them.[21]

It was nothing less than an attempt at genocide: Bruce urged South Australia to accept babies, as 'they would not know in later life that they had Aboriginal blood and would probably be absorbed into the white population and become useful citizens'. Less controlled forms of violence also continued: in August 1928 a Northern Territory police party led by William Murray massacred as many as a hundred men, women and children near Coniston in revenge for the killing of a white settler; Murray was exonerated by a federal Board of Enquiry. At this time William Cooper, an elder from Echuca in Victoria, formed the Australian Aborigines League to fight for Aboriginal franchise, parliamentary representation and land rights.[22]

As these historic images of the Other were being solidified in Australia's cultural lexicon, disciplinary machinery and strategic planning, another was being conjured from the deepening crisis in industrial and economic management. Previously a vague outline, this 'enemy within' was taking on a solid mythical form, in a premonition of its future presence at the very core of the Australian identity. Its name was communism – and in its spectre conservatives found a threat to social order, morality, progress and the sacred institutions of property and entrepreneurial risk. Earlier Bruce had worried that 'Bolsheviks' might thwart efforts to force down wages, efforts that were meant to make Australian industry more internationally competitive. Again the liberal problematic of 'government' appeared: the radicals might utilise the freedoms of a democratic society and the resentment of workers to foment revolution.[23] Yet in the angry mood of the time, Bruce's 'businessmen's government' eschewed the co-optive liberal strategy of Deakin and Reid which had previously sought to contain and moderate class antagonisms.

In June 1925 Bruce tried to amend the Immigration Act, to create powers that would enable the deportation of immigrants who engaged in industrial militancy. His language – and the Bill's whole conceptual framework – brought into play the totalising and individualising technology of subjectivity that was central to *security* as a modern strategy of power. One clause enabled the deportation of any immigrant convicted of 'an offence against the laws of the Commonwealth relating to trade and commerce or conciliation and arbitration', particularly if the minister felt the immigrant's actions hindered the transport industry or were 'injurious to the peace, order and good government of the Commonwealth'. Another enabled the deportation of anyone who advocated the overthrow by force of 'the established government of the Commonwealth' or preached 'the unlawful destruction of property', and even extended to anyone who was 'a member of or affiliated with' an organisation with such goals.[24]

Bruce claimed these were merely emergency measures which would 'only be applied in times of great industrial turmoil'. Declaring that the 'amendments are designed entirely to benefit the community as a whole', he pitted a harmonious collective identity against a pernicious and alien otherness:

> . . . among those coming into Australia are a number of persons of alien race and blood who, although we offer to them the opportunity to enjoy our citizenship, refuse to become Australians, do not recognise our ideals, and are not absorbed into our national life . . . they voice here false doctrines and ideas and refer to social conditions in a language that is absolutely inapplicable to any that exist in Australia. Being thus prejudiced, they carry on a propaganda of a most insidious nature . . . it is absolutely dangerous to the national life of our country.[25]

Although Bruce's words were deliberately vague, he was clearly speaking of communism. The Bill was a brazen attempt to build an unscaleable legal and ideological fence around a possible 'Australian' subjectivity, and to trigger the use of force against those deemed to exist outside its boundaries. They and their 'poisonous propaganda' could be expelled from the social body, much as 160 000 convicts were removed from Britain and sent to Australia during its first hundred years. A month after the assent to the new Act George Pearce, Minister of State for Home and Territories, invoked its powers during a waterfront strike. In November two officials of the Seamen's Union were marked for deportation. The High Court later ruled that the legislation was unconstitutional.[26]

In January 1926 Bruce's Attorney-General, J. G. Latham, introduced another Bill to amend the Crimes Act. This Bill provided for the deportation of seditious aliens or, if Australian-born, their imprisonment for up to two years. Proscribed were organisations which advocated the violent overthrow of any state or Commonwealth government, the 'injury of property of the Commonwealth or of property used in trade or commerce with other countries or among the states'. Most alarming was a fantastically sweeping clause which provided – in the event of a proclamation of a 'serious industrial disturbance' by the Governor-General – for the deportation or imprisonment for up to a year of anyone involved in a lock-out or strike 'in connexion with' the transport of goods or passengers in overseas or interstate trade or in 'the provision of any public service by the Commonwealth'. Labor's Matthew Charlton, after hearing this clause read, rightly protested that 'every trade union leader can be brought in under that section'.[27]

For all the state violence and activism, there was nonetheless an air of desperation about the measures, as the liberal consensus was swept away and the labour movement responded with greater militancy: between 1924 and 1927 the number of working days lost annually rose from 900 000 to 1.2 million, and reached a phenomenal 4.5 million in 1929. Security – as an effective tool in the management of industrial populations, social order and economic prosperity – was beginning to look like a chimera. Rising unemployment was paralleled by a steady fall in commodity prices which, coupled with the vast loan obligations, put untenable pressure on the nation's foreign reserves. In 1929, as the destructive wave of the Depression built and stood ready to break, Bruce proposed to remove the Commonwealth entirely from the realm of conciliation and arbitration, only retaining jurisdiction over the maritime industry and the public service. Despite his hope that it might strengthen the hand of employers, this measure split his party and was defeated on the floor. Labor – now able to portray itself as the defender of living standards, sound finance and industrial peace – won the ensuing election.[28]

Yet Labor's day in the sun was short-lived. With the economy already in grave trouble, the Wall Street Crash heralded a storm from which no society could hope to take shelter. Wheat and wool markets plunged by 50 per cent – export incomes fell 30 per cent between 1929 and 1930 alone. Multiplier effects surged through the economy causing job losses, business failures and a vast contraction in demand. Unemployment exploded to over 30 per cent by the middle of 1932. Between 1929 and 1930 GDP fell 10 per cent, and by August 1930 short-term debt had ballooned to £38 million, long-term overseas debt being £567 million. Reserves were pitifully low.[29]

Australia's level of borrowing and its exposure to international commodity markets had made it particularly vulnerable, and as the crisis wore on it became bitterly clear that security – whether that of the daily welfare of individuals or of the 'economy' as a whole – lay hostage to the whims of foreign bankers and the vicissitudes of global economic forces. In Australia class conflict only deepened as British and domestic capital both fought to stem their losses, while internationally the Depression slid inexorably into global war.

In the ensuing years Australia's political life became paralysed by a bitter struggle over the direction of economic policy. In 1931 the Labor government split and Scullin's Treasurer, Joe Lyons, won the ensuing elections at the helm of the new conservative United Australia Party (UAP). He immediately imposed the deflationary medicine demanded by foreign bankers and agreed to at that year's Premiers' Conference – cuts in public expenditure of 20 per cent across all programs and 12.5 per cent for pensions. By that time as few as half the workforce had full-time jobs and two-thirds of all breadwinners received an income less than the basic wage. Unemployed families lived on *half* a basic wage – already pegged at their 'minimum essential requirements' – and that was made up largely of ration coupons. Eviction riots became common.[30] While the economy was technically in recovery by 1932, high levels of unemployment and vast social misery continued for the rest of the decade. At Ottawa and in London the States' managers had had to beg for new markets and the conversion of loans, while at home the new millions of poor remained at the mercy of the same wolves. More and more, 'security' seemed to hinge on the caprice of a vast, opaque and systemic impersonality which mocked the age's Cartesian pretence at mastery.

The riddle of the sphinx: Japan's frustrations and ambitions

The economic disasters of the 1930s were shadowed by a steady drift to war. In Australia this focused attention on Japan – as the Chiefs of Staff's 1920 report showed, Japan had emerged early as Australia's foremost potential antagonist. Yet by the time Australians were fighting and dying on the Asian mainland, in Papua New Guinea or at their own borders, few would appreciate the systemic forces which drove Japan to colonisation – the very same desire for economic progress and security which Australian elites had marked out as their own. Ironically enough, it was Hughes who issued a prescient early warning in 1921:

> [Japan] wants both room . . . and markets for her manufactured goods. And she wants these very badly indeed. America and Australia say to her millions 'Ye cannot enter in'. Japan, then, is faced with the great problem which has bred wars since time began . . . [she] sees across a narrow strip of water 400 million Chinese gradually wakening to an appreciation of Western methods, and she sees in China the natural market for her goods . . . But other countries want the market too, and so comes the demand for the 'Open Door' . . . This is the problem of the Pacific – the modern riddle of the Sphinx, for which we must find an answer.[31]

Prescient enough, if stubborn in its refusal to pose a solution to its own 'riddle' and betraying the general Western inflexibility which, by 1941, would bear as much responsibility for the outbreak of war as did the ruthlessness of Japan's military rulers. The causal chain in the drift to war is a complex one, and is further complicated by the desperate struggle for economic survival unleashed by the Depression. Yet by the time Western countries were seriously seeking to restrain Japanese militarism after the invasions of China, Korea and Indochina, the League-style sanctions on strategic materials appeared indistinguishable from economic self-interest.

During the 1920s many felt Japan was safely contained within the League of Nations, the Washington Agreements and the Kellogg Pact; by 1934, when Japan had taken control of Manchuria, Jehol and Shanghai and withdrawn from the League and the Washington Agreements, there were stronger grounds for alarm. In 1935 the Director of the Prime Minister's Department, Pacific Branch, E. L. Piesse, said the Royal Navy would be inadequate, and advocated greater defence preparations – particularly land and air forces – but remained presciently calm about Japan's intentions towards Australia. While it was likely Japan would 'extend her Empire towards Australia', that was 'far short of saying that she plans to annex Australia. For that there is scarcely any evidence; and in our view of her needs it would seem most unlikely that she has any such plan'.[32]

By 1935–36 Australia's trade surplus with Japan funded over a third of Australia's interest payments. The 1936 Trade Diversion policy, biased towards London, could not have failed to annoy Japan, and was implemented at a time, according to the historian C. A. Hawker, when 'credit difficulties had filled the public mind of Japan with an almost feverish sense of the urgency of making overseas sales'. Likewise, official historian Lionel Wigmore has argued: 'Australia had contributed to the fear on which Japan's expansionists were able to play that she was being excluded from the world's markets, and might be deprived of means of existence as an industrial nation.'[33]

The Lyons government responded to Japanese imperialism in Manchuria with appeasement. According to T. B. Millar, it did so because they were 'relieved that Japan had struck north-west rather than south. Subsequently the Lyons government assured a visiting Japanese mission that Japan had *carte blanche* in Manchuria.' Anxious that the US would not come to Australia's aid in a crisis, now External Affairs Minister George Pearce told the US Consul-General that Australia had to be 'friendly with Japan, to give her no excuse to adopt an aggressive policy vis-à-vis the Commonwealth, and to rejoice (irrespective of the moral aspect) every time Japan advanced more deeply into Manchukuo and North China. [We] hope that her energies would be absorbed there for a generation.'[34]

When war broke out in Europe, the enduring fact of the imperial tie was underlined by Menzies, who told Australians on 4 September 1939: 'It is my melancholy duty to inform you officially that in consequence of the persistence of Germany in her invasion of Poland, Great Britain has declared war upon her, and that as a result, Australia is also at war.' Labor, while reaffirming 'its traditional horror of war', stated that it would 'do its utmost to maintain the integrity of the British Commonwealth'. Menzies' action derived from no personal revulsion at the Nazi regime. Both he and Lyons had supported appeasement of Germany, and after visiting Berlin in 1938 he wrote to Lyons of his fears that 'Czechoslovakian President Edward Benes, egged on by France, will refuse to do the fair thing and trouble may ensue'.[35]

Strategic anxieties about the Pacific and Indian ocean areas immediately affected Australian decisions on its commitment to the war in Europe. Two RAN cruisers and five destroyers were placed under control of the Royal Navy, despite anxieties about Japan using the opportunity to launch attacks on Australian Pacific dependencies. Australia believed that Singapore would be at risk should Britain not reinforce it, and that the Netherlands East Indies (NEI) would be an attractive target for Japan if Germany invaded the Netherlands. By 1940 Australia had decided to declare war on Japan if it invaded the NEI, and allocated some of its expanding war production to New Zealand and the Netherlands. In February 1941 Roosevelt told the British that the US would be unlikely to enter the war if Japan attacked only British or Dutch possessions, and that if they did, they would fight a 'holding war' in the Pacific while sending forces and materiel to the Atlantic theatre. Soon after this statement was made, the US transferred part of its Pacific fleet to the Atlantic. Australian commitments to the Atlantic theatre were also dictated by British strategic interests: three Australian divisions were deployed to the Middle East to reinforce the Mediterranean–Suez–Indian Ocean route, and to help Britain maintain its control over Palestine, the Iranian oilfields and the north-west frontier of India. Australian troops were reluctantly deployed to Malaya and Singapore in late 1940.[36]

As 1941 wore on, Japan – obsessed with access to oil supplies as a guarantee of its naval power – became antagonised by the US tactic of 'using appeasement to mask slow strangulation', backed by an oil embargo and restrictions on shipping which would limit its ability to import oil. Japan sought guarantees of access to supplies from the NEI, serving notice on the NEI administration in September 1940 that it would need three million tons of oil per year over the next five years, and demanding concessions that would make it independent of Stanvac and Royal Dutch Shell. The attacks on Pearl Harbor, and later on Darwin and Broome, were designed to neutralise threats to the Japanese Navy and provide 'six months to secure the oil and refineries of the Netherlands East Indies'. Japanese forces landed in Borneo on 21 January 1942 and in Sumatra on 15 February, only to find that workers at the Stanvac refinery in Palembang had burned the plant, sealed the wells and cut the pipelines.[37]

The Pacific war: Security, identity and the Other

The automatic declaration of war in 1939, the faith in the Royal Navy and the swift dispatch of forces to protect the lifelines of imperial trade and capital, suggest that Australia's immersion in the greater subjectivity of the imperial body politic was still an overwhelming fact. Once again, Australians had been sent to defend 'peace and order' in Europe, even as Menzies feared that 'millions of French and British lives will be lost, and . . . the economic force which will be our ultimate weapon will tend to affect us as severely as it does Germany'. As he had made clear in his correspondence to Lyons earlier that year, the conflict was not a moral one: 'it is really quite indefensible for us to be dictating to the German people what sort of government they shall have'.[38] Labor supported the declaration of war, yet opposition leader John Curtin opposed the immediate dispatch of the AIF for Europe, with a major element of his concern being Australia's own defence, particularly if the Netherlands were invaded and a vacuum thus appeared in the East Indies.[39]

Memories of the Great War and its effect on the labour movement also weighed on his mind. He was concerned by the possible impact of the new National Security Act, under which the government was already deciding which meetings could be held, and in November 1939 he warned:

> The paramount thing in this war is that, however the war ends, its termination must see in Australia a united, well-organised, clear-thinking Labor movement, so that the trophies of victory won't just be for non-workers . . . war might smash this party again – conscription would tear us apart as before – we may get our political opportunity and wedges will be driven in our ranks by every militant, every militarist, every politician, every opportunist. We, Australia, you, the party, me, the movement, we're all threatened.[40]

Earlier that month he spoke of his concerns about the effects of the war on the class structure, both internationally and in Australia. Aware of the potential of war and nationalism to strengthen the hand of Capital, he outlined Labor's vision of the postwar political and economic order, at least as it stood in 1939:

> It is not the reshaping of maps and territories that is our concern.
> Our concern is for peace, security and safety, and economic order of
> the type that Labor believes is the foundation upon which peace is
> practicable . . . Our conception of national unity, which we regard as
> imperative in ensuring the maximum strength in time of war, does not
> imply that we condone profiteering and exploitation, or any violation
> of the civic liberties of the people . . . we must not allow the instruments
> of production and exchange to be used to build up economic power
> for a privileged class in our own country.[41]

This discourse – with its rhetoric of unity, its concern for governmental reason and strength, and its belief in a war for freedom – is clearly recognisable as a vision of *security*, but it was one with important differences from the one harboured by the conservatives. It will be worth recalling later, when the government led by Curtin's successor, Joseph Benedict Chifley, was in a position' to influence the postwar order – with the objective of realising just this vision of security. Then Australia would still struggle to assert its voice and autonomy in international affairs, whether in their diplomatic, economic or strategic dimensions.

A revealing account of what was at stake in 1939 has been provided by official historian (later Liberal Minister for Foreign Affairs and Governor-General) Sir Paul Hasluck. Opening the first of his two volumes, *The Government and the People*, he argued that as *security* had now become so crucial, national identity was a paramount political consideration. The major significance of the war, he declared, was that 'it made Australia face up to the double challenge of national survival':

> the two great practical tests of economic and social responsibility and
> of national security, and the far more searching test of the strength
> of those spiritual forces which hold a people together as a nation,
> giving the nation a reason for its being, an identity and purpose . . . Its
> people had to come together as one people in one effort. It came to
> understand in more brutal terms what its claim to nationhood meant
> and to meet the stark and single issue of survival.[42]

In 1939, he argued, 'Australia' stood on the edge of the conflict as a problematic unity. While nationalism had been 'fervent' in

1914, 'nationhood was still the bold outline of an idea rather than a completed structure, a manifesto rather than a fact'. Twenty-five years later, the Depression had dramatically weakened the sense of 'pride' and 'accomplishment' achieved by the spirit of Anzac: the ideal of 'mateship' was dimmed by the new meaning given to the 'class struggle', while the punishing interest paid to London made Australians see 'the overseas investor, usually a British investor, as unfriendly'. Of particular concern was the new class-consciousness which, 'when carried to the point of class antagonism, tend[ed] to undermine mutual trust, to set the claims of class above the claims of all the people, and thus to weaken the identity of common interests and purposes on which national loyalties are nurtured'.[43]

Nationalism was above all a political technology, with implications both for the conduct of the war and for a future societal order. In its turn, the way in which the war was conducted, experienced and narrated could affect national unity. The anxiety was over class and national power, and over a task of administration which stretched from the vast mobilisation of national populations and resources to the inner beliefs of individuals – beliefs which now, aggravated by the 'personal hardship and disappointment' of the Depression, were poisoned by 'bitterness, resentment, and a cynical lack of enthusiasm'. How was such a population to be roused? How could such a disparate array of interests and subjectivities – not to mention their leaders – be convinced of their responsibilities to 'the precarious existence of a small nation in a world of power'?[44]

Japan's invasion of Indochina in 1940, and its attack on Pearl Harbor and landings in Malaya in December 1941, were particularly disturbing to the Australian strategic imagination. Prior to that, a sense of security had hinged on the promise of the British fleet based in Singapore and on the continuity of French control in Indochina, British in Malaya, American in the Philippines and Dutch in the Indonesian archipelago. Imperialism represented both political stability and the natural order of things; the brutalities meted out by colonial powers were of little moment. Thus the long-feared rise of an Asian power was as much a potent psychological shock as a geopolitical setback.

Australia's constitutional immersion in the imperial body politic, and its identification of security with the Western imperial status quo, coalesced in the declaration of war with Japan on 9 December 1941. It was made, Curtin said, because 'Japanese naval and air forces launched an unprovoked attack on *British* and *United States* territory' (emphasis added). Further reasons were, he added without irony, 'because our vital interests are imperilled and because the rights of free people in the Pacific are assailed'. The psychological trauma became even more acute after the fall of Singapore on 15 February 1942, with the accompanying loss of 18 000 troops as prisoners of war, and the consolidation of Japan's hold on the NEI over the ensuing months. It had long been a belief of the Australian Chiefs of Staff – confirmed in a strategic analysis of December 1941 – that the capture of both territories would 'enable the Japanese to invade Australia'. As if to emphasise that crucial questions of identity hinged on the confrontation, Curtin declared: 'The fall of Singapore opens up the battle for Australia. On its issue depends not merely the fate of this Commonwealth but the frontier of the United States of America and, indeed, all of the Americas, and therefore in large measure the fate of the English-speaking world.'[45]

In response, 2500 AIF were dispatched to Koepang (West Timor) and Ambon, including an Independent Company of 250, which landed in Dili on 17 December 1941 against the express wishes of the Portuguese government. The Japanese landed 1500 troops a month later. The Australians remained on the island for twelve months, carrying out guerrilla-style raids on the Japanese with the crucial aid of local tribes. The consequences of the Australian presence were devastating. With their NEI perimeter breached at its very centre, a 20 000-strong Japanese occupation force fought ongoing Timorese and Portuguese resistance for the next four years, carrying out terrible reprisals in areas where the Australians had been active. At least 40 000 Timorese died from the combined effects of Japanese violence, famine induced by crop destruction, and devastating Allied bombing from bases near Darwin. In his book *Timor: A People Betrayed*, James Dunn speculates that had the Australians not landed, the Japanese may have deployed only a token force or none at all, while official historian Gavin Long argues that the Japanese High Command feared that the Allies were planning an all-out attack on the Indies, and it was this that

provoked them to reinforce so heavily.[46] This experience was to
initiate a long history – felt most intensely again with the Indonesian
invasion of 1975 – in which the fate of the Timorese became captive
to an interpretation of how the island was crucial to Australia's
security. After the Australian commandos left in January 1943,
leaflets were dropped over the island saying: 'We will never forget
you.'[47]

Even two months before the fall of Singapore, as news from
Malaya worsened and the Japanese expanded their perimeter east
by capturing Rabaul, there were intense anxieties in Australia
about invasion. US troops en route to the Philippines during the
Pearl Harbor attack were diverted to Australia, and Curtin asked
Churchill for the return of a division from the Middle East to reinforce either the NEI or the Australian mainland. At the end of
December Curtin made his famous broadcast, which some have
read as a 'strategic turn' to the US, in which he appealed for a
'solid and impregnable barrier of democracies', including the Soviet
Union, 'against the three axis powers':

> We refuse to accept the dictum that the Pacific struggle must be treated
> as a subordinate segment of the general conflict . . . the United States
> and Australia must have the fullest say in the direction of the democ-
> racies' fighting plan. Without any inhibitions of any kind, I make it
> quite clear that Australia looks to America, free of any pangs as to our
> traditional links or kinship with the United Kingdom. We know the
> problems that the United Kingdom faces . . . But we know, too, that
> Australia can go but Britain can still hold on.[48]

The anxiety in the statement was palpable, and at its heart was the
claim for the fullest participation in the higher direction of the
Allies' war effort. During this period the Australian government
struggled to gain access to the highest Allied councils, with a particular anxiety being the agreement reached between Churchill and
Roosevelt that the European and Atlantic theatres would be first
priority, and that substantial resources would not be committed to
the Pacific until Germany was defeated.[49]

These concerns were also the theme of an extraordinary national
broadcast by Curtin on Australia Day 1942, a speech which drew
on the whole panoply of national myths in an effort to rouse his
people and assert Australia's claim to international subjectivity:

> The whole philosophy of the way of life for which we are fighting means that in wartime it is more important even than in peacetime that consultation as equals should mark the activities, firstly of those charged with the government of a democracy, and secondly those jointly representing the several democracies . . . Our men have shown the stuff of which we are made on many a death-charged battlefield . . . We, therefore, claim the right to bring to the collaborating council table the same fighting calibre, the same passionate determination which is our heritage from the past and our possession in the present.[50]

Here Curtin, the man gaoled as a conscientious objector for five days in 1917, invoked the terms of the Anzac tradition – without a shiver of irony. In turn he introduced it into a mythic patchwork which might bind the present moment into a seamless narrative ideal:

> The flame of freedom lit in this land by our first settlers, and kept aglow by the generations which followed, is not extinguishable by any enemy . . . I pay tribute to intrepid explorers, hardy pioneers, great citizens, statesmen, industrialists, men and women of the land, heroic warriors, and all those nation-building spirits whose works have come down to us. We dedicate ourselves to their noble aspirations.[51]

He could not be accused of lacking a sense of occasion. On a day marking the anniversary of Phillip's establishment of a British colony at Port Jackson in 1788, Curtin sought to draw together all the narrative threads of Australian identity and subjectivity, and bring them to bear with all the force of a noble and irrefutable tradition – past, present and future welded into an organic unity, in which prior acts of work and colonisation might inspire others to secure the anxious linkage between soil, sovereignty and identity against its gravest-ever danger. In turn, their example would be the basis for a future vision of progress when the crisis was over.

The speech was a significant landmark. With its emphasis on freedom, colonisation, citizenship and productivity, it was a potent culmination of the 'political double-bind', the linked images of individual, national and international subjectivity which had been central to the 150-year-old Australian politics of *security*. It marked a point when the war, via its integration into a larger mythic trajectory, might be able to reunify an atomised community: identity secured by a defining structure of otherness in which the Asian enemy threatened the anxious claim of British civilisation to the continent, while the land's true owners – absent from the list of 'nation-building spirits' – functioned yet again as a silence at the heart of the idealist movement of nationhood.

Of note too was the appearance of a phrase that would become commonplace as a signifier of identity, especially in the war on terror: the 'way of life'. The historian Richard White suggests that, from the 1940s on, it replaced the idea of a racial or national type as the basis of the Australian identity.[52] While this account may be too stark – Curtin's address suggests that 'way of life' was being combined with older 'types' rather than merely replacing them – the phrase may have been effective in that it imagined identity as a *process* rather than an achieved state, as a series of everyday practices that included the most humble persons and tasks, rather than as a pantheon of unattainable myths. Thus individuals might be made more accessible to power, and their immersion in the collective identity more natural. In the language which spoke of 'the way of life for which we are fighting' the smallest daily activity – the preparation of a meal, a game of backyard cricket – could be linked with the terrible abstraction and responsibilities of a global war.

The period between the attack on Pearl Harbor and June 1942 was a genuinely frightening one. Japan's intentions were unknown, and its successes alarmingly swift. At the fall of Singapore Australia lost one of its four AIF divisions, and felt utterly unable to repel any concerted attack. It watched as Japan bombed Darwin, Wyndham and Broome, causing hundreds of casualties, took Rabaul, Lae and Salamanua in Papua New Guinea, and consolidated control over Malaya, the Netherlands East Indies, the Philippines and the North Pacific islands. In February 1942, immediately after the fall of Singapore, the Australian and New Zealand Chiefs of Staff argued that Australasia was 'in danger of attack . . . not so much from the aspect of economic exploitation as from a desire to deny these territories to us as bases for future Allied counter-offensive action'. Possible lines of attack were from the NEI to northern Australia or down the west coast, or through Papua New Guinea to eastern Australia. Such views fed later beliefs that the Japanese drive on Port Moresby – thwarted in the Coral Sea and on the Kokoda Track – was a prelude to an invasion of the mainland.[53]

Yet while later strategic appreciations (official assessments of the strategic situation) – whether of the British, the Australian Chiefs of Staff or MacArthur – tended to play down the danger of invasion in force, political leaders consistently placed this prospect before the public as an impending fact. In late February Curtin warned Australians that their country was 'in imminent peril'; a month later MacArthur's first strategic appreciation suggested that a general invasion, beyond raids or an attempt to secure air bases, was unlikely. Neither Washington nor London ever saw invasion as probable – they thought Japan would seek to isolate Australia by occupying a chain of bases from Papua New Guinea to Samoa. While the occupation of Darwin and raids on the coast were possible (to neutralise strategic threats and divert Allied forces), it was thought that Russia would be the next major offensive if Japan's position improved. While Curtin accepted such analysis, at the end of April he continued to assert that 'an outright attack on Australia remains a constant and undiminished danger'.[54]

Even after the naval battle in the Coral Sea – which seemed an indecisive engagement at the time, but was later interpreted as crucial to finally securing the Australian mainland – Curtin expressed fears about invasion:

> If Japan should move in force against Australia and obtain a foothold, as threatened to occur last week with the Coral Sea action, it may be too late to send assistance. Possibly in the long run the territory might be recovered but the country may have been ravished and the people largely decimated.[55]

At the battle of the Coral Sea in May Japan's seaborne drive on Port Moresby (*not* Australia) was defeated. Japan lost one carrier and sustained damage to another; the Allies lost a carrier, a destroyer and an oiler. Yet the battle of Midway Island (4–7 June), in which Japan lost four carriers and a cruiser, was a more decisive blow to the Japanese Navy – it had lost the majority of its carrier fleet and would never recover. These two actions, and the arrival of twelve US divisions, had made a Japanese invasion of Australia impossible. Yet on 17 June, in a radio broadcast appealing for subscriptions to the second liberty loan, Curtin again spoke of 'the menace that Japan presents at our very threshold . . . I say it flatly that Australia can be lost . . . Had the outcome of the Coral Sea battle been adverse, who could give guarantees as to the consequences for Australia? That battle was crucial with fate.'[56]

Out of such untruths myths are made. In this case, the Battle of the Coral Sea would be abstracted from the chaos of the war as a defining moment in Australian history, and used by conservatives ever since as a legitimising narrative for Australian adherence to the US alliance. Much of this centred on the Australian American Association's sponsorship of the annual Coral Sea Week celebrations. Evatt could have contributed: in a March 1945 speech he said that had 'the Japanese triumphed in the Battle of the Coral Sea either Australia would have been heavily invaded, or at least the key islands commanding the southern Pacific sea and air routes would have been occupied by the enemy'. As Humphrey McQueen suggests in his book *Japan to the Rescue*, by repeating the fiction that the Japanese had been intent on taking Australia, and emphasising an event in which the RAN played little role, the battle became 'the ideal clash of arms through which to demonstrate how dependent Australia had to be on the US military'.[57]

To this narrative was added a series of emotional declarations about the fraternity between Australians and Americans in which mutual interest, shared values and cultural affinity converged. Yet the US decision to defend Australia was coldly strategic. In December 1941, soon after the attack on Pearl Harbor, General Marshall had asked Eisenhower (then a brigadier on his staff) to recommend a course of action if the US were driven from the Philippines. Eisenhower replied that Australia was

> the base nearest to the Philippines that we could hope to establish and maintain, and the necessary line of air communications would therefore follow along the islands intervening between that continent and the Philippines. If we were to use Australia as a base it was mandatory that we procure a line of communications leading to it. This meant that we must instantly move to save Hawaii, Fiji, New Zealand and New Caledonia, and we had to make certain of the safety of Australia itself.[58]

Having failed to take Port Moresby by sea, the Japanese sought to do so by land, launching an ultimately abortive drive across the Owen Stanley Range in July 1942. They managed to drive the Australians to within 30 miles (48 km) of the coast before withdrawing their starving and exhausted troops. An Australian counter-attack, assisted by US Air Force and Army units, then drove the remaining Japanese from the Papuan mainland – with 625 Australians killed and 1055 wounded. This was the fabled four-month Kokoda campaign, which has since passed into mythology. In his history of the campaign, *Blood and Iron*, Lex McAulay argues that it 'has taken its place in Australian history alongside the landing at Gallipoli, the charge at Beersheba, and the siege of Tobruk . . . [It] marked a pivotal point in Australian awareness. It was that occasion when, for the first time, Australians were fighting for their own homeland without the protection of large and powerful friends.'[59]

The mythic significance of the Kokoda campaign – which occurred at the same time as Australians repelled a force attacking Milne Bay near Port Moresby, and the US Navy inflicted a grave defeat on the Japanese at Guadalcanal – turns on a combination of strategic perception and potent imagery. The first hinges on the way the campaign was interpreted, then and since, as narrowly preventing a Japanese takeover of Port Moresby and then Australia. In September, Curtin, in a national broadcast opening his campaign for austerity, argued: 'Our fate is in the balance as I speak to you. The battle of the Solomons is not only vital in itself, but . . . represents a phase of the Japanese drive in which is wrapped up invasion of Australia.' If Port Moresby and Darwin fell, Australia would be faced with 'a bloody struggle on our soil, a struggle in which we would be forced to fight grimly, city by city, village by village, until our fair land might become a blackened ruin'. Yet Curtin would have known Japan had no plans to invade Australia by this time, as US communications intercepts had revealed this as early as April.[60]

Curtin's colourful and alarming imagery, cutting through the fog of censorship which limited Australians' knowledge of the war, would have seized the public imagination and emphasised the significance of the later victory. In this fear of direct invasion Kokoda had something over Gallipoli, while sharing its images of bravery and hardship and the struggle to prevail against the great odds posed by not merely a fanatical enemy but also the steep terrain, the heat and jungle and the difficulties in obtaining supplies and evacuating wounded. The New Guinea campaign also gave Australia some moving images, among them Damien Parer's film of a blinded digger being helped across a river by a mate.[61] In this, one of the most repeated and enduring images of the Pacific war, Australians saw a portrait not merely of victory and heroism but also of suffering and pain; its effect was not to encourage militarism but rather to illustrate Australia's sense of vulnerability in the face of an implacable and alien enemy.

In this way Kokoda, like Gallipoli, became a crucial event in the reinterpretation of the national identity. Humphrey McQueen goes further, arguing that '[i]n place of the Anzac legend' of national birth, the Australian nation was born on the Kokoda Track; or at least Kokoda formed 'the focal point in a decade of rebirth'. It provoked an 'enormous upsurge of race patriotism' and had a unifying potential which was lacking in the class war of the 1920s and the heartbreak of the Depression.[62] My view is that Kokoda appeared as evidence of direct Asian threat, fulfilling fears which had coursed through the Australian identity for decades – an identity then strengthened around the scene of its bloody confrontation and narrow defeat. What was left, however, was a residue of vulnerability, and a consequent strategic dependency. The binary structure of (vulnerable) identity versus threatening otherness thus took on great force, enabling it to later be emptied out and replaced with new actors and threat scenarios. Insecurity, as much as national pride, would be the event's enduring legacy.

Preparing for the postwar order

As the tide of battle turned against the Japanese at the end of 1942, the minds of Australian leaders became focused on the postwar period. Here the question of Australia's international subjectivity would bear on anxieties about its future influence on Pacific affairs, the terms of peace and the postwar system of global military and economic order – anxieties that would influence Australia's military deployments and diplomacy till the end of 1945. During 1943 and 1944 Australian units fought on Wewak and New Britain, and relieved US forces on Bougainville and the Solomon Islands – forces then diverted to the main axis of the US drive against Japan across the North Pacific. In June 1945 the Australian government made a formal request to the US Chiefs of Staff to associate Australian forces with 'the forward movement against Japan under General MacArthur', but met with firm US opposition.[63]

Australia's limitation to a South Pacific role was determined by its subordination to a US commander, its strategic obsession with the area, and its postwar ambitions. The strategic historian Coral Bell argues that having accepted MacArthur's leadership in 1941, the government lost 'leverage on the strategic control of the Pacific war, and on the choice of role for Australian troops. That in turn meant loss of control of campaigns in Bougainville and elsewhere, which seems to have entailed many pointless deaths by battle and disease.' She also quotes John Dedman, a member of the war Cabinet, as saying that Evatt 'kept reminding his colleagues that if Australia was to have a say in the peace negotiations, its troops must take the offensive in some major operation'.[64]

Australian postwar anxieties were also aroused by Australia's exclusion from the Cairo Conferences of 1943, which included China, the US and Great Britain. They settled the terms for peace with Japan and discussed the disposal of the territories under its control. Evatt said in Parliament in October 1943 that 'Australia has done her fair share in putting out the fire that was kindled in Europe', and spoke of a proposal to call a conference of governments interested in the South-West Pacific to consider defence, native welfare, postwar development, trade, air routes and communications. He also protested to Truman at Australia's exclusion from the peace settlement talks with Germany and Italy, despite its 'effective and at times decisive role in portions of the campaign against both Germany and Italy'.[65]

By now it was clear the Western powers were all self-consciously jockeying for position. Curtin had acknowledged this in 1944 when, wanting to involve British and Australian forces in moves on the Philippines and Borneo, he cabled Churchill asking for the dispatch of British naval forces to the Pacific. While MacArthur supported the request, Curtin betrayed more antipodean anxieties when he wrote of his concern 'at the position that would arise in our Far Eastern Empire if any considerable American opinion were to hold that America fought a war on principle in the Far East and won it relatively unaided while the other allies including ourselves did very little towards recovering our lost property'.[66]

Australia's response to Cairo was to meet with the New Zealand government in January 1944 to discuss the postwar Pacific order. The text published at the end of the meeting, the ANZAC Agreement, asserted that as the two governments had 'vital interests' in the armistice, they should share in its planning, and that 'as a matter of cardinal importance' they should be involved in the planning and establishment of the 'general international organisation' referred to in the 1943 Moscow Declaration. The US was deeply annoyed by an article of the Agreement which asserted that the construction of bases did not 'afford any basis for territorial claims or rights of sovereignty or control after the conclusion of hostilities'. To remove any ambiguity, the text also declared that the 'ultimate disposal of enemy territories in the Pacific . . . should be affected only with [Australia and New Zealand's] agreement'.[67]

The attitudes to the Pacific Islands in the Agreement seemed an odd mixture of imperialism, paternalism and idealism – there were clauses asserting the need to encourage missionary work, health and education, and 'material development including production, finance, communications and marketing'. While suggesting that trusteeship should be the most suitable form of control, the Agreement also recommended increasing native participation in decision-making, with a view to eventual self-government. The Pacific was also seen as crucial to regional security, with a clause promoting 'within the framework of a general system of world security, a regional zone of defence . . . based on Australia and New Zealand stretching through the arc of islands north and north-west of Australia, to Western Samoa and the Cook Islands'. Greg Fry has commented that this proposal, strongly pushed by Evatt elsewhere, was a reappearance 'in all but name' of the Australasian Monroe Doctrine.[68]

This was a kind of modernist, security-minded benevolence that asserted overwhelming Australasian interest and influence in the Pacific, would accept a US presence as ultimate security guarantee, and sought to promote economic 'development' and eventual decolonisation within those frameworks. Tensions over multilateralism aside, this policy appears broadly consonant with US postwar plans to reorganise the Asia-Pacific economies around Japan after 1947, and which the 1950 Colombo Plan was designed to initiate. Further efforts to influence postwar outcomes saw Australian troops participate in the Allied occupation of Japan, and General Blamey (after early US opposition) signed the surrender instrument on behalf of Australia during the ceremony held on the USS *Missouri* in Tokyo Bay on 2 September 1945.[69]

The Chifley government also took this activism to the San Francisco conference which established the United Nations in 1945. Australia's delegation – nominally led by Deputy PM Francis Forde but effectively by Evatt – was intensely prepared, and lobbied for 38 amendments to the draft agreed upon by the great powers at Dunbarton Oaks in August 1944. The amendments were 'idealistic' on both security and economic questions, but nevertheless implied a subservience to dominant meanings of security. While Australia wanted 'a pledge from all members to respect the territorial integrity and political independence of other members' and a declaration that 'justice and the rule of law shall be the principles guiding the action of the Security Council', it also sought

> to see that the Security Council is in fact composed of 'security' powers i.e. powers which by their past military contribution to the cause of world security have proved able and willing to assume substantial security responsibilities, or which are willing, and by virtue of their geographical position in relation to regions of primary strategic importance are able to make a substantial contribution to the maintenance of international peace and security.[70]

This implied that whatever the projected role of the UN in resolving international disputes, realist military frameworks and territorial coverage would provide an ultimate security guarantee, and that the strategic control of space and its denial to 'hostile' powers were necessary operations. While Labor resisted the demonisation of communism that came with the Cold War, they deferred to this more general strategic principle when they compromised their initial plans for the British Commonwealth Occupation Force (BCOF) in Japan out of sensitivity to the US, which feared that offering a separate area to the British might provoke a similar request from the Soviet Union. Evatt's statement also reflected his desire for the Security Council to be configured in a way that would allow

Australia to participate: notwithstanding the claims of the 'Big Four', Australia was, in his mind, clearly such a 'security power'.[71]

The conventional nature of Evatt's thinking stood in contrast to his prescient desire to democratise the voting and membership structures of the new international organisation. Successes included Article 73, which required colonial powers to report to the Secretary-General on the conditions of their territories, but Evatt's efforts to have full employment included as an obligation failed. While Australia also failed to prevent permanent members of the Security Council having a veto power – the very power that paralysed the organisation until the late 1980s and remains deeply problematic – it was able to prevent great powers using their veto to stifle discussion. The White Australia policy was protected, much as it was by Hughes in 1919, by modifying Article 2 so that the UN could not intervene with force over an issue within the domestic jurisdiction of a state. Although John Curtin was now dead, struck down by a lung illness in July, the ambition he declared in 1941 had been achieved: 'We shall hold this country and keep it as a citadel for the British-speaking race and as a place where civilisation will persist.'[72]

Conclusion: War, justice and subjectivity

This chapter has sought to trace a second crucial period in the imagination of a unified and progressive Australian subject – from its dark postwar achievement in the Anzac tradition, through the failed vision of 'Australia Unlimited', the terrible division and hardship of the Depression, to its reconsolidation in the patriotic struggle against Japan in the Pacific war. While conservatives had previously sought to deploy the force of the Australian subject against the labour movement, between 1942 and 1945 the reconstruction of identity would occur under a Labor administration which sought to ameliorate social division in a common cause, and proclaimed its dual objective as bringing justice to the workers and security to the nation as a whole – a vision in which, as Curtin's biographer Lloyd Ross has pointed out, 'social security and national security were indivisible'.[73] As the rhetoric and conduct of the war showed only too starkly, it was thus a vision in which the 'political double-bind' was the fundamental operative principle. It would be accompanied, however, by a potent new claim: that in the Labor vision, and in the achievement of victory over Japan, security and justice would coalesce. Henceforth this would be a crucial element of Labor's 'governmental' rhetoric, revived by the governments of Gough Whitlam, Bob Hawke and Paul Keating, and in the revised platforms developed by Labor opposition leaders Kim Beazley, Mark Latham and Kevin Rudd.

Thus to the claims of one philosophical universal – security – were added those of another – justice. Together they provoke some disturbing questions, which undermine the promise of their idealist unity. Much of what Labor had sought to preserve – a white Australia, economic progress, the correspondence between soil, sovereignty and identity – had its roots in an older system of discourse with a problematic and violent history. The understandable anger at the treatment of the Allied POWs, the narrations of Kokoda and Coral Sea, and Curtin's repetition of invasion fears well into 1943 had entrenched a fear and revulsion of Japan with crucial future effects. In this way the ontological purchase of the Australian subject had been strengthened, but only through an intensification of the historic image of the Other that lay at its centre. Aborigines remained a silence in the story of progress and heroism that Curtin evoked in 1942, without status as citizens and still subject to a sinister machinery of slow annihilation. Yet some had even sought to defend the subject that dispossessed them, in the face of army regulations restricting enlistment to those 'substantially of European origin or descent'. In 1939 William Cooper had urged Aborigines to boycott the war: 'We have nothing to fight for but the privilege of defending the land which was taken from him by the white race without even compensation or kindness.'[74]

Ignoring this continuing history, and the sufferings of those who had endured the full force of Japanese occupation, many Australians drew from the war a sense of unique moral injury. Although over 7000 Australian POWs – a third of their total number – had perished in the camps at Changi, Sandakan and on the Thai–Burma railway, it was by no means the worst experience or the most terrible atrocity of the war. Japan had made victims all through Asia, and on the Allied side Indians and Timorese had also surrendered thousands of lives in the defence of imperial territory. The murder of over 400 000 Japanese civilians during the fire bombings of Tokyo and the atomic destruction of Hiroshima and Nagasaki were cruel acts of terror with little strategic rationale – yet, told by their leaders that the atrocities were necessary to bring about surrender, few in the West questioned the war's shocking final acts.

Out of these fears and ambiguities Labor proposed to bring Australians into an order in which domestic reconstruction would merge with the international 'creation of a permanent system of general security'. Invoking a seductive vision of human enlightenment Curtin told Australians in 1943 that 'the principles of the Atlantic Charter, on which the hopes for a new international order are based, are a pledge that national policies will be directed to the betterment of mankind'. The next decades would fall far short of such ideals, but not without some valiant protest from Labor. In seeking to understand why, my analysis will consider the political and discursive conditions under which governments would seek to realise them. Domestically, Labor's visions of social justice, full employment and economic prosperity would turn on political and ideological struggles over the respective roles of public and private capital, while internationally Australia would seek to trade into a system ravaged by war and in which far more powerful actors were now laying down the rules. Similarly, Evatt's dreams of an international order based on law and justice were hostage to the same 'Big Four' whose armed strength Curtin hoped would 'be used as a trust for all mankind'.[75]

While an Australian subjectivity had been reworked and strengthened, its history and its ontological structure left a dark legacy; and the 30 000 lives it had sacrificed, in virtually every theatre of the war, would be of little assistance in the difficult task of asserting an independent voice in postwar diplomacy. Poised between the carnage of the first truly global war and the unknown promise of a new international order, *security* more than ever hinged on the bleak continuum linking the individual, national and geopolitical – a monstrous calculus of being, seemingly without escape.

3

Cold War against the Other 1946–69

Australians live in a potentially dangerous area; we are a Western outpost hard
by Asia in revolution, and we need allies.

Howard Beale[1]

By the end of 1945, after six years of a war which consumed more
space, more technology and more human beings than any in history, as many as 85 million were dead – 20 million combatants and
65 million civilians. They included some 6 million Jews brought
from all over Europe to German extermination camps, 5 million
more Gipsies, dissidents and homosexuals, and hundreds of thousands of victims of Japanese brutality and of Allied firebombing in
the closing stages of the war against German and Japanese cities.
Twenty-five million more were refugees. The Soviet Union alone
lost as many as 50 million people. The conflict had seen the development of terrifying new weapons and techniques of warfare and,
in a terrible evolution of the total organisation of resources and
populations inherent in *security*, the obliteration of any distinction
between combatant and civilian. Further, in the war's sickening
denouement, the United States had demonstrated a weapon which
appeared to unlock the very laws of nature, and which Secretary of
War Henry Stimson later feared would utterly transform the rules
of the international system and destroy the earth.[2]

Taken as a whole, this historical moment seemed to hold together
the irreconcilable: an experience of carnage, murder and fear played
out on an unprecedented scale, and fantastic new dreams of human
destiny and material progress. At San Francisco a new international
organisation had been formed, promising co-operative efforts

to ensure universal security, prosperity and welfare. A Universal Declaration of Human Rights had been made, and institutions established to eliminate poverty, ignorance and disease. In the United States, publisher Henry Luce had already outlined his postwar vision of a 'vital international economy' and an 'international moral order' in which the US would provide the capital, technical expertise and cultural model for a new global order based on freedom, justice and progress. In similar fashion, at the Japanese surrender ceremony on USS *Missouri* MacArthur spoke of his hope that 'a better world shall emerge out of the blood and carnage of the past, a world founded upon faith and understanding, a world dedicated to the dignity of man and the fulfilment of his most cherished wish – for freedom, tolerance and justice.'[3] In such visions, which many Australians shared, the war appeared as a trial, even a close call, but was also an enabling, ground-clearing event, which could not be allowed to sully their image of a future without contradictions. As Evatt told the Paris peace conference, in July 1946, 'By united efforts and common sacrifices we have overthrown great tyrannies and won a new birth of liberty.'[4] Rightly enough, many argued that the Allies had saved humanity from enslavement and terror; yet looking back through another half-century, we may wonder if they were ever banished at all – simply given new names and forms, of which our own *security* was one.

Standing on the threshold of a new global order, the Australian subject breathed these contradictions like a harsh wind. While the destruction wrought in Europe, the USSR and Asia may have made Australia's experiences seem trivial in comparison, this is to underestimate the vast cultural, political and economic transformations on whose edge Australia stood and in which it would be a major actor – less in terms of the volumes of capital, aid, or force it could deploy than in terms of the ideas, activism and fear it would bring to the process. As the final stages of the Pacific war and Evatt's diplomacy in San Francisco had shown, this activism was already a marked feature of Australian statecraft and strategy. Speaking in March 1945 of the need for postwar US and Australian co-operation to realise the idealist vision of the Atlantic Charter, Evatt argued: 'The destiny of our countries is bound up with the future Pacific Order.'[5]

Labor's own visions of security and justice hinged on how it could both achieve a reconstruction of Australian society and intervene in the new strategic, economic and cultural spaces being formed around the globe and particularly in its region. In these exceptionally mobile contexts Australian foreign and defence policy took on a new sweep and intensity, with Evatt continually seeking to assert 'disproportionate' influence as new hegemonic formations took shape. Over the next twenty years Australian policy became conscious of operating over larger fields of action and influence, and strategic appraisals became more detailed and encompassing, prefiguring the later development (and projection) of more detailed and mobile administrative and security formations into the region. Thus this period saw a vast expansion of the 'strategic imagination' – which married new institutional techniques with new technologies of communication, surveillance, transport and warfare – to match that being extended by other powers.

As the political and economic landscape of the Pacific changed, difficult and morally profound problems for policy emerged. Old assumptions were challenged, while others were strengthened or transformed. The two most weighty issues were the reconstruction of Japan and the challenge posed by the movements which now confronted the European powers attempting to return to their colonies after the Japanese withdrawal. Up to this point Australian governments had associated certitude and stability with the continuity of colonial power, and the postwar decades would see them attempting to recover this lost sense of security in difficult new contexts, contexts which required adding the claims of new nationalisms for justice to their calculations. The struggles in the Netherlands East Indies, Malaya and Indochina, and the way in which Japan was rebuilt and integrated into a new Asian economy, would have enormous and far-reaching effects which are still with us today. These effects include the future of Indonesia, a thirty-year war in Vietnam and the tragedy of Cambodia. Here fantastic and barely foreseeable levels of economic growth and prosperity, along with profound cultural changes, were parallelled by crises involving the death and dislocation of millions, with flow-on effects which transformed the global political economy. Australia would be deeply involved, over decades, in all these events.

Important principles had already been set out, by both the major global powers and the Labor governments of Curtin and Chifley. The Atlantic Charter, drafted by Roosevelt and Churchill in August 1942 and later signed by a further twenty-nine states, committed the Allies to renouncing territorial aggrandisement, to the principles of democracy and self-determination, to the achievement of fair trade and economic prosperity, and to economic and social security. The final principle projected, 'pending the establishment of a wider and general system of general security', the 'abandonment of the use of force' and a lightening of the 'crushing burden of armaments'. Labor consistently invoked the Charter during the war, as both an underpinning for its war aims and a blueprint for the future, with Evatt stating in 1943 that 'the declaration is universal in its scope and application' – its principles should underpin a postwar Pacific order which allowed for 'the legitimate aspirations of the peoples' and formed 'a basis for economic development which [would] provide improving standards for all the peoples of the Pacific'.[6]

Yet within a few months of Japan's surrender many of the Charter's ideals had already been abandoned. Preoccupied by its interests in Europe, the United States acquiesced in the British return to Malaya and Burma, the Netherlands' return to the East Indies, the French return to Indochina, and had itself retaken the Philippines and staked a claim to a chain of islands stretching from Hawaii to the east coast of Japan. The Soviets were determined to control those nations they occupied. Cold War tensions were already in play as the US attempted to exclude the Soviet Union from Japan, where the use of the two atomic bombs – just as the USSR entered the Pacific war – had been crucial. Similarly, the Truman administration's decision, against the advice of retiring Secretary of War Stimson, to further develop and refine the Bomb shattered forever the Charter's final dream of a world without arms.[7]

Those who died, either in the terrible heat of the blast or later, in the slow agony of radiation poisoning, were the Cold War's first victims, and occupied Japan was a crucial space in which its economic and strategic dimensions converged. Contrary to myth, during 1945 US officials knew of Japanese efforts to surrender on terms which preserved the Emperor, and that clarifying the surrender terms or Soviet entry into the war might bring about that surrender. An important factor in Truman's decision was the desire to brandish the terrifying new weapons at the USSR. Stimson wrote, 'let our actions speak for words. The Russians will understand them better than anything else', while Secretary of State Byrnes told Truman that 'the atomic bomb might well put us in a position to dictate our own terms at the end of the war'. The US wanted leverage against the Soviets in Europe, and to prevent them making territorial claims on China or having any effective role in the occupation of Japan. On the other hand, Stimson later wanted co-operation with the USSR in the control of a force he feared was 'merely a first step in a new control by man over the forces of nature too revolutionary and dangerous to fit into the old concepts'.[8]

This was a function of the United States' broader strategic objectives: to build an integrated capitalist world economy subject to the rules of multilateralism – currency convertibility and free trade, investment and resource access – in which the US dollar would be the pre-eminent currency. US policy in Asia became directed towards the military and economic strengthening of a 'Great Crescent' from India to Japan, with Indonesia as its 'southern anchor', and with Japan's economic recovery underwritten by a trade and investment triangle between itself, the US and (a non-communist) South-East Asia. In turn, under the influence of Cold War intellectuals such as George Kennan, the US abandoned many of the reforms it had previously planned for Japan, in order to speed its economic recovery and integrate it into a global system of 'containment'. Australia's economic, foreign and strategic policies, and its possible forms of identity, would now evolve within these constraints. Yet whatever the weight and inertia of these constraints, many dramatic choices were still available.[9]

Cold War premonitions: Labor faces the world

Labor's vision of postwar justice, played out in a context of international ruin and upheaval, and beneath which remained many of the historic cleavages in Australian society, which had been merely papered over by wartime unity, would strike real difficulties. With Asian and European markets in chaos and Australia's foreign reserves at a low ebb, the government feared another depression, and with it further political setbacks of the kind which had split the party's ranks during the 1930s. Memories of the Depression – chief among them how the Australian economy had foundered on its overseas dependence – reinforced the government's fundamental commitment to full employment and its suspicion of banking capital, along with its conviction that the key to 'security' lay in effective macroeconomic management. Security now depended upon finding a combination in which the productivity and price of labour, the control of investment and consumption, and new techniques of state intervention into both the domestic economy and the evolution of the international system, could coalesce into the engine of a broadly based prosperity in which contradictions between private capital and public interest could be virtually eliminated. It was a vision, according to political scientist Carol Johnson, of 'social harmony', a 'humanised capitalist society rather than a radical socialist one' – which sought to give systemic form to the unity of a collective subject.[10] Given the sweep of such claims, much would be at stake. Could capitalism be humanised as Labor hoped, and the historic divisions between classes mitigated and resolved? Could the new international order be moulded into a medium for universal justice and prosperity?

In many ways Labor's vision of security – linking sovereignty, economy and population – was similar to that harboured by previous governments, and confronted many of the same historic problems. Like the proponents of 'Australia Unlimited', Labor wanted to develop Australia's resources and industries, and populate its empty spaces, both to increase its domestic market and to make the still tenuous link between sovereignty, soil and identity more secure. Immigration Minister Arthur Calwell predicted that within 25 years, there would be another challenge 'to our right to hold this land'.[11]

At the same time as it sought the immigration of Eastern European refugees, British settlers and southern Europeans, Asian refugees in Australia were deported, without exception. The

Philippines closed its consulate in Sydney in protest and the national legislature in Manila considered expelling all Australians. Turning the moral complacencies of the Australian identity neatly on their head, the *Manila Evening Chronicle* argued that the policies drew on 'the natural sadism that springs from Australia's penal origins'. While Curtin warned that Australian industries would have trouble finding Asian markets while 'refusing them access to an empty Australia', he maintained that Asians harboured an essential 'antagonism to the white man'.[12]

The problems inherent in Labor's drive for security and justice were compounded at the interface between the domestic and international, where policies of race, development and economics confronted the constraints imposed by the international political economy, Western strategic policy and calls for decolonisation. The grand visions of international co-operation, universal values and general prosperity soon struck demoralising obstacles. Other problems lay in the limits of Labor's own thinking. Its vision of international economic justice, and an economically secure Australia within it, turned on the possibility of being able to trade into a system which was growing steadily and in which full employment was an agreed objective. Yet the government had failed to have a commitment to full employment included in the UN Charter, and delayed joining the International Monetary Fund (IMF) because the US resisted a full employment clause. Chifley convinced his party to join the IMF in 1947, declaring: 'I have been an ardent advocate of all international organisations because I believe that through them, we are engaging in a great human experiment, which is designed to prevent the catastrophes that result from wars and financial and economic depressions'.[13]

However anxious Labor was about a potential loss of economic autonomy, it would nonetheless stake its future on the development of a multilateral economic order. As the historian David Lee argues, Labor's overwhelming imperative in the postwar years 'was to establish Australia's economic security' and avoid another depression like that of the 1930s. Yet by the end of 1947, because of a massive dollar shortage caused by the US refusal to run trade deficits to speed European recovery, multilateralism was dying. Australians had been reminded once again of their precarious dependence on the international economy and on decisions over which they had little influence. There was also some naivety in Labor's approach – however hard they had had to fight for Australian 'interests', they too easily spoke as if capitalism were a politically neutral form which, once deployed for growth in employment and prosperity, could benefit all equally. As the crisis ground on through 1949 the government found itself arguing, like many Cold War liberals, that the US should reduce tariffs and 'increase investment in backward areas, especially Asia'.[14]

Labor also struck obstacles to its vision of international order in the way the US sought to remake Japan. There the Australians were locked out of occupation decision-making, which was monopolised firstly by Supreme Commander of the Allied Powers (SCAP) Douglas MacArthur and, after 1947, by Cold War conservatives in the US Department of State. Driven by fears of a future Japanese military resurgence, Australian desires for sweeping political reform, welfare measures and the dissolution of the Zaibatsu foundered on the US government's Cold War priorities. While MacArthur accepted the land reform proposed by Commonwealth representative W. MacMahon Ball, he largely ignored the four-power Allied Council for Japan (ACJ). Postwar Japanese governments successfully resisted SCAP's Zaibatsu reforms, and after 1947 the US administration dismantled the anti-monopoly and reparations programs, and advocated the strengthening of the Japanese police and the establishment of a small defence force to resist 'subversion'.[15]

The US's objectives now were to rebuild Japan as a military and economic bulwark against Soviet 'penetration' of north-east Asia, even if it meant retarding Japanese democratisation. In 1948 SCAP began encouraging the Japanese government to arrest unionists and strip workers of their right to organise – reacting to criticism from Ball's successor on the ACJ, Sir Alvary Gascoigne, MacArthur accused the Commonwealth of 'siding with the Kremlin' and 'betraying' the US. The Chifley government, presumably anxious to preserve relations with the US, which it was endeavouring to draw into a Pacific security pact, chose not to confront them. In May 1948 Chifley signalled Australia's accord with the new US industrial strategy in Japan, and signed a new agreement allowing trade between Japan and the sterling area countries. Australia reaped 10 per cent, some £6 million, of the total share to June 1949.[16]

By now the Labor government was increasingly concerned by several trends: US and British anti-communism, the growing hostility between the superpowers and the abrogation of Labor's dreams of collective security under the United Nations in favour of an older (and with atomic weapons, increasingly dangerous) balance-of-power model. At Yalta Roosevelt had hoped that collective security might 'spell the end of the system of unilateral action, the exclusive alliances, the spheres of influence, the balances of power, and all the other expedients which have been tried for centuries', but the dream was fading fast.

In 1947 the Truman Doctrine was declared, and in August the Australian Legation in Moscow suggested that 'the next four to six months will determine the final success or failure of attempts to secure Russian co-operation in solving world problems'. It argued that the US's obsession with security could 'have serious effects' on 'Australian interests in Asia and the Pacific', and that because the US saw

> communist hares behind every Asiatic bush . . . there is some danger that the United States may regard genuine and legitimate aspirations in Asia towards self-government as necessarily Soviet inspired or controlled, and try therefore to restrict or suppress nationalist movements. This could have the opposite effect . . . to make nationalists see in Russia their only hope of salvation, and to regard the United States and supporting powers as antipathetic and ignorant.[17]

A more prescient account of future events in Vietnam, or Sukarno's Indonesia, could not have been made; from this point, feeling that its own 'interests' were being damaged by the US obsession, the Australian government strove for a more independent course in South-East Asia, especially Indonesia. There its approach was a mixture of morality and pragmatism: sympathy for the Indonesian nationalists combined with security concerns and the promise of economic gain.

Three months after the nationalists' declaration of independence of 17 August 1945, Australian envoy W. MacMahon Ball wrote that Australia had to prevent the NEI becoming 'a focus of conflict between East and West. And from that focus the infection may spread with menacing speed to many other countries in South-East Asia.' Yet it was only after the Netherlands' July 1947 'police actions' – in which 100 000 troops were thrown against republican forces in Java and Sumatra – that Australia helped sponsor a Security Council resolution calling for a ceasefire and negotiations. Evatt's departmental secretary John Burton justified Labor's intervention by saying that 'only by retaining initiative in this respect can Australian economic and security interests be promoted'.[18]

After the resolution was finally passed and a ceasefire in place, Australia (through its representation on the Security's Council's 'good offices' committee on behalf of the Indonesian Republic) acted strongly to seek a settlement fair to the nationalists, to control Dutch infringements and assert Indonesian interests in the UN, against the consistent opposition of the Europeans, Canada and the US. Even after the second Dutch 'police action' of December 1948, the US frustrated Australia's efforts to support the republicans.[19] By this time concerns about security were gaining the upper hand: in April 1948 the Department of External Affairs argued that the 'fundamental considerations underlying Australian policy . . . are that there should be order and stability throughout Indonesia and that oil and other Indonesian products should as soon as possible become available to relieve current world shortages'. After the uprising by the newly formed Indonesian Communist Party (PKI) in August at Madiun in central Java, which was quickly crushed by the nationalist government of Sukarno and Hatta, Australian policy focused on fears that a delay in decolonisation would strengthen the PKI against the pro-Western republicans. Similarly, the government was relieved when West New Guinea (WNG) was left out of the new Indonesian Republic established in 1949. Thus two potent themes for future Australian policy – hostility to communism and the fate of West New Guinea – were established even before the new Indonesian nation was brought into being.[20]

Labor was also strong, at least initially, in resisting the ossification of Europe into two hostile blocs. Labor opposed the formation of the North Atlantic Treaty Organization (NATO), and criticised Western policies which supported reactionary governments (such as the junta in Greece) merely because of their anti-communism. Burton warned that such policies would be interpreted as another move to encircle Russia and would bring about just the set of circumstances the establishment of NATO purported to be attempting to avoid.[21] Labor also resisted such tendencies in Commonwealth defence policy, while otherwise clearing some crucial areas of common discursive ground. As early as 1946 the UK had pressed for an integrated Commonwealth defence plan, directed against the Soviet Union, but Labor refused to either commit Australians to serving outside the South-West Pacific or designate the USSR as enemy.[22]

This was a direct rebuke to the Australian Chiefs of Staff, whose 1947 strategic appreciation was preoccupied with the USSR and recommended a defence vote of £90 million a year. This document introduced some discursive themes which would eventually drive and obsess Australian policy. It showed anxiety about the consequence of growing third world nationalism: uncertainties, they said, had been created by independence in Burma, by the division of India, by the civil war in China, and by Indonesia's decolonisation. They argued that Indonesia posed 'a security problem as well as an economic problem' and, in a formulation that would echo through Australian policy to the present day, argued that Indonesia was 'of great strategic importance. It is most desirable that this region should be administered by strong and stable governments with whom Australia could establish friendly relations, since the only route by which an aggressor weak in sea power could approach Australia is through this region.'[23]

A March 1947 analysis by the Joint Intelligence Committee also betrayed an early version of the thinking that would later coalesce into the 'domino theory':

The real danger to Southeast Asia, and therefore to Australia will arise from the Far East if Russia should combine with China. Under these circumstances China could be well placed, and indeed might be prompted on her own account to embark on operations in Indochina, Burma,

Siam, Malaya or elsewhere in the region. In such an event she would derive substantial assistance from the large groups of overseas Chinese who honeycomb these countries.[24]

While significant differences between Labor and the Defence Chiefs remained, an important watershed had been breached: Asia had been designated an area of prime strategic interest, and communism an emerging threat; military commitments to Malaya, Korea and Vietnam could now follow.[25]

The Malayan crisis was an important test of Labor's attitude to colonialism and the gathering Cold War. The British, heavily dependent on the dollars earned by its exports of rubber and minerals from Malaya, portrayed the uprisings as directed by the Malayan Communist Party (MCP) at the Kremlin's behest. Australian business also held interests worth £6 million in twenty-one of Malaya's eighty-six tin mining enterprises and £2 million in gold and rubber. Malaya also had a key strategic location.[26]

Australian diplomats at the Singapore High Commission portrayed the uprisings as a prelude to Malaya becoming a 'Chinese Communist republic', and said that a communist success would strengthen the communist parties in Indonesia and Burma, 'place control of our outer zone of defence in Chinese hands' and 'prevent any effective use by us of Indonesia as a strategic barrier between us and the populous countries of the Asian mainland'. Chifley, however, regarded the conflict as an anti-colonial revolt, but nevertheless acquiesced to pressures to provide military aid. In July and August 1948 Australia sent 500 weapons and 160 000 rounds of ammunition to Singapore, but ruled out the dispatch of troops.[27]

External Affairs Minister Evatt, however, had been more receptive to the High Commission's arguments, and later moved closer to the US and British positions on Europe, supporting the formation of NATO at the Commonwealth Prime Ministers' Conference of October 1948. According to David Lee, Evatt 'talked of the necessity, in some cases, of abandoning "just" conclusions, arrived at after consideration of individual problems in isolation, because of the "overriding claims of expediency"'.[28] On the other hand, he and his Prime Minister refused to see in the shifting sands of

Asia a general conspiracy: Evatt argued that nationalist movements were not all acting in unison, that 'the majority of nationalists in South East Asia are not communists; there is plenty of evidence that they resent being identified with communism . . .'. The West 'should not be dogmatic in relation to the future of China . . . [if] we give the Chinese communists any ground for thinking that they can never expect international co-operation from the West in future, that very declaration might lead them to adopt an extreme course and to sever all their traditional contacts with the democracies'.[29]

Thus as the Cold War was rapidly spiralling out of the control of any one 'idealistic' small power, Labor had made a series of ambiguous interventions. As Labor watched the dying vision of a world system based on justice and collective security, Evatt's faith in the possibilities of the UN system should perhaps have been tempered by the earlier warnings of his first Prime Minister. In 1938, in a formulation that would perfectly describe NATO as a vehicle of so-called 'collective security', Curtin had said:

> As an ideal collective security is admirable. But as a practical policy in a world based upon imperialism it is . . . a highly dangerous idea which can be seized upon to excuse the very forces it is intended to defeat. When governments are co-operating in the economic field on an anti-imperialist basis, collective security will become a very practical method of dealing with aggression . . . The workers do not control the governments of the world. Until they do, it would be suicidal for the workers of Australia to join in supporting pacts, treaties, understandings or obligations of any sort which would involve them in war against the workers of any other nation . . . at the dictate of capitalist governments.[30]

Multilateralism may have been portrayed by the US as a general good, but its aims were clearly to preserve (while diversifying) imperial economic patterns – now secured less by direct colonial control than by economic integration and indirect forms of influence. By 1947 the reconstruction of both Europe and Asia became inseparable from the formation of an economic bloc that could resist the Soviet Union and counter the growth of domestic socialist forces. Most tellingly, the halting by SCAP of Japanese reparations payments (which were to include technology and industrial machinery) reflected a deliberate effort to postpone Asian industrialisation and integrate the region into a traditionally imperial pattern in which Japanese manufactures would be traded for Asian raw materials. In turn the Japanese could pay for US imports and Western corporations could exploit opportunities for resource extraction and agricultural industry in South-East Asia.[31]

From Other to Same: Cold War architecture

At the December 1949 federal elections Labor was swept from office. Although it retained a slim majority in the Senate, the Liberal-Country Party coalition won the House of Representatives by a staggering twenty-seven seats, beginning a conservative dominance of government that would last until 1972. The parties led by Menzies and Arthur Fadden conjured alarmist visions of 'socialist regimentation', and promised to reduce taxes, eliminate petrol rationing and ban the Communist Party of Australia (CPA). While Chifley had been trying to protect Australia's scarce stock of US dollars, voters were frightened by the spectre of communism and seduced by visions of the good life. Fadden even claimed in Queensland that the 'platform of the Labor party' was 'paving the way for a communist regime'. In 1948 the US chargé d'affaires had written to Washington of 'the strength of communism in the present Labor Government' and accused Burton of being a 'fellow traveler'.[32]

Within five years the architecture of a vast new discursive formation would be in place, centring on the Menzies government's attempts to ban the CPA during 1950 and 1951, the initiation of the Colombo Plan and the deployment of forces to Korea in 1950, the signing of the ANZUS and Japanese peace treaties in 1951, and the establishment of the South East Asia Treaty Organization (SEATO) in 1954. From then on Australians could be sent to fight 'Communism' in Malaya and Vietnam, according to a 'forward defence' doctrine which extended Australia's frontiers – and thus the very borders of a vulnerable national subject – to mainland South-East Asia. What Manning Clark had said of the founding fathers was true also of this time: there was a constant incitement of 'the enemy without and the enemy within'.[33]

That anti-communism was central to a policing of identity was clear when Menzies introduced the Communist Party Dissolution Bill to Parliament in April 1950. Framed 'to outlaw and dissolve' the CPA and 'to pursue it into new and associated forms', Menzies defended it in a language which replayed the same images of security and subjectivity present in Hobbes, Bentham and Hegel, and deployed them into an Australian constitutional structure. First, the Bill claimed to derive from the Constitution's *defence* powers because, 'in a most special and important sense, [it] is a law relating to the safety and defence of Australia. It is designed to . . . give the government power to deal with the King's enemies in this country . . . a self-defending attack on treason and fifth-columnism wherever they can be found'.[34]

In turn this enemy was linked with the global threat Australia's strategic planners were already preparing to fight. Menzies conceded that if communism were merely 'militant unionism, opposed to arbitration but determined to alter the law by lawful means' the Bill would not be justified. However, as it was 'an international conspiracy against the democracies, organised in a prelude to war and operating as a fifth column in advance of hostilities' we must 'fight them wherever we find them, leaving no immunity and no sanctuary'. In a radio broadcast in September Menzies announced the establishment of a national service scheme and a Citizen Military Force of 50 000 in which recruits would be liable for service anywhere in the world. In March 1951 he told Australians to prepare for a new global war in three years.[35]

His objective was clearly to produce a heightened atmosphere of fear and crisis that would strengthen the government's authority, make the population more credulous, and destroy the enemies of his party and his class. Yet the High Court ruled the Communist Party Dissolution Bill unconstitutional on the grounds that Australia was not in a state of war, and it was further rejected in a referendum held in September 1951 (if by a slim margin of 53 000 votes). Crippled by the growing strength of the anti-communist 'movement' in its ranks, the ALP did not vote against the Bill in the

Senate. However, Evatt acted as counsel for the CPA and unions in the High Court, and campaigned heroically for a *No* vote at the 1951 referendum.[36]

The entire discursive matrix for this vision of domestic and international order was set out by Minister for External Affairs Percy Spender in a speech to the Australian Parliament in March 1951. While he would only remain in the ministry for eighteen months, Spender's role in the Colombo Plan, the negotiation of the ANZUS Treaty and in formulating strategic priorities established a structural and conceptual blueprint for Australian defence and foreign policy for the next two decades. Here the disciplinary ambition of the political project Australia was engaged in became starkly visible. The stakes were nothing less than the nation's future, the forward movement of progress which gave the Australian subject its form and destiny: 'Geographically Australia is next door to Asia,' Spender said in January 1950, 'and our destiny as a nation is irrevocably conditioned by what takes place in Asia. Our future to an ever increasing degree depends upon the political stability of our Asian neighbours.'[37]

Thus the achievement of security, of subjectivity, the progressive movement of reason which would express and complete Australia's being, was anchored in the truth of a space here named 'Asia'. 'No nation,' he declared, 'can escape its geography. That is an axiom which should be written deep into the mind of every Australian.' Yet if land had been held out as the fundamental anchor of identity, as its basic empirical fact, it was only through an act of deception. What was precisely at issue here was space itself – space and the whole network of bodies, meanings and economic flows that gave it form and life. Space was *not* an axiom, but was itself under construction and in dispute. 'Asia' became not a neutral index of the real but a highly charged semiotic entity, at once passive and turbulent, which was liable to intervention yet loomed over Australia like a vast, threatening sea. As Labor leader Arthur Calwell was to recognise when Menzies committed two combat battalions to Vietnam in 1965, it was a logic in which 'the very map of Asia becomes a kind of conspiracy of geography against Australia'.[38]

Creating the illusion of a single rhetorical unity, the speech turned on a series of interrelated operations: a projection of geostrategic uncertainty, of immediate vulnerability and insecurity, and a partitioning of sameness and otherness according to a mobile set of boundaries. While many years ago, Spender argued, Australians could feel isolated from threat, now their security 'has become an immediate and vital issue because changes since the war have resulted in a shifting of potential aggression from the European to the Asian area, and our traditional British Commonwealth and United States of America friends have not yet completed their adjustments to the new situation'.[39]

Sameness was initially projected in the importance of Western alliance and commonality: Australian security was dependent upon the 'strength and influence' of Britain, with whose 'interests and safety' we must 'be vitally concerned'. Second was the 'common tradition, heritage and way of life' shared with the United States which, by virtue of its status as 'the greatest Pacific power' required that Australia 'carry out [its] Pacific policies as far as possible in co-operation with it'.[40] This thinking had the effect of smoothing over the deep differences – of interest, sensibility and means – between the Western powers, to narrow the scope for independent decision-making and tie Australia more closely to the strategic imperatives and outlook of the United States.

Next came the imagination of otherness and threat. At the pinnacle was the Soviet Union, whose 'foreign policy is essentially global in character', whose 'ultimate objective is world communism' and whose 'immediate purpose is to work towards its ultimate objective by Communist infiltration in all democratic countries' through 'peace offensives, propaganda and industrial dislocation' – which was to tar all domestic dissent with a Stalinist brush. Setting out the great binary opposition, the umbilical antagonism between Self and Other, Spender stated that while Europe had been 'the main focus of the conflict between democracy and communism', the same situation was 'now developing throughout Asia and the Pacific'. The communist takeover in China had 'fundamentally changed the whole picture in Asia', and would give fresh heart to 'the efforts of international communism to control and direct the new spirit of nationalism in these countries'. While conceding that there was 'still doubt and uncertainty about the way China is likely to act', he quickly closed it off:

> But even without actually invading neighbour states, or engaging in
> open intimidation of them, China, either in order to secure markets
> and raw materials, or as part of communist aims, without much expen-
> diture of resources, could foment dissatisfaction in other countries.
> The Chinese have a ready-made instrument in the form of the many
> millions of Chinese scattered throughout all countries of South-East
> Asia.[41]

This formulation would reach far into the future: in Indonesia it
would legitimate the killings of Chinese during the great slaughter of 1965–66, and it would appear again in the period leading
up to, and immediately following, the Indonesian invasion of East
Timor. Already in Malaya it was being used against the guerrillas of the Malayan Communist Party and as a slur upon Malaya's
Chinese communities. Spender again followed this with a partial
(and short-lived) discursive opening. He said first that 'we do not
accept the inevitability of a clash between the democratic and communist way of life' and hoped 'that the Chinese communists would
look for the sympathetic help of the Western democracies in the
work of uniting and rehabilitating their country'. Yet China had
supposedly blocked this avenue: 'the communists' behaviour to
date, including their treatment of United States property and citizens, and their eager recognition of the rebel forces in Vietnam,
leaves us uncertain whether the Peking Government will conduct itself in accordance with recognised principles of international law and refrain from interfering in the affairs of neighbour
states'.[42]

As later US actions in Vietnam, North and South Korea, and
many other third world states would show, 'principles of international law' were to become a highly flexible matter of interpretation.
And to assert them in favour of South Vietnam's Bao Dai government, scarcely independent and only a few months old, was deeply
misleading. French colonial power – in conflict with Ho Chi Minh's
Democratic Republic of Vietnam (DRV) in the north and represented by a surrogate in the south – was still in place, if looking
vulnerable. To make the test of peaceful coexistence with China its
support of the DRV was to deny to Ho with one hand what was being
offered to China with the other. This was, of course, a function of the

intense emotional significance already being placed upon Vietnam. The key to this was the domino theory, which, while not formally enunciated by Eisenhower until 1954, had already appeared – a National Security Council (NSC) document endorsed by Truman in 1949 argued:

> it is now clear that Southeast Asia is the target of a co-ordinated offensive directed by the Kremlin . . . motivated in part by a desire to gain control of Southeast Asia's resources and communication lines, and deny them to us . . . The extension of Communist authority in China represents a grievous political defeat for us; if Southeast Asia is also swept by communism we shall have suffered a major political rout the repercussions of which will be felt throughout the rest of the world, especially in the Middle East and in a then critically exposed Australia.[43]

Spender echoed this thinking, expanding it into a detailed causal chain centred on the preservation of Western power in Vietnam:

> [Vietnam] is the great present danger point in the South-East Asian area . . . Should the forces of communism prevail and Vietnam come under the heel of Communist China, Malaya is in danger of being outflanked and it, together with Thailand, Burma and Indonesia, will become the next direct object of further Communist activities. The establishment of Communist control over Vietnam – and over Laos and Cambodia, which could scarcely be expected to offer much resistance – would bring Thailand next in line as a target of Communist pressure.[44]

A key weapon in this conflict was the Colombo Plan – established in September 1950 – which provided for a program of economic and technical assistance to non-communist Asian nations. Australia pledged £30.25 million over six years, and by 1952 the US, Cambodia, South Vietnam, Burma and Nepal had joined the original signatories. Spender argued that the plan would 'stabilise government and create conditions of economic life and living standards under which the ideological attractions which communism exerts will lose their force'.[45]

Western governments were putting into place a series of strategies directed to a vast disciplinary project: that of securing, across the region, a certain kind of interdependent economic, political and cultural order. The scale, and enormous transformative power, of this project was not lost on Western leaders. Speaking of the Colombo Plan, Spender later remarked:

> Politically Southeast Asia had lagged far behind the movements which had characterised the civilisation of Europe. Centuries of history had excluded this vast part of Asia from the liberal influence of European thought and political ideas . . . south and Southeast Asia had to face the immense task of creating a new economic structure. The natural wealth had to be tapped by the introduction of modern methods or the improvement of old ones. Almost entire populations had to be taught new methods of work and production, indeed new ways of thinking.[46]

Difference, then, became more closely delineated. Absolute otherness was reserved for movements named 'communist'; they were to be confronted, contained and eliminated. For the different kind of otherness represented by Asian adherence to pre-modern political, cultural and economic forms, was reserved a strategy of transformation, a movement of integration and towards sameness. In their practical operation these coercive and transformative strategies were closely co-ordinated and mutually reinforcing. The claim that ancient societies had to shed their backward traditions and learn entirely 'new ways of thinking' betrayed the disciplinary operation of the 'political double-bind', the conviction that spaces, populations and subjects could be simultaneously directed, managed and transformed into the substance of a new societal order. This was a conviction echoed by the *Current Affairs Bulletin*, which argued in 1952 that the Cold War in Asia was less a strategic contest than 'a struggle for the hearts and minds of men'.[47]

The government moved quickly to back its rhetoric with force. In 1950 they sent 2000 Owen guns to Malaya, along with a squadron of Dakota aircraft, and another of Lincoln bombers, to 'saturate jungle targets'. In 1955 Menzies announced the deployment of an infantry battalion, two fighter and one bomber squadrons, plus a naval force of two destroyers and an aircraft carrier, to a new Commonwealth Strategic Reserve available for service anywhere on the Asian mainland. Menzies argued that if communism over-ran South-East Asia, Australia's existence as a free country would be at risk. Evatt, now opposition leader, opposed the use of Australian troops in the Emergency, instead advocating negotiations, a faster move to self-government and the improvement of working conditions in plantations. When we think of future deployments to Vietnam, his opposition was prescient: the draft directive for the use of the force stipulated a role 'in operations against the communist terrorists'.[48]

Even a relatively uncontroversial deployment – of forces to South Korea under United Nations authority to resist the North Korean invasion of June 1950 – was twisted retrospectively into an illustration of the domino theory and the conspiracy of international communism. In his radio broadcasts of September 1950 Menzies chose to interpret the North Korean attack as 'a new technique of world aggression':

> The communists undermine or over-run some European or Asiatic country. They set up a puppet government . . . then inspire their new puppet or satellite to make an attack under circumstances which impose the greatest military difficulty . . . The purpose of this strategy . . . is to disperse the democratic forces, to weaken the democratic reputation and authority, to maintain nervous tension, to force up costs and prices in democratic countries, and to create, in the minds of people like ourselves, a feeling that as any of us may be attacked we had better keep all our forces at home.[49]

Without humour or irony, he then pleaded: 'These are not heated fancies on my part. Men of authority all round the world know they are a true picture of this new and deadliest and subtlest form of aggression the world has seen.' We might wonder at his sense of history, but his fevered logic also contradicted more considered accounts of the war's origins. While the North Korean offensive was clearly naked aggression, South Korean leader Syngman Rhee had also repeatedly threatened to reunify Korea by force. Official historian Robert O'Neill has carefully weighed the actions of both the USSR and China, and concluded that neither was responsible for initiating the attack. Even where other accounts had suggested

Kim Il Sung sought prior Soviet and Chinese approval, the initiative and timing clearly came from his government.[50] Even China's entry into the war in November 1950, provoked by the UN forces' counter-attack north of the 48th parallel to within fifty miles of their border, was portrayed as further evidence of deliberate expansionism and of a general conspiracy, rather than a discreet defence of its north-eastern flank.[51] Instead the Americans and Australians chose to view the second stage of the war as direct evidence of the domino theory. As Menzies was to say in 1955, the threat to Australia came from an 'expansionist and aggressive communist China, as demonstrated first by the conflict in Korea, then by that in Indochina.'[52]

Sovereignty, alliances and dominoes

Where the Australian Labor Party had responded to the early challenges of decolonisation with some sensitive (if problematic) diplomacy, the Menzies government now saw only turmoil, threat and uncertainty – uncertainty they immediately sought to tame with both the ultimate in material force and the most rigid ontological categories. In turn, through treaty arrangements such as ANZUS and SEATO, the formation of Malaysia and considerable artifice in South Vietnam, they sought to bind such ontologies into an unassailable juridical form that would also facilitate further intervention. In short, ambiguity and doubt could not be countenanced or tolerated.

The Indonesian takeover of Dutch West New Guinea (WNG) was a particular source of anxiety, feeding into a triangular structure of military deployments and fears which joined the fates of Malaysia, Indonesia and South Vietnam into a volatile index of Australia's future security. Channelled together in this way, these fears would see Australians fighting Indonesians in North Borneo, support US intervention in the Sumatra rebellion of 1958, affect both Australian and US decisions to deploy large ground forces to South Vietnam and play into Australian diplomacy following the so-called 'coup' in Indonesia in October 1965. Permeating all these decisions were deep anxieties about the future of British power in South-East Asia and the commitment of the United States, not only to the area but also to Australia's own security. This matrix of assumptions was most tellingly visible in the explanation given by the Australian Ambassador to the United States, Howard Beale, for the deployment of Australian forces to Vietnam. He said that 'it had to do with our relationship with the United States and our right or expectation to receive assistance from her in the event of serious difficulty overtaking us in our part of the world. Australians live in a potentially dangerous area; we are a western outpost hard by Asia in revolution, and we need allies'. It seemed that little of substance had changed since Billy Hughes had worried, during the Great War, that the Australian people 'were but a tiny drop in a coloured ocean'.[53]

Australia thought it had found a new white protector when the ANZUS Agreement was signed in 1951, linking the two Anzac nations with the United States in a mutual defence treaty. (Australia resisted the inclusion of the Philippines, Japan and Indonesia, whom the US wanted to include in order to prevent the ANZUS Treaty from appearing to be a 'white man's pact'.) It contained provisions for 'mutual aid' to assist the three parties to 'develop their individual and collective capacity to resist armed attack' and, ironically enough, obligations on the parties 'to settle any international disputes in which they may be involved by peaceful means'. Article IV, described by US negotiator John Foster Dulles as 'the meat of the treaty', stated that 'each Party recognises that an armed attack in the Pacific area on any of the Parties would be dangerous to its own peace and safety and declares that it would act to meet the common danger in accordance with its constitutional processes'. Article V stated that an 'armed attack' on any party would be 'deemed to include an armed attack on any of the Parties, or on the island territories under its jurisdiction in the Pacific or on its armed forces, public vessels or aircraft in the Pacific'.[54]

While Article IV provided a trigger for an automatic response (not necessarily military), it also gave great sweep to the territories and facilities it would potentially cover – including the US-controlled Pacific Island groups, Australian and New Zealand island dependencies such as New Guinea, and military facilities, vessels and troops forward deployed into South-East Asia. After resisting such a pact for nearly ten years, the US agreed to it to draw Australia into signing the lenient Japanese Peace Treaty, while also seeing in Australia's commitment to South Korea a sign that they might be persuaded to involve themselves more heavily in South-East Asia in future. Yet the US also sought to limit its own obligations: Dulles emphasised that '[ANZUS] does not commit any nation to action in any part of the world . . . the United States can discharge its obligations . . . in any way and in any area that it sees fit'. To this day the terms of the ANZUS Treaty have never been specifically invoked; yet it was effective in pulling Australia more closely towards US positions in Asia and facilitated an increased strategic and economic integration.[55]

ANZUS symbolised the way in which the Menzies 'development' strategy for Australia would involve large amounts of new US investment, draw Australia more closely into the US economy and into the Asian economic bloc centred on Japan, and in turn help strengthen the US-dominated regional security framework. Building on the historic discourse which viewed Australia's economic development as an essential buttress against a threatening Asia, the government argued, in defence of its request for a US$250 million World Bank loan (to build new industrial, transport and communications infrastructure), that 'potential security advantages . . . would accrue to the US from having an industrially stronger ally on the southern rim of Southeast Asia'. The US accepted this argument and supported the World Bank decision to grant an initial US$100 million; by 1962 total borrowings were US$418 million. By 1970 Australia was the fifth-largest global recipient of US investment, with over US$2360 million.[56]

Mirroring this strategy were the construction of supra-national networks of *sovereignty* which might simultaneously enable greater Western intervention and efface its scandal. As leaders like Sukarno denounced Western interference in Asia as neo-colonial and imperialist, the images of political sovereignty and subjectivity dating from Hobbes were called upon to fashion an image of general will linking Asian and Western powers in a common project and identity. If the Colombo Plan acted as a bedrock economico-political strategy of this type, the South East Asian Treaty Organization (SEATO) was intended to combine a mechanism for co-ordinated military planning and deployments with an incontestable juridical form.

South Vietnam in particular became a space in which the construction of an apparently stable 'sovereignty' was sought through an elaborate combination of diplomacy, performance and political manipulation. After the Viet Minh's defeat of the French at Dien Bien Phu in 1954, the Menzies government sought observer status at the Geneva Conference on Indochina. The Geneva Accords, signed in July the same year, provided for the military partition of Vietnam at the 17th parallel, a ceasefire, and free elections in 1956 for a reunified Vietnam. They proscribed the stationing of foreign military bases or forces in either zone. The 17th parallel was to form a military demarcation line, *not* a political or territorial boundary. The DRV (North Vietnam) clearly hoped the 1956 elections would lead to a reunified Vietnam under their control, while the US and Bao Dai governments refused to endorse the Accords. The US hoped that at least the two zones could be turned into separate states, such as had happened in Germany and Korea.[57]

US policy thus became concerned to strengthen the South Vietnamese (RVN) regime under the new Catholic Prime Minister Ngo Dinh Diem, to assist him to eliminate his political enemies, and to scuttle the coming elections. Menzies said that 'Our own security in Australia depends upon converting a temporary halt into a permanent one', while Labor's Arthur Calwell argued that communism had been brought 350 miles (563 km) closer to Australia, and that the ceasefire was an attempt to save Europe by sacrificing South-East Asia. If a South-East Asian defence pact were achieved, he said, its headquarters should be in Darwin.[58]

Diem could not have been a more unlikely candidate for a Vietnamese popular hero – carefully chosen and imported by the United States to replace the French-sponsored Emperor Bao Dai, his regime was supported with vast amounts of US and military aid; US officials under the command of Edward Lansdale supervised the construction of his intelligence agencies, police and armed forces (ARVN); and US advisers were present in the regime's bureaucracy and closely supervised military planning and operations against the Viet Minh. By the early 1960s his regime had an unparalleled reputation for corruption, nepotism and repression, and was both deeply hated in Vietnam and seen as an obstacle by the West. He was assassinated, with the explicit connivance of the US Embassy, in November 1963.[59]

Yet between 1955 and 1961 Diem was widely hailed as a champion. He visited Australia in September 1957, at the close of a massive two-year program of repression directed against the Viet Minh which saw the killing and torture of tens of thousands and the imprisonment, without charge or trial, of another 50 000–100 000. The Australian government was unconcerned that this program entailed the gross abuse of the most basic human and civil rights, or that its impact on the guerrilla organisation provoked the National Liberation Front (NLF) to resume its military struggle and call on support from northern Vietnamese – thus beginning an escalation of the civil war which would eventually see the deployment of Australian and US ground forces in 1965. In May Diem had visited the US, where he had been hailed by Eisenhower as a 'miracle man', and in Australia his visits to Canberra, Sydney and Melbourne were marked by twenty-one gun salutes and military guards of honour. He was awarded one of the highest imperial honours – a Knight Grand Cross of the Order of St Michael and St George.[60]

A telling photograph taken during his visit captures its elaborate and calculated theatre. Diem stands on the tarmac at Canberra airport, walking from a Qantas aircraft. He wears traditional Vietnamese dress; behind him stands Menzies, wearing tails, and to his right is Governor-General Sir William Slim in military uniform, chest blazing with medals. Around them, in full military regalia, is an escort from the Australian and South Vietnamese armed services. Carefully assembled here were all the signs of sovereignty, identity and cultural authenticity that were being invoked to persuade Australians of the legitimacy of Diem's regime and the Western order in South Vietnam – with a sleek technological display of mobility and modernity looming in the background. In turn, Diem's legitimacy was linked to those figures (Menzies, Slim and the army leadership) who personified the Australian subject and the project of its *security* – a security which had already been inextricably paired with the survival of the South Vietnamese state.[61]

The *Sydney Morning Herald* said Diem was 'one of the most remarkable men in the new Asia . . . incorruptible and patriotic . . . authoritarian in approach but liberal in principle'. *The Age*, just as incredibly, argued that he was 'not a morally equivocal figure, like Chiang Kai-Shek or Syngman Rhee'. Evatt joined the chorus, saying at a parliamentary lunch that peace and democracy had been achieved in Vietnam. This powerful semiotic performance of sovereignty was parallelled by other actions. In 1959 the Australian diplomatic mission in Saigon was elevated into an embassy: Australia now regarded the 17th parallel as a political boundary. In June 1962, the special report of the International Control Commission (ICC), in 'a diplomatic victory for Saigon and Washington', confirmed this view. The report was thus the culmination of a long series of verbal, visual and material performances of 'sovereignty' aimed at building the legitimacy of the RVN regime and entrenching the partition of Vietnam.[62]

SEATO sought to build on such efforts. By signing the treaty, which came into force at the beginning of 1955, the Menzies government wanted reassurance: that the US could be drawn into South-East Asia more deeply; that Britain would remained committed to the security of the whole South-East Asian region, not merely to Malaya; that France's military strength might be retained as a factor in the regional balance after its colonial role had ended; and that these major Western powers could be co-ordinated with Australia, New Zealand and as many Asian countries as possible in a collective defence system.[63] The treaty was signed by Australia, New Zealand, the US, Britain, France, Pakistan, the Philippines and Thailand, and was effective over 'the general area of Southeast Asia, including also the entire territories of the Asian parties, and the general area of the South-west Pacific' south of 21 degrees north. Its key article (Article IV) included a provision for 'subversion':

If . . . the inviolability or the integrity of the territory or the sovereignty or political independence of any Party in the treaty area or of any other state or territory . . . is threatened in any way other than by armed

> attack or is affected or threatened by any fact or situation which might endanger the peace of the area, the Parties shall consult immediately in order to agree on the measures which should be taken for the common defence.[64]

This section was extremely broad and ambiguous, leaving governments great scope to interpret events as threatening across a wide variety of situations and a wide geographical area. This was of great significance for the Indochinese states, which, while prohibited under the Geneva Accords from entering into military alliances, were designated under a 'Protocol' to the Manila Treaty as being territories to which Articles III and IV were applicable. Thus the three areas were not formal parties to the treaty organisation, but were 'unanimously . . . designated' by the parties as being within its scope.

Just as the US was trying to create the illusion of a unified body politic in South Vietnam, SEATO was an attempt to give juridical form to an even vaster aggregation of sovereignty – an attempt which, in combination with the detailed administrative techniques deployed through military and economic aid programs, could transform the subjectivity of individuals while policing a 'non-communist' identity which both derived from, and exceeded, the meta-subjectivities of its member nations. It was the vision of security presaged in Hobbes writ large: a *super-Leviathan* whose aims and purposes would be One and which would be arrayed against a monolithic Other, who might appear at any place in the vulnerable flesh of this new political body. As George Kennan argued in 1946, 'world communism is like a malignant parasite that feeds only on diseased tissue'.[65] Hence the significance of 'subversion' to the treaty – its injunction to its members to 'counter subversive activities directed from without against their territorial integrity and political stability' created an apparatus that could now portray Western intervention as a self-protective reflex coming from the very interior of the political body.

Many, however, were not fooled. Sukarno denounced the pact as neo-colonialism, and instead sponsored his own conference of Afro-Asian nations (a precursor to the Non-Aligned Movement), held in Bandung in 1955. India's Mrs Pandit said sarcastically that

SEATO was a 'South-East Asian alliance minus South-East Asia', and India's Prime Minister Nehru argued that the US proposals for the organisation 'came near to assuming protection or declaring a kind of Monroe Doctrine unilaterally over the countries of South-East Asia'.[66] In response, the Western powers became even more convinced that SEATO should perpetuate and extend the stark ontological divide between democracy and communism. Thus neutralism – with its connotations of independence, decolonisation and opposition to foreign military bases – was to be seen as a scandal. Australian Minister for External Affairs R. G. Casey declared:

> Australia will respect the decision of any country to follow a policy of neutrality. We feel, however, that we have the right to expect neutral countries to follow a policy of genuine neutrality . . . They should not criticise or work against SEATO and other democratic countries, while pulling their punches when dealing with the communists . . . They should not allow international communism to use the umbrella of neutrality to protect domestic communist subversion.[67]

SEATO could also be seen as an attempt to solidify an imperial system in a world in which its overt form was no longer tolerated. The same anxieties drove the United Kingdom's decision to decolonise its possessions in Malaya, Singapore and North Borneo in a way that would ensure its interests were preserved. The 1956 Anglo-Malayan Defence Agreement ensured that British forces (including the Commonwealth Strategic Reserve) could remain after the British had wound up their administration, and in May 1961 Malayan leader Tunku Abdul Rahman proposed the federation of Malaya, Singapore, Sabah, North Borneo and Brunei into the new state of 'Malaysia' (an idea the historian Gregory Pemberton asserts 'was almost certainly of British inspiration'). The UK wanted to preserve access to its £600 million investments in oil, tin and rubber – which were by 1963 the greatest source of US dollars in the sterling area – and the highly strategic port of Singapore. Australian External Affairs Minister Garfield Barwick told Cabinet that Malaysia 'was the only hope of a bastion against China', and anticipated new commercial opportunities in an integrated Malaysian economy.[68] The establishment of the new state, he said, 'would contribute to the stability of the region . . . it deserves support as a major act of *orderly* decolonisation' (emphasis added). Similarly, US President John F. Kennedy said it was 'the best hope for *security* for that very vital part of the world' (emphasis added).[69]

Following Britain's violent suppression of the December 1962 rebellion in Brunei (with the help of two Australian Hercules aircraft), Indonesia declared its policy of 'Confrontation' against the new federation. Sukarno denounced it as 'an attempt to save the rubber, tin and oil of the area for the imperialists'. Australia was alarmed: it had deployed much of its overseas force in Malaya under its 'forward defence' doctrine, and saw Singapore as a strategic port. The Defence Committee's 1962 *Strategic Basis* document, in enunciating forward defence, argued that 'while Southeast Asia is held, defence in depth is provided for Australia'. It laid out an alarming scenario in which the decline of British strength and commitment, the divisions within SEATO, and the precarious Indonesian balance between the Army and the PKI raised the spectre of 'the full threat of a communist Asia and a communist Indonesia'. Menzies supported Britain's push for a fast decolonisation: by 1965 an SAS squadron and a regular battalion of Australian troops were fighting an undeclared war against Indonesia in Borneo. Thirty Indonesians were killed. An Australian battalion was also put into operation against the Malayan communists so that British troops could be diverted to fight Indonesia. David Lee has since argued that 'a policy which turned out to have no serious consequences for Australia could easily have turned into a tragic blunder' – only the (unforeseeable) destruction of the PKI and the removal of Sukarno averted an escalation in which prolonged Indonesian intervention in Borneo could only have been countered 'by an attack on Indonesia itself'.[70]

The Vietnam War

Here, the attempt to construct a seamless new body politic amid the turmoil of decolonisation had again been challenged, and countered with a potentially disastrous deployment of military force. As Malaysia was consolidated after the Indonesian coup of October 1965, the military efforts to solidify the fragile sovereignty of South Vietnam escalated. Australia insisted on seeing the problems together: Country Party leader John McEwen wrote to Harold Wilson that Confrontation and Vietnam were 'coming to form a common pattern and a common threat'. In August 1962 thirty military advisers of the Australian Army Training Team Vietnam (AATTV) arrived in Saigon. Half had experience in the jungles of Malaya. That year a squadron of Sabre jet fighters was also loaned to Thailand to fight their communists. In September Cabinet approved defence budget proposals of nearly £650 million over the next three years, bringing Australian defence expenditures to a peak of 4.6 per cent of GNP by 1968. This coincided with a rapid escalation of US involvement – in February 1962 the US Military Assistance Advisory Group (MAAG) in Vietnam was replaced with the Military Assistance Command Vietnam (MACV) under General Harkins; by the end of the year 11 000 US personnel would be in South Vietnam.[71]

In January 1964 Cabinet allocated £250 000 of its SEATO defence aid to the 'strategic hamlet' program, which Barwick had seen when visiting South Vietnam in 1962. After this visit Barwick, invoking the vulnerability of the Australian subject, told Cabinet that 'we should regard Vietnam as our present frontier'. As the war continued to escalate, and a succession of military regimes grew weaker, French President de Gaulle floated proposals for the 'neutralisation' of Indochina. In March 1964 Barwick told the Parliament that 'neutralisation' would be 'a course of despair', requiring the removal of all Western bases and conventional forces. Betraying a ridiculous Cartesian hubris, he argued that the West needed to retain the option of 'controlled and graduated resistance'. In June Cabinet approved a doubling in the size of the AATTV to sixty – with approval for its members to accompany ARVN units into battle – along with six RAAF Caribou and crews. The AATTV was eventually increased to a hundred.[72]

August 1964 saw the passage through the US Senate of the Gulf of Tonkin Resolution, which freed the US administration to escalate the war without recourse to Congress. In the Australian Parliament, opposition leader Arthur Calwell called for UN intervention and a reconvention of the Geneva Conference, and questioned the lack of clear and public treaties to cover the deployment of Australian troops overseas. He argued that the conflict was essentially a civil war, and that the 'Vietcong' drew 'its basic strength from the support it receives within South Vietnam itself'. Gough Whitlam, however, supported the government and the US Navy's actions in the Gulf of Tonkin and, referring to the bombing raids Lyndon Johnson had ordered, said that military action was necessary to enable the US and the RVN to negotiate from a position of strength![73]

Labor MP Jim Cairns, while happy for the US to retain a 'sea and air cordon' around South-East Asia, opposed US intervention because it would only make the 'national revolutionary movement' more oppressive. No speaker advocated the withdrawal of Western forces or aid; the overriding theme was a questioning of the legal basis of the Western commitments. Minister for External Affairs Hasluck admitted that the RVN had not requested Australian help under the SEATO protocol, but asserted that the Australian commitment 'flowed from' the general obligations assumed under the Manila Treaty. Thus while Western commitments did not directly invoke SEATO (due to the divisions among its members), the deployments still drew on the discursive and juridical illusions embodied in the Treaty.[74]

On 2 March 1965, 3500 US Marines landed in Da Nang, and the carpet bombing of North Vietnam ('Operation Rolling Thunder') began. On 2 April the meeting of the US National Security Council approved two more Marine battalions, an air squadron and 18 000– 20 000 more support troops; the Marines were authorised to conduct counter-insurgency operations outside their bases. The meeting also decided that the deployment of forces from South Korea, Australia and New Zealand should be sought urgently. On 5 April the Defence Committee recommended sending a combat battalion because it was in Australia's strategic interests to have a strong American military presence in South-East Asia, and on 7 April the Cabinet's Foreign Affairs and Defence Committee met. McEwen, Menzies and Defence Minister Paltridge argued that Australia should commit the battalion in support of the US, who had intervened in Vietnam partly because they 'knew the security of Australia would be at stake if South Vietnam fell'.[75]

After three weeks of convoluted diplomacy aimed at soliciting a 'request' from the RVN government, Menzies made the announcement in Parliament on the evening of 28 April. Both Whitlam and Calwell were absent. His statement included the famous claim that the communist takeover of South Vietnam 'must be seen as part of a thrust by Communist China between the Indian and Pacific Oceans'.[76] However fanciful, this drew on a series of historic images of threat from Asia: just as Pacific war posters of Japanese arrows thrusting towards Australia had segued into Fadden's 1949 image of 'red spearpoints' bearing downward yet again, it traced an easy mutation of the yellow peril into a lurid shade of red. It was a monumental deceit, which nonetheless found its mark in the Australian population. A year later Harold Holt, riding on the euphoria of Johnson's visit to Australia, would win an unprecedented electoral majority on the back of the war in Vietnam.

A week after Menzies' announcement, Calwell replied in federal Parliament. In one of the most remarkable speeches ever made there, he denounced the deployment as unwise, untimely, and politically and morally wrong. It was based, he said, on a flawed analysis of Vietnamese society, the nature of the struggle, and the strategic situation in South-East Asia. While Menzies had argued that the force was needed for Australia's security, Calwell asserted that the deployment would *damage* that security. Thus while a basic ontology of political strategy and being was agreed, the two men were totally at odds regarding its form and achievement. To call the struggle that of democracy against foreign aggression, Calwell continued, was wrong; destroying the whole sovereignty effect attached to the RVN, Calwell pointed out that the South Vietnamese had suffered nine military juntas since the murder of Diem, half of which the US had supported and half they had opposed: 'The Government of South Vietnam does not base itself on popular support. Yet this is the government at whose request, and in whose support, we are to commit a battalion of fighting men. And we are told we are doing this in the name of the free and independent Government and People of South Vietnam. I do not believe it.'

The majority of South Vietnamese, uncommitted to either side, 'watch uncomprehendingly the ebb and flow of this frightful war around them, and as each day threatens some new horror, they become even more uncomprehending. And because this is so, our policy of creating a democratic anti-communist South Vietnam has failed.'[77]

He went on to argue that the obsession with the domino theory had generated an obsessive and dangerous militarism:

> It blinds and obscures the real nature of the problem of communist expansion. It lends support and encouragement to those who would see the problem in purely military terms, and whose policies would, if ever adopted, lead to disaster . . . Preoccupied by the fear of a military Munich, we have suffered a score of moral Dunkirks . . . Preoccupied with fear of communist revolution, we have supported and sought to support those who would prevent any sort of revolution, even when inevitable; even when most needful.[78]

Seeing also the enormously divisive potential of the decision, and the need for the conscription of reinforcements as Australia sank deeper into the quagmire, he concluded with an appeal for the 'dispute to be settled through the councils of the United Nations', and with a profound warning to all the war's opponents:

> This course we have agreed to take today is fraught with difficulty. I cannot promise you that easy popularity can be bought in times like these . . . When the drums beat and the trumpets sound, the voice of reason and right can be heard in the land only with difficulty. But if we are to have the courage of our convictions, then we must do our best to make that voice heard. I offer you the probability that you will be traduced, that your motives will be misrepresented, that your patriotism will be impugned, that your courage will be called into question. But I offer you the sure and certain knowledge that you will be vindicated . . . [79]

The goal of a democratic South Vietnam had failed; escalation threatened a world-destroying war; and the defence policy which generated the decision was based on a damaging series of strategic fallacies. Furthermore, in stating the need for social revolution in Asia, and the determination of the Western powers to frustrate that, Calwell recognised an economic fact of the postwar order whose basic truth had eluded mainstream Labor, and which would quickly be forgotten. It was an utterly damning critique, but one that would go unheeded, as he knew: 'when the great weight of Western opinion calls for a pause, Australia says there must be no pause for reflection, no pause for reconsideration'.[80] In August the size of the force was raised from 800 to a battalion group of 1050, and in March 1966 to a task force of 4500. At the end of July President Johnson affirmed that the US was now deeply committed to the war, and would deploy forty-four battalions (50 000 troops), increasing total US forces to 125 000. The US presence in Vietnam would reach a peak of 560 000 troops in 1968. Johnson visited Australia in October 1966, but Australia's commitment was not increased again (and this was for the last time) until October 1967, when troop numbers were increased to 8000. Over 50 000 Australians were to serve in the conflict.[81]

Australia's support may have seemed militarily insignificant but, as Pemberton argues, it was of enormous political weight – it helped the US administration counter its domestic and Congressional critics, and its 'support as a fellow SEATO member was also crucial ... because America's obligations under the Manila Treaty constituted an important element of the juridical basis of the Tonkin Gulf Resolution and ultimately for direct US involvement'. On a smaller scale it was also militarily important: Australian special forces officers worked in the CIA's 'Phoenix Program', which, through the capture of 28 000 and the killing of another 20 000, decimated the NLF clandestine government in the years after 1968; similarly, US Colonel David Hackworth praised the Australians' counter-insurgency skills and sent his own officers to train with them.[82]

The war to which Australia gave unstinting diplomatic support, and which Holt's Minister for the Army Malcolm Fraser[83] would decades later maintain was a just cause, would drag on until April 1975 and claim as many as 4 million Vietnamese lives, 58 000 American lives and 508 Australian lives. South Vietnam was turned into a vast military and social laboratory, in which horrific new weapons were tested and deployed, populated areas designated free-fire zones and subjected to incessant bombing, strafing and napalm bombing, and the environmental and genetic order poisoned for generations by the use of defoliants. Millions were made refugees, while during the most intense years of the war, between 1963 and 1969, at least 25 000 civilians were killed every year and another 50 000 were seriously wounded. Hundreds of thousands more were killed in combat and during the bombing of the north, or were assassinated (by both sides). One hundred and fifty thousand Cambodians were also killed by B52s as the war expanded into Cambodia in 1973.[84]

The conflict that government leaders asserted lay on Australia's frontiers was a cruel and brutal display of techno-scientific murder, a terrible apogee to the systemic chain which married the most rigid ontology of being with the Cartesian hubris that led to the belief that spaces, populations and resources could be easily moulded, controlled and exploited. Confronted by its failure – which was visible as early as 1962 and most conclusively after the Tet Offensive of 1968 – the machine simply ground on, destroying everything in its path. In short, the war was a moral disaster of major order, recalling the Holocaust in its marriage of industrial modernity with an amoral rationality that systematically demonised, and dehumanised, its victims.[85]

The Indonesian killings

If Vietnam was an event felt later in global economic upheaval and far-reaching transformations in Australian society, the enormous turmoil in Indonesia after 1 October 1965 would have equally profound – and disturbing – consequences. More than any other event, Sukarno's downfall and the destruction of the PKI helped determine the coming shape of the South-East Asian economic and geopolitical order, and in turn played into a politics which sought to reinterpret and strengthen the linked Australian structure of subjectivity, security and identity – yet another powerful exercise of the strategic imagination. As before, it was the *interpretation* of events, rather than their illusory 'essential' quality, which was most important. Affirming the centrality of the Indonesian New Order to Australian international policy, by 1992 Paul Keating was arguing that Australia and Indonesia had 'joined destinies'. Thus the political vicissitudes of Indonesia were drawn into a vision of security which saw a reinterpretation of the Australian movement of culmination, within the greater achievement of a stable geo-political ideal. It had been no different for the governments of Holt, McMahon, Whitlam, Fraser or Hawke.

Since at least 1941 Indonesia had been seen as a space essential to Australia's security, a view which drove the wartime decisions to occupy Portuguese Timor, confront the Japanese in Borneo and join the British reoccupation of Java. After 1945 Labor had responded, with one eye on economic and security considerations, to the challenges of decolonisation; yet an important precedent had been set with their obvious relief at the quick suppression of the PKI's rebellion at Madiun in 1948. In 1958 the Australian government secretly supported CIA assistance to rebels in Sumatra with the use of airfields, navy logistic and medical support, and the use of the Christmas Island base by US submarines. Yet the US had a parallel strategy of providing large sums of aid and training to the Indonesian army and police, with the hope either of drawing Sukarno closer to the West or bolstering forces which could eventually confront the PKI, which by 1955 had the fourth-largest national vote and in 1957 won regional elections in central Java.[86]

Australia's opposition to the takeover of West Papua foundered on this US strategy, which aimed to resolve an issue which was preventing the divisions between the PKI, the Army and Muslims from sharpening into a deeper (and more useful) antagonism. In 1950 Spender had argued against the takeover because the area was strategically vital to Australia and its people had a natural cultural affinity with the Papuans, rather than with Asians. Uncertainty about the future role of communism in Indonesia deepened such fears. By 1961 the US, using those same fears, sought to persuade Australia to accept the takeover as a *fait accompli*. The NSC's Robert Komer, in a classically racist formulation, argued that the US needed 'to sell [Australia] on the proposition that a pro-bloc (if not communist) Indonesia is an infinitely greater threat to them (and us) than Indo possession of a few thousand square miles of cannibal land'. In contrast, Spender's argument that 'it hardly seems consistent with modern ideas that a million people who have not yet reached a stage of political consciousness and maturity should be transferred from one nation's sovereignty to another without their will having been ascertained' appeared a shining example of humanitarian virtue. A more pragmatic Barwick persuaded the government to accept the Bunker settlement of 1962 under which control reverted to Indonesia in 1963, with provision for a plebiscite by 1969.[87]

As Confrontation escalated, the hostility between Sukarno and the West deepened. In March 1963 the Soviet defence minister visited Jakarta, followed by Chinese officials a month later. In June a new agreement on profit shares was reached with US oil companies Caltex and Stanvac – only two weeks before they were to have been expelled. After the British embassy was sacked in September, US arms shipments were cancelled and US$50 million in IMF drawing rights was revoked; but crucial aid for the army's civic action program was continued, as was training for army officers and the police mobile brigades. On 17 August 1964 Sukarno warned of a coming 'year of dangerous living', and in January 1965 Foreign Minister Subandrio announced the formation of a 'Peking–Jakarta axis'. As Sukarno's health became more uncertain, the PKI was now the largest communist party outside the Soviet Union – although it still had only a small and symbolic presence in the Cabinet. Visible symbols of US power, particularly United States Information Service (USIS) offices, came under attack. In February workers seized Goodyear rubber plantations, which were then expropriated by the government. By the end of April Sukarno had signed a decree ordering the confiscation of all foreign-owned enterprises, including all US assets and oil interests.[88] The 'last domino' seemed in danger of falling.

On the night of 30 September 1965 six of the army's most senior generals were murdered, including armed forces head Achmad Jani. Defence Minister Nasution escaped, but his daughter was killed. The murders were the work of elements of Sukarno's palace regiment, led by Lieutenant Colonel Untung; neither Sukarno nor the PKI was directly involved or previously informed. The motives appeared to be resentment against the generals for their corruption, their close links with the United States, and their covert resistance to Sukarno's policies. Both Kostrad Commander Soeharto (intriguingly left off the killing list)[89] and Nasution – who seized the initiative by directing operations to capture the conspirators – saw the opportunity to move against the PKI. The party was blamed for the coup, which was said to have been directed against Sukarno's authority; in November PKI leader Aidit was killed and in March 1966 the party was banned. In late October a campaign of archipelago-wide massacres began, directed by the army and carried out mainly by soldiers and Muslim and Catholic youth. 'Very soon', wrote Humphrey McQueen, 'there were too many corpses to bury. So many bodies were thrown into streams that they formed log-jams, turned the waters red and polluted the drinking supply. Orphaned children crowded railway stations begging for food.'[90]

By March 1966, when the level of killing declined, between 500 000 and a million people were dead, most of them communists, leftists and Chinese. In November Soeharto asked the US for assistance: communications gear and small arms were delivered as 'medicines'. CIA operatives complied a list of 5000 PKI cadres, which was passed on to army headquarters. At the end of October, US Ambassador Marshall Green cabled Secretary of State Dean Rusk that the army was resisting Sukarno's efforts to stop the slaughter, and Rusk cabled back that the 'campaign against PKI' must continue as 'the army are only force capable of creating order in Indonesia'. A week later Green wrote that 'we have made it clear the Embassy and USG generally sympathetic with and admiring of what Army doing'. In December he reported that between 100 000 and 200 000 people had been killed in northern Sumatra and central and eastern Java alone.[91]

The Australian government viewed the massacres with admiration and relief. Declassified files reveal that the Jakarta embassy was aware of the level and scale of the killings, and took heart from the army's determination to systematically crush the PKI. On 20 October Ambassador Keith Shann cabled Canberra: 'The Army, as of today, is refreshingly determined to do over the PKI.' Another cable spoke of the 'brutality of [the Army's] methods now clearly revealed, and probably absorbed by the population as a whole ... We will never know how many people have lost their lives. We think it is a lot.' A Canberra-based information officer, Richard Woolcott, worked with Shann to ensure that Radio Australia broadcasts gave every assistance to the army's efforts to destroy the credibility of Sukarno and the PKI.[92]

Prime Minister Harold Holt was quoted as saying in July 1966 that 'with 500 000 to one million communist sympathisers knocked off, I think it is safe to say a reorientation has taken place', while in February 1967 the new Labor leader Gough Whitlam wrote: 'If the coup of 18 months ago had succeeded, as it nearly did, we would have had a country of 100 million dominated by communists on our border. We can only imagine the additional and crippling sums we would now be spending on defence. Yet our aid to Indonesia and abroad generally is trifling and ineffective.' Thus there was acute awareness of, and bipartisan support for, the radical transformations that took place during what have since become known as 'the Indonesian killings'.[93]

With the PKI destroyed, Sukarno removed and Confrontation ended, a whole raft of threats to Australian visions of security, prosperity and order had been removed – at a truly terrifying human cost. While the historian Peter Edwards argued that the events 'undermined much of the rationale for the Vietnam commitment', the Coalition government's psychological investment in the RVN was too deep to reverse course. Nevertheless by the end of the decade, with the Vietnam War heading towards stalemate, US forces being drawn down and the war's geopolitical verities under challenge, there was a sense that the certitude the Australian government craved had largely been achieved. Having been wagered on the most rigid, antagonistic ontology, with the elimination of the PKI *security* could finally complete its own circle, return to its claustrophobic truth. In the death-clogged rivers of Java and the smashed paddies of Vietnam *security* found its meaning, its comfort, and its promised prosperity – which were ours also.

Conclusion: The price of stability

This chapter has traced a new achievement in the story of the Australian subject – less now a story of its growth than one of its refinement, narrowing and solidification. Drawing on the historic fears of Asia, a modern pattern of class war and the stubborn imagination of identity based upon the threatening strangeness of the Other, it reduced Australian security and *being* to a fear-soaked core in which only the most rigid and coercive relation with difference was possible. In short, it sought a violent consolidation of the Same, at a time when new democratic, nationalist and anti-capitalist forces and aspirations strove for recognition. The 'way of life' that Spender had declared 'uppermost' in the determination of Australian foreign policy was now simply assumed, even it was itself just another policing of difference, another reduction of variety, dissent and resistance to a single vision of existence – for which the quarter-acre block, the white picket fence and the Holden car stand as slightly surreal cartoons. As always, Australia's first people were excluded from this seductive index of Australia's being, and their children were still being removed from Aboriginal homes in the hope that they could be remoulded, their identities erased and their links with kin and land irrevocably severed. Around Maralinga their lands were fenced off for the testing of British atomic weapons and became poisoned wastelands from which nature was banished.[94] Similarly, in remote areas all over the continent their lands were developed, without consultation or compensation, by transnational resource capital as the basis of the easy prosperity which liberals since Smith had been proclaiming as the highest aspiration of modern human society.

Thus the extension of the 'political double-bind' to a vast disciplinary formation which merged individuals with the immense spaces and flows of geopolitics was paralleled by the passage of the 'Australian' story of progress into a 'global' movement of reason that would be the glittering face of the new post-colonial imperial order. In this way former US Ambassador to Vietnam General Maxwell Taylor could say in 1972 that Indonesia's 'freedom from an internal communist threat is attributable, to a large degree, to what we've accomplished in South Vietnam'. The entry of substantial US ground forces after 1965, he maintained, emboldened the Indonesian generals 'to run the risk of eliminating President Sukarno and destroying the Indonesian communists'.[95] Likewise, on returning from his Asian tour in 1967, Prime Minister Holt told Australians that they should look beyond the horrors of the Vietnam War 'to a prosperous and secure future in Asia'. Others have more recently argued that US intervention in Vietnam provided a 'shield' for the rest of South-East Asia to develop, free from communist influence.[96]

Under its carefree, prosperous sun, Australia was simultaneously experiencing some of its darkest hours and profiting from them. Yet even as a comforting new 'stability' was being established over the ashes of the PKI and the establishment of new regional organisations such as ASEAN and the Five Power Defence Arrangement, the ground was irreversibly shifting. At elite levels geopolitical truths were under challenge – by seeking détente with China the US broke apart the monolithic image of international communism, while Nixon's proclamation of the Guam Doctrine in 1969 (which ruled out future US military intervention in South-East Asia) was parallelled by External Affairs Minister Gordon Freeth's comments that Australia 'need not panic whenever a Russian appears'. A year before, John Gorton had ordered a complete review of Australia's defence strategy.[97]

The social upheavals were even more sweeping. Along with the rise of a broad-based movement to oppose conscription and the war in Vietnam were a whole series of new claims and struggles – of women, indigenous peoples, the third world. The social transformations of what historian Coral Bell has called 'a slum of a decade' would act as a catalyst for new forms of dissent which challenged longstanding structures of power, identity and thinking. Already their effects were being felt in the mainstream – Labor had removed the White Australia plank from its platform in 1965, while Holt also disavowed it during a visit to Asia in 1967.[98] In the hope that new communities, identities and modes of life might be recognised and heard, the public unity of nation and being was increasingly being questioned. In time, elites would recognise the threats this posed, and seek new rhetorics, tactics and modes of disciplinary power to counter them. The next decades would be permeated by this confrontation. Yet something had undoubtedly changed, in ways which have largely made my own speech possible: beneath the great movement of culmination, a reality of struggle, dissent and counter-truth had been revealed – discourses were breaking apart with the inexorable momentum of tectonic plates.

4

Realpolitik beyond the Cold War
1970–95

All Australians must realise how damaging and dangerous a reputation
Australia's present policies produce. We are a European nation on the fringe
of the most populous and deprived coloured nations in the world. What the
world sees about Australia is that we have an Aboriginal population with the
highest infant mortality rate on earth, that we have eagerly supported the
most unpopular war in modern times on the ground that Asia should be a
battleground for our freedom, that we fail to oppose the sale of arms to South
Africa, that the whole world believes that our immigration policy is based on
colour and that we run one of the world's last colonies.

E. G. Whitlam, January 1971[1]

Anyone hearing Whitlam's words could have been forgiven for
thinking a revolution in progress, given their dramatic challenge
to longstanding modes of Australian identity, policy and belief.
Whitlam made the statement on his second visit to Papua New
Guinea as leader of the federal opposition, where he was pressing
his case for the early decolonisation of a territory Australians had
long seen as absolutely essential to their security. The obsession
with New Guinea had been one of the most enduring themes in
Australian diplomacy, from the earliest attempts at annexation in
the 1880s, Hughes' appearance at Versailles as the living voice of
60 000 dead, to the Kokoda Track in 1942 and the failed attempt
to keep West Papua out of Indonesian hands. In 1961 Hasluck, as
Minister for Territories, had maintained that Papua New Guinea
would not be ready for independence for at least twenty years,
perhaps even fifty. Now Whitlam was proposing self-government
immediately on the election of Labor, and independence by 1976.[2]

As radical as this seemed, the idea of Papua New Guinea as a
bulwark of Australian security would remain central to Australian

policy, as the vast subsequent flows of military and economic aid, even for the Bougainville war, would attest – what Whitlam was suggesting was that Australia's security could be preserved with Papua New Guinea as an independent state. As Sir John Guise was to say as the Australian flag was lowered at the independence ceremony in 1975, 'It is important that the people of Papua New Guinea and the rest of the world realise the spirit in which we are lowering the flag of our colonies. We are lowering it but not tearing it down.'[3]

Not that the statement came out of nowhere. It had its roots in a series of broader political, cultural and discursive shifts: the failure of US strategy in Vietnam, the rise of third world militancy and dissent in the West, and a corresponding re-evaluation of US foreign policy. Indeed the strategic implications of Whitlam's New Guinea proposals – which saw the indigenisation of the Pacific Islands Regiment under Australian tutelage and with Australian aid – were more or less consistent with the dramatic shift in the strategic imagination marked by US President Nixon's statement to reporters on the island of Guam in July 1969. There, introducing a concept later formalised as the 'Nixon' or 'Guam' Doctrine, he announced that while the US would continue to stand by its treaty commitments, it would increasingly expect Asian nations to assume responsibility for their own defence and security. The speech marked a new US reluctance to make *extended* military interventions in the third world: although these were not ruled out, economic and military aid would now be the preferred mechanisms. Nixon remarked that 'the objective of any US administration would be to avoid another war like Vietnam any place in the world' – a deeply disingenuous comment when we consider the then ongoing operations in Vietnam, Cambodia and Laos, and later US interventions in Chile, Nicaragua, El Salvador, Cambodia and Afghanistan. As the historian Gabriel Kolko argued, the intent of the Guam Doctrine 'never fully adjusted to the new economic and political structural context in which decisions had to be made, or the heritage of interests and attitudes that were inherent to American imperialism'.[4]

In 1971 Nixon's 'Vietnamisation' of the war was already underway, and within twelve months a new détente with China would also have been initiated. Whitlam himself travelled to China in

June 1971, only weeks before Nixon's National Security Advisor Henry Kissinger made a secret visit to Peking. In Australia the first tremors of change had been felt in August 1969, when Minister for External Affairs Gordon Freeth told Parliament that 'Australia has to be watchful, but need not panic whenever a Russian appears'.[5] This marked a shift in the discursive structure of Australian security thinking, in which a link between strategic policy and national identity was no longer formed around a single axis of confrontation. Instead, the interplay between identity, otherness and fear – while remaining – would be structured by a series of more nuanced cleavages, which nonetheless owed much to the geopolitical models of the preceding thirty years. Citing Australia's defence co-operation programs, Freeth continued to hope for 'an appropriate international framework of co-operation for security and development'. The Five Power Defence Arrangement (FPDA) with Malaysia, Singapore, the UK and New Zealand, which took effect in November 1971, was crucial, and enabled Australian forces to remain on the Asian mainland.[6]

Thus Australia was already moving to establish a new regional order which might deal with the anxieties which had drawn them into Vietnam – fear that US commitment to South-East Asia (and thus Australia's own security) would wane, and in turn be compounded by the British withdrawal from its historic security role 'East of Suez'. The FPDA would lock the UK into the defence of Malaysia and Singapore and eventually, through the Integrated Air Defence System (IADS), offer a security umbrella to the broader South-East Asian region. Military aid and training would strengthen regional forces, reinforce their pro-Western orientation, and help with the confrontation of internal dissent and 'instability'.[7] Thus while 'forward defence' had receded as a doctrine, along with the cruder versions of the domino theory, policy had largely reverted to a pre-1962 status quo.[8]

Consolidating the Indonesian New Order

Of enormous significance to this order were the changes in Indonesia after October 1965. As Soeharto slowly consolidated his power, a rash of ministerial visits and exchanges were combined with a vast expansion of Australian aid to the new regime – with the aim of cementing Indonesia's integration into the new international economic and strategic spaces which for many would become synonyms of 'stability' and 'progress'. The ending of Confrontation in August 1966, plus the formation of ASEAN (among whose objectives was to strengthen 'the economic and social stability of the region') and of the Asian Development Bank underlined the dramatic regional transformations wrought by the PKI's destruction.[9]

Australia would have a crucial role in protecting the New Order's position in Indonesia and securing the broader regional order it had enabled. External Affairs Minister Hasluck visited Jakarta in August 1966, only a few months after the killings had subsided, returned in January 1967 to open the new Australian Embassy, and again in January 1968, just prior to Soeharto's appointment as President. Indonesia's Finance Minister, Dr Frans Seda, visited Australia in October 1967, followed by Foreign Minister Adam Malik in December for Holt's funeral.[10]

Added to the covert support Australia had shown the generals in eliminating their political enemies during the turmoil of October and November 1965, were aid and diplomacy which sought to help the army revive the economy – this was crucial both to alleviate widespread misery and to consolidate the army's political gains, which Australian officials feared 'could be eroded by economic discontent'.[11] Australia immediately began a program of direct aid and also participated in the international consortium, the Inter-Governmental Group on Indonesia (IGGI), formed in 1967 after earlier IMF missions gave the new regime their approval.[12] In March 1966 Soeharto obtained sweeping powers from Sukarno to 'restore security and order', powers which he immediately used to dissolve the PKI; he was appointed Acting President by the People's Consultative Assembly (MPR) in March 1967, and President a year later. In May 1967 Sukarno was stripped of all official titles, and was placed under house arrest; he remained confined until his death in June 1970. Soeharto had purged the armed forces, bureaucracy and political parties of leftists and Sukarnoists, and in

1971, only a few months before his visit to Australia, his close ally General Ali Moertopo engineered a crushing electoral victory for the army's new parliamentary vehicle, Golkar.[13]

Australian political leaders were neither disturbed by the vast slaughter which had underpinned Soeharto's rise to power, nor by the blatant fraud of the 1971 elections. Indeed they responded, as one, with an extraordinary personal endorsement of his leadership. At the state luncheon held for Soeharto at Parliament House during the 1972 visit, McMahon expressed frank gratitude for Soeharto's actions following the events of 1 October 1965. He gave thanks for Soeharto's decision to enter the Army, and for his role as Kostrad (Strategic Reserve) commander on the night of the killings, saying:

> I believe . . . that Providence intervened and placed you in a decisive position and one in which you were able to exercise your power and influence on the future in a way that no other person in the history of Indonesia has been able to do. And, Sir, because of those two actions . . . you [were able] to make the decision that saved Indonesia and I think has brought peace, order and goodwill to your own country.[14]

Gough Whitlam was also there – he praised Soeharto, recalling a meeting in August 1966 at which he (Whitlam) 'was immediately struck by the determination and the decorum of the General, the future President'. His speech also prefigured later accounts of Indonesia's strategic importance to Australia: the need for Australia's maritime trade and aircraft movements to use Indonesian waters and airspace, and the resource and security interests that apparently made seabed agreements a priority.[15]

On the eve of Labor's election victory in 1972, a series of complex political and discursive currents were in play. Longstanding forms of identity, policy and belief were under challenge, from those who opposed both the Vietnam War and the postwar thrust of Western imperialism, and – differently – from conservative attempts to retain hegemonic manoeuvrability amid a more turbulent economic and geopolitical context. The conservatives held the upper hand: a new consensus and a new regional order were successfully being shaped, in ways which preserved the same interests which had driven the Cold War and strengthened its underlying discursive and political architecture. Here the public incitement of fear which had characterised the Menzies era was giving way to the long-term objective of managing 'stability'. The Defence Committee's 1971 opinion, that Australia faced no immediate or obvious threat, was no longer radical – a deeper continuity with Spender's vision of security and development existed in the politics of coercion and transformation that would underpin the new regional order. As McMahon said of Indonesia, 'security and stability [go] hand in hand with economic improvement and development. Australia's programmes of assistance w[ill] help strengthen the capacity of the administration, the networks of communications and transportation, and the security of the neighbouring countries.'[16]

Meanwhile, drawing in part on the impetus and vision provided by the anti-war, women's and indigenous people's movements, Whitlam was promising further sweeping change. However, his disturbing response to Soeharto suggested that this change might also have its limits.

Power politics or new identity?

The Whitlam government's vision of the future, outlined during the election campaign of 1972 and swiftly implemented once it took power, would share much with that of its Labor antecedents, the Curtin and Chifley governments. In the broad outlines of its domestic and international policies, it promised the same reconciliation of security and justice – at home *and* abroad – which could be found in Curtin's wartime speeches and Evatt's energetic postwar diplomacy. In this it married a potent evolution of the 'political double bind' – the simultaneous achievement of social and national security – with a new extension of universal justice and principle. As Whitlam declared in his policy speech at the Blacktown Civic Centre in November 1972, 'We have a new chance for our nation. We can re-create this nation. We have a new chance for our region. We can re-create this region.'[17]

The Labor vision thus involved a dramatic reimagination of the national identity – at least rhetorically – which departed from both the verities associated with the previous thirty years of conservative rule and from many held dear by 1940s Labor. The Chifley government had struck problems confronting the evolving structures of the postwar international order, but in 1972 Labor took office in a context in which those structures were now deeply entrenched, and in which Australia was closely allied with the very power most aggressively seeking to preserve them. To these obstacles were added the limitations of the government's own thinking.

In assessing its record, particularly in the light of Whitlam's own retrospective and more recent attempts to identify a 'Labor tradition' in foreign policy, some key questions emerge.[18] Beneath its dramatic rhetorical reimagination, were the fundamental ontological structures of the Australian identity really changed? How different was the politics of security that sought to safeguard and realise it, and was it consistent with its other claim – to justice?

To conservatives still grappling with the implications of détente, the end of the White Australia policy, the decolonisation of Papua New Guinea or the irritation of the Aboriginal tent embassy, much of what Whitlam espoused must have seemed shocking. In its first months the new government withdrew Australia's remaining forces from Vietnam, recognised the People's Republic of China and freed gaoled conscientious objectors. It began moves to legislate land rights for Aborigines, to establish a universal health system, raise pensions and abolish tuition fees for tertiary education, and reopened the case for equal pay in the Conciliation and Arbitration Commission. It cancelled wheat exports to Rhodesia and closed down Rhodesia's information office in Sydney, and banned racially selected sporting teams from visiting Australia. More radical moves included the restoration of a passport to the journalist Wilfred Burchett, which symbolised the rejection of what Whitlam in his policy speech had called the 'eighteen years of bombing, butchering and global blundering' in Indochina.[19]

After much personal equivocation on the Vietnam War, Whitlam had now firmly set his face against it, and it would be one of the most strident notes in the government's new foreign policy. Along with the decisions on conscription and Aborigines, it boldly proclaimed the beginning of new era – and a new meaning for the

Australian nation. At the Blacktown Civic Centre Whitlam declared
the necessity of the new path: 'We cannot afford to limp along with
men whose attitudes are rooted in the slogans of the 1950s – the
slogans of fear and hate. If we made such a mistake, we would make
Australia a backwater in our region and a back number in history.
The Australian Labor Party – vindicated as we have been on all the
great issues of the past – stands ready to take Australia forward to
her rightful, proud, secure and independent place in the future of
our region.'[20]

In contrast to the rhetoric of an absolute break with the past, and
more revealing of the contours of the general ontology he was constructing, Whitlam's foreign policy goals were more conservative.
Taking a pose between the verities of power politics realism and
the neo-Kantian dreams of liberal internationalism, he maintained
that:

> a nation's foreign policy depends on striking a wise, proper and prudent
> balance between commitment and power. Labor will have four com-
> mitments commensurate to our power and resources. First to our own
> national security; second to a secure, united and friendly Papua New
> Guinea; third to achieve closer relations with our nearest and largest
> neighbour, Indonesia; fourth to promote the peace and prosperity of
> our neighbourhood.[21]

Many will notice the same indexes of national power, and political
'prudence', which had marked Hans Morgenthau's political realism,
and which seemed to sit oddly with Whitlam's reputation as an
internationalist – here power politics formed the underpinning to
a rhetorical idealism.

This was most comprehensively underlined when Whitlam
made his first visit to Jakarta as Prime Minister, in February 1973.
Whitlam used the occasion to outline his government's approach
to foreign policy, which aimed for 'a more independent Australian
stance in international affairs firmly based on national identity,
social justice, human rights and peaceful regional co-operation,
and not open to suggestions of racism'. During this address to the
state banquet held in his honour Whitlam again, and without irony,
declared his admiration for Soeharto's achievements:

> This region . . . is entering a new and more hopeful era. There are
> three principal reasons for my optimism. The first is the ceasefire
> in Vietnam, which has brought to an end 20 years of bloodshed,
> suffering and turmoil. The second . . . is in the progress Indonesia
> herself has made – under your guidance, Mr President – to achieve
> peace and development, and to restore fully the principles of harmony
> and justice, democracy and freedom embodied in your Constitution
> of 1945. A just and prosperous Indonesia is an essential condition of
> a just and prosperous Southeast Asia. We in Australia have looked to
> you to set an example to our neighbourhood of progress and social
> transformation.[22]

Given what was known of Soeharto's rise to power, the fraud
of the 1971 elections, and the 55 000 political prisoners still lan-
guishing in camps and gaols across the archipelago, this is a truly
astonishing statement.[23] I am sure I am not the only person to
have read it two or three times, in utter disbelief. That words such
as 'peace', 'justice', 'democracy' and 'progress' could be plausibly
used in this context strains credibility, tearing asunder the already
tenuous principle linking language and reality that again recalls the
perverse world of Orwell's *1984*.

Yet at the time they probably passed as an unproblematic description of the changes Soeharto had forced, and which Australian elites
found so comforting. Furthermore, the formulation was absolutely
germane to Whitlam's co-ordinated vision of security, identity and
diplomacy, of which 'justice' (as a possibility of general teleological
achievement) was the crowning jewel. Soeharto's Indonesia would
be essential to the new ontology Whitlam was in the process of
constructing – after all, the region could only be 're-created' in the
context provided by the destruction of the PKI. Later in 1973 he
underlined this to the Australian Institute of International Affairs:

> The importance of Indonesia to Australia is indisputable. We need,
> however, to see the development of our relations with Indonesia in a
> broader South-East Asian regional context . . . our standing in other
> regional countries is not irrelevant to the importance which Indonesia
> will attach to Australia . . . as our destiny is inseparable from Indone-
> sia, so Indonesia cannot separate her own destiny from those of her
> immediate neighbours to the north in ASEAN.[24]

Whitlam quickly moved to back such rhetoric with action – affirming his commitment to the three-year aid program announced by McMahon, ratifying the seabed agreement between the two nations, and concluding an agreement on the border between Papua New Guinea and West New Guinea (now called Irian Jaya). This agreement underlined Whitlam's conviction that Dutch control of West Papua was an anachronism, regardless of the brutal way Soeharto's government had engineered the so-called UN 'Act of Free Choice' in 1969 – again orchestrated by Soeharto's key to the 1971 elections, General Ali Moertopo. The voting process involved using 1025 hand-picked community leaders to represent 700 000 Papuans, and was riddled with threats and intimidation. Moertopo personally threatened to shoot those who voted against Indonesia 'on the spot'.[25]

After 1962 the Indonesian military fought uprisings from the new Free Papua Movement (OPM), and systematically imprisoned, killed and tortured the more politically active. Despite the highly critical report of the UN observer mission, the General Assembly voted to accept the plebiscite as a genuine demonstration of the West Papuans' wish to integrate with Indonesia. The legacy would be an ongoing guerrilla war, bloody counter-insurgency operations and the movement of a vast number of refugees into Papua New Guinea. After the vote the *Sydney Morning Herald* editorialised prophetically that 'we are helping to prepare the ground for a Papuan irredentist movement and laying up grave trouble in store for New Guinea and consequently for ourselves. Where else in today's world would the dictum be accepted that a people was too primitive ever to be free?'[26]

Whitlam also stepped up military aid to the New Order (it had been resumed in October 1967). A major component of the three-year program of technical assistance and defence aid totalling A$20 million announced by McMahon in June 1972 was an operational squadron of sixteen Sabre jet fighters. Military aid also included work by Australian Army surveyors, who mapped Kalimantan in 1970 and the whole of Sumatra during 1971 and 1972 – although portrayed as a 'foreign aid' project, the mapping was no doubt used to progress the Indonesian government's internal security operations. Indonesian Army officers were also among regional allies who trained in counter-insurgency and jungle warfare techniques at Canungra (Queensland), and in 1974 joint naval exercises were also held off the east coast of Australia. The close strategic and political ties certainly helped the rapid expansion in trade and investment – between 1972 and 1974 trade with Indonesia rose fourfold, from A$21 million to A$97 million, and by 1974 there were fifty Australian corporations with Indonesian investments. As historian Greg Pemberton has pointed out, such a continuation of military aid to repressive governments helped support 'coercive approaches to the region's problems' despite the doctrine of forward defence having been formally abandoned.[27]

New strategic challenges: The end of certainty I

As disturbing as Whitlam's Indonesia policies already were, their full meaning would not be revealed until the invasion of East Timor in December 1975; meanwhile, the political and alliance relationship with the United States displayed the same tensions between continuity and change. Whitlam was an admirer of the United States, and had softened his criticism of the Vietnam War by saying his opposition was aimed at helping end 'America's agony'; similarly, he affirmed support for ANZUS and for US facilities on Australian soil. As his memoirs explain, he was also aware of how the evolution of the strategic imagination (which paired perennial Cold War tensions with rapid advances in military, space and communications technologies) had bound the two nations more closely, even as the Vietnam War drew to a close: 'The US is important to Australia as it is the most powerful and vital nation on earth. Australia is important to the US as it occupies a crucial position on the earth's surface and in relation to the heavens above and the waters beneath.'[28] Yet almost as soon as it took office, the government was faced with a dramatic increase in tension with its closest ally.

The Nixon administration reacted angrily to Labor criticism of the 1972 'Christmas bombings' of Hanoi and Haiphong, criticism which provoked a black ban on all US shipping by maritime unions and a letter of protest from Whitlam to Nixon.[29] Cairns described it as a 'brutal, indiscriminate slaughter' and Clyde Cameron as an 'act of virtual genocide'. Marshall Green (now Assistant Secretary for Far Eastern Affairs) warned that the bans might provoke 'retaliatory action' from US unions and 'affect Australia–US relations on a broad range of subjects'. In a meeting with US Ambassador Rice, Whitlam said that if the US tried to place further pressure on the government, the US facilities 'would become a matter of contention here'.[30]

However, Whitlam was supportive of the US in other ways. He held few concerns about the satellite ground stations at Pine Gap and Nurrungar, and despite his concern about North West Cape's role in US nuclear strategy – he remarked that the bases could be used to begin a third world war without Australia's knowledge – only cosmetic changes were made. Australia failed to achieve scrutiny of messages passed through the station, and in 1978 the Fraser government found out from the press that the US was planning to build a new ground station there. He also supported US plans for the Omega station in Victoria, which would be crucial to communications with US ballistic missile submarines. However, the government consistently opposed US plans to expand the air and naval base at Diego Garcia in the Indian Ocean, which amounted to a challenge to the whole strategy of deterrence which underpinned US naval doctrine. However, not wanting to side with the USSR or undermine ANZUS, Australian protest was almost inaudible when Congress eventually voted funds for the base in July 1975.[31]

Whitlam's goodwill towards the United States did his government few favours, if the hysterical reaction from elements of the US intelligence community was any guide. They were disturbed by the criticism of the Hanoi–Haiphong bombings, Attorney-General Lionel Murphy's raid on the Melbourne premises of ASIO and, most significantly, by public questions about the role and function of the bases – especially the CIA's (then secret) control of Pine Gap. Serious questions still remain about the role of the CIA and the US government in the dismissal of Whitlam's government in 1975. Citing former CIA Deputy Director Ray Cline and agent Victor Marchetti, John Pilger argues that there was a fully formed conspiracy to remove Labor; Brian Toohey does not claim a general conspiracy, but both maintain that Sir John Kerr *was* briefed on the contents of an alarmist ASIO cable, sent two days before the dismissal, listing US concerns about Whitlam – a claim the Governor-General denied. What is uncontested is CIA Director William Colby's assertion in his memoirs that Australia and its 'left-wing and possibly antagonistic government' was one of the three greatest crises the CIA faced at the time.[32]

However paranoid the CIA may have seemed, its actions formed only a small part of the United States' attempts to find responses to its gravest foreign policy crisis in the postwar era. Not only was it dealing with a looming defeat in Vietnam, but the inflationary stimulus of the war's massive US$173 billion expenditures had flowed into the global economy with devastating effect.[33] By 1975 the Bretton Woods system – in which global exchange rates were pegged to the US dollar and its value held at a level which would encourage exports into the US – was a memory. The OPEC countries' response to the inflationary pressures (and US support for Israel in the Yom Kippur War) was first a complete oil embargo and then a vast price hike that cost the US an extra $21 billion in imports over three years. This setback was crowned in May 1974 with the call by a group of seventy-seven third world countries for a New International Economic Order (NIEO) which would raise and stabilise raw materials prices, waive debt, increase development aid and, most alarmingly, allow them to nationalise foreign-owned assets.[34]

This challenge, which followed Mexico's and Venezuela's attempts to develop OPEC-style commodity associations and the election of the socialist Salvador Allende in Chile, energised US efforts to avert demands that analyst David Denoon described as an attempt to 'reorganis[e] the character of world economic relations'. If achieved, he wrote, these changes 'would be as fundamental a change in structure as occurred with the establishment of the Bretton Woods system or the shift from mercantilism to liberal trade in the nineteenth century'. The Chilean coup was one possible response to the new third world assertiveness – others came in the form of denying trade preferences to countries joining commodity associations, and aggressive resources diplomacy which mixed efforts to play off suppliers against each other, foot-dragging on North–South dialogue and 'divide and rule' tactics with third world states wanting access to global capital markets.[35]

Disgusted by the CIA's role in Chile, Whitlam had withdrawn ASIS officers and, speaking in the UN General Assembly in September 1974, he made a veiled criticism of the US by denouncing the attempt by certain states 'to bring about political or economic change in another through unconstitutional, clandestine, or corrupt methods' – words that would come to haunt him as Indonesia's subversion of East Timor gathered pace over the next year. He had established policies to secure 'greater Australian and government control and supervision of the use of our national resources', endorsed greater co-operation between countries producing raw materials, yet was lukewarm about the NIEO. He assured the UN that 'Australia is not in the business of resources blackmail'.[36]

At the same time, his government's ability to manage the economy (in a way consistent with its declared social program) was being sorely tested by the transformations in the world economy wrought by Vietnam and the oil shocks. The government confronted for the first time the phenomenon of stagflation – rapid inflation *and* stagnating growth – which had been thought impossible. In turn the Keynesian consensus which had underpinned the global economic order since 1945 came under challenge. Australian inflation was 7 per cent by 1971, and hit 13 per cent by December 1973 in response to international pressure on food prices. A 31 per cent growth in adult male wages in 1974 saw inflation top 16 per cent. Whitlam's belief – expressed in the John Curtin Memorial Lecture of 1961 – that socialists no longer had 'to ration scarcity but plan abundance' had been shattered. His response to the crisis was to institute a deflationary policy; this, though it included some important caveats, marked the beginnings of the Chicago School's supremacy in economic thought in Australia.[37]

Cultural historian Lindsay Barrett has suggested that these events – within the broader context of Vietnam and the abandonment of Bretton Woods – destroyed the modernist project of 'Whitlamism', which had hinged on the ability of governments to plan and spend amid unproblematic growth and easy Keynesian interventions. Now economists were saying that growth merely fuelled inflation, and that hitherto unacceptable levels of unemployment had to be sustained to keep it in check. In particular, Barrett suggests that the Hayden Budget of July 1975 – which dramatically reduced the deficit in accord with monetarist 'inflationary expectations' thinking – was 'a much neglected watershed in Australian social, political and cultural history' which 'signalled that the era of certainty was over'.[38]

East Timor: *Realpolitik* or Labor tradition?

While this crisis was building through 1974 and 1975, amid escalating political turmoil for the Whitlam government, the government simultaneously faced one of the most profound and far-reaching foreign policy dilemmas in recent Australian history: East Timor. It would be a major test of Whitlam's declared idealism, and come to dominate the relationship with Indonesia. It was also a case where the drive for a new national identity fused with much older – and more coercive – ways of thinking about security. The fate of the Timorese people hinged on how that security was interpreted and achieved.

In April 1974 Portugal announced that it would decolonise its overseas possessions, provoking the formation of three new Timorese political organisations: the Timorese Democratic Union (UDT), the Timorese Social Democratic Association (ASDT, later Fretilin) and the Timorese Popular Democratic Association (Apodeti). UDT initially favoured a gradual transition to independence over fifteen years, Fretilin a slightly faster process over eight to ten years, while Apodeti favoured integration with Indonesia.

While foreign affairs officials developed a policy of support for self-determination, when Whitlam met with Soeharto in Central Java later that year he told Soeharto that 'an independent Timor would be an unviable state and a potential threat to the stability of the area', adding that 'the people of the colony should have the ultimate decision on their future'.[39] It was simple, colourless bureaucratese, but its significance was world-shaking: as the journalist Peter Hastings wrote, 'Despite the rider about self-determination processes, there is a highly unfortunate construction to be placed on the two statements. The Prime Minister seems virtually to be saying that the tidiest solution to Portuguese Timor is to incorporate it within Indonesia, if means acceptable to international and Australian public opinion can be found.'[40] Indeed the official record of the meeting, made public in September 2000, shows that Whitlam told Soeharto of his 'basic' belief 'that Portuguese Timor should become a part of Indonesia' and that 'for the domestic audience in Australia, incorporation into Indonesia should appear to be natural process arising from the wishes of the people'.[41]

Emboldened by Australia's response, Indonesia's subversion operation, Operasi Komodo (again under the direction of Ali Moertopo) was begun in October 1974, and in November the *National Times'* Andrew Clark wrote of 'an upsurge of "reds under the bed" stories . . . a dressed-up scenario of Chinese Communist infiltration into Portuguese Timor would pose a huge security threat which could not be allowed to continue'.[42] The Australian Department of Foreign Affairs, fearing that Jakarta was planning an invasion, warned Indonesia that 'Australia would not condone force'. Secretary Alan Renouf claims that at these talks he also argued that 'an independent East Timor should not necessarily concern Indonesia. By mutual co-operation and with the help of the UN and other ASEAN countries, Indonesia and Australia could ensure that East Timor freely chose integration with Indonesia or, if she chose independence, could ensure a stable and friendly East Timor.'[43]

Such arguments were put to Indonesia only twice more: at meetings in Townsville in April and in a letter from Whitlam to Soeharto in February, after military exercises in Sumatra provoked renewed fears of an invasion. Yet they were never strongly pursued: Whitlam still asserted to Soeharto that integration was his preferred option. By August 1975, when a civil war provoked by Indonesian subversion broke out between UDT and Fretilin, Australian diplomacy had sunk into the worst kind of complicity. In Parliament Whitlam said that Timor was 'in many ways a part of the Indonesian world', that Australia understood 'Indonesia's concern that the territory should not become a source of instability on Indonesia's border' and that Indonesia 'may thus be turned to as the only force capable of restoring calm in the territory'.[44] According to the journalist

Hamish McDonald, Whitlam even withdrew his injunction against the use of force, sending Soeharto a private message saying that 'nothing he said earlier should be interpreted as a veto on Indonesian action in the changed circumstances'. McDonald's claim is substantiated by a record of a meeting between Whitlam and the Indonesian Ambassador, Her Tasning, on 26 August 1975. Whitlam told him that if Portugal requested Indonesian intervention, Australia would not be 'seeking to exercise a veto on the Indonesian response'. This was said despite an earlier cable from Australia's Ambassador in Lisbon, Frank Cooper, which emphasised Portugal's reluctance to make a request because they 'foresee a bloodbath in Timor unless there can be some supervision of Indonesian actions on the ground'.[45]

Whitlam's statements were preceded by an extraordinary cable from Jakarta Ambassador Richard Woolcott, ironically dated 17 August 1975, the anniversary of Indonesia's declaration of independence. Woolcott counselled silence as Indonesia moved to take over:

> We are dealing with a settled Indonesian policy to incorporate Timor . . . From here I would suggest that our policies should be based on disengaging ourselves as far as possible from the Timor question; getting Australians presently there out of Timor; leave events to take their course; and if and when Indonesia does intervene act in a way which would be designed to minimise the public impact in Australia and show privately understanding to Indonesia of their problems.[46]

At the same time Woolcott unwittingly underlined how influential Australia could have been in deterring Indonesian aggression: 'Australia has been singled out by the Indonesians in their planning discussions as the country (along with China) that will be most vocal in the event of Indonesian intervention in East Timor. They know that reaction in Australia – unlike other ASEAN countries and New Zealand – will probably be their main problem.'[47]

He concluded with his by now infamous comment, since widely quoted, which focused on the broken seabed border between Indonesia and Australia, believed to contain enormous oil and gas potential: 'closing the present gap in the agreed sea border . . . could be much more readily negotiated with Indonesia . . . than with Portugal or independent Portuguese Timor. I know I am recommending a pragmatic rather than a principled stand but this is what national interest and foreign policy is all about.'[48] This complicity was deepened by the private briefings he and his staff received from key Indonesians in advance of operations across the border from West Timor – including the operation in which five Australian and New Zealand journalists were executed. In 1991, former Whitlam Minister John Wheeldon also claimed that Australian officials had been secretly urging Indonesia to invade.[49]

Recently declassified records provide a revealing window into Whitlam's thinking at this crucial time. On 14 August 1975, a few days after the UDT coup, Woolcott cabled a report of a meeting he had had with General Yoga Sugama, the head of the BAKIN intelligence agency co-ordinating Operasi Komodo. Sugama had graphically portrayed Indonesia's paranoia about a possible Fretilin takeover, and Woolcott concluded the report by saying, in Paragraph 29: 'I am fully aware of our consistent and public support for self-determination which is both enshrined in the government's platform and in our general stance at the United Nations. But . . . in the final analysis we need to make a pragmatic, practical, hardheaded assessment of our real long-term interests . . . I know I am suggesting that our principles should be tempered by the proximity of Indonesia and its importance to us and by the relative unimportance of Portuguese Timor but, in my view, this is where our national interest lies.' Whitlam was not angered by this repudiation of Labor principle: a foreign affairs cable to Jakarta five days later began by saying, 'The Prime Minister wishes Woolcott to be advised that he agrees generally with paragraphs 28 and 29 of Jakarta telegram O.JA1201'.[50]

In desperation at their international isolation, Fretilin made a unilateral declaration of independence on 29 November. Xavier Do Amaral, when sworn in as the new President, said: 'We have had to fight alone against UDT in Dili and against Indonesia at the border. We direct our appeal for peace to Indonesia but we will live by the slogan: "Independence or death".' The same slogan was still being shouted by young protesters twenty years later. On 5 December Adam Malik visited the Jakarta embassies of eight key nations (including Australia) saying they 'should not be surprised at any steps Indonesia should take'. Cartoonist Bruce Petty summed up Australia's role, and Timor's coming years of horror, when he drew a convoy of tanks labelled '1966 massacre of PKI' headed in the direction of a sign saying 'East Timor'. In the foreground was an Australian diplomat hiding under his desk.[51]

If East Timor were now to suffer because of Indonesian and Australian fears about their *security*, that dreadful irony is underlined by the lengths to which the Timorese were prepared to go to assuage Indonesia. In February 1975 UDT and Fretilin had cabled Australia begging for Australia to support talks between themselves, Australia and Indonesia 'for cooperation towards peace stability SEA [South-East Asia]'. This request was ignored by Whitlam. Years later Jose Ramos-Horta despaired at how 'all our assurances of friendship, co-operation, membership of ASEAN, a foreign policy that was tantamount to Finlandisation of East Timor – all fell on deaf ears. In retrospect, I cannot see what assurances and concessions we could have offered to buy our own survival.'[52]

The Indonesian invasion of East Timor was thus the final act in the saga of Whitlam's problematic and troubled efforts to 're-create' the nation and its region. Enjoying unrivalled authority in international policy-making, he had ignored policy set by his own Department of Foreign Affairs, and ignored several crucial opportunities at which it may have been possible to stop the Indonesians in their tracks. In particular, had he stood firm in November 1974 the basic structure of the relationship with Indonesia could have been preserved, along with the ability of the East Timorese to shape their own future. Instead he, Defence Minister Bill Morrison and key bureaucrats such as Woolcott encouraged an interpretation of the crisis which drew on the same murderous fantasies which had given birth to the New Order and underpinned the hegemonic images of Australian security and identity through thirty years of conservative rule. Despite Whitlam's disavowal of the 'racist' anti-communism of Dulles, Menzies and Spender, what was revealed here was an essential continuity with the past – the rhetorical abandonment of racism and a new sensitivity to Asian aspirations was a mere gloss over a power politics *structure* which had itself been violently achieved.

Worse, the decisions on Timor were deeply interlaced with the images of security, identity and culmination which gave form to a newly totalised image of the Australian subject. Indonesia, and the favour of the New Order regime, had now been designated essential to the security of Australia's very *being* and the realisation of its larger project. These were the conditions in which Whitlam's vision of a 're-created' region and 're-created' Australia would coalesce. Having ignored the moral lessons of Vietnam, 'forward defence' could be abandoned while a proxy army, maintained and directed by Soeharto's New Order regime, was trusted to protect Australia's 'security' throughout the Indonesian archipelago. Thus the safety, aspirations and freedom of the Timorese were to be sacrificed so that Australia could remain secure. This was the meaning of Whitlam's judgement that a small neighbouring territory, with indigenous traditions and forms of life, was too backward to ever constitute a 'viable state' and that an independent Timor would have left Australia with 'a weak, unstable, left-leaning' neighbour. This formula may seem far-fetched, but it was still being incited by Richard Woolcott twenty years later, when he argued that 'sentimental notions of self-determination for the East Timorese or Bougainvilleans . . . threaten our national security'.[53] In this impoverished view, difference and uncertainty were to be dealt with in much the same way as they had been for thirty years.

The second Cold War: Timor, Cambodia and Fraser

The invasion of Dili, East Timor's capital, began in the early hours of 7 December 1975, ironically enough the anniversary of the Japanese raid on Pearl Harbor. By virtue of its excellent signals intelligence and its exchange agreements with the US, the Australian government was aware of it as it happened. In August Woolcott had revealed that he had been promised 'at least two hours' notice' of the operation; by 3 December the CIA was telling the US administration that Soeharto had approved 'the idea of full scale intervention' but that they were unlikely to move until President Ford and Secretary Kissinger had left Jakarta on 6 December. Despite the Army's belief that it could quickly wipe out Fretilin resistance, the CIA wrote that Fretilin had been 'building up defences near the capital and moving supplies and weapons to the interior to wage guerrilla war against an Indonesian occupation'.[54]

At around 2 am the Indonesian Navy began bombarding positions to Dili's east and west, and Kopassandha special forces paratroopers were dropped just before dawn in the waterfront area. Some of the paratroopers were dropped short and fell into the sea, where they drowned under the weight of their equipment. Fretilin fighters withdrew from Dili at around noon, and over the next week the invading troops murdered hundreds of Chinese along with hundreds more Timorese, including pro-Indonesian supporters of Apodeti. They murdered whole families in their homes, and held numerous mass public executions. A group of 150 were shot before a crowd at the harbour, where their bodies fell like stones from the jetty into the water. One of the victims was Isabel Lobato, wife of Fretilin's military commander, Nicolau. Many women associated with Fretilin were also imprisoned, then raped repeatedly and tortured with cigarettes burned into their breasts. At least 2000 Timorese were killed during those few days – the bishop was to say later that the paratroopers had drifted from the heavens like 'angels' and then behaved like 'devils'.[55]

By April there were 35 000 troops in East Timor. When the towns of Liquica and Maubara were captured the Indonesians murdered nearly the whole of their Chinese populations; when Aileu was captured in February its entire population was slaughtered, save children under four, who were trucked to Dili and later placed in a Jakarta orphanage under the care of a foundation owned by Soeharto's wife, Tien. By May the Indonesians still controlled only Dili and a few major towns – the countryside was Fretilin's; Fretilin now had responsibility for some 500 000 people, most of them refugees.[56]

In public the caretaker Fraser government condemned the invasion, but was already acting duplicitously. In the UN General Assembly Australia sought, with Indonesia, to head off a Guyanan draft that 'strongly deplore[d]' the Indonesian invasion and called for the complete and immediate withdrawal of all its forces. After trying (with India, Iran, Saudi Arabia and other ASEAN states) to delete references to Indonesia's military intervention, Australia eventually voted for the Guyana draft, abstaining on the paragraphs referring to Indonesia.[57] While Australia supported sending Security Council envoy Winspeare Guicciardi to Timor, it refused his request for an aircraft to reach Fretilin-held areas. This followed a meeting between Adam Malik and new Australian Foreign Minister Andrew Peacock on 20 January, at which Peacock remarked that 'differences of attitude . . . should be seen in the context of the long-term importance to both countries and the region as a whole of close and co-operative relations between Australia and Indonesia'.[58]

Prime Minister Fraser visited Indonesia in October 1976, just after Australian Federal Police seized a radio transmitter near Darwin being used by activists to communicate with Fretilin. Fraser's official communiqué following the talks stated that 'the important thing now was to look to the future, and to alleviate as far as possible the human suffering which had come with the fighting . . .'. After he had left Indonesia, an adviser to Soeharto, Lieutenant General Sudharmono, told journalists that 'although Indonesia saw Australia as agreeing with the steps Indonesia was taking in relation to East Timor, nonetheless Australia had other domestic interests of its own'. Fraser was said to have been angered by the implication that Australia's policy was two-faced. This view of Australia's behaviour was confirmed, however, by former Indonesian Foreign Minister Dr Mochtar Kusumaatmadja, who told the author that while 'secretly both the US and Australia were applauding what Indonesia did, publicly they were outraged'.[59]

In the UN General Assembly sessions of 1976 and 1977 Australia abstained on the East Timor motion. By January 1978 it had formally provided *de facto* recognition of the annexation, and in 1979 this was made *de jure*. Shortly after, negotiations over the Timor Gap oil and gas reserves began. At no point did Australia protest against the abuses carried out by the Indonesians; furthermore, the recognition of Indonesian 'sovereignty' over East Timor was made while Indonesian authority in Timor was weak and bitter fighting was still taking place. In June 1976, 2000 people were massacred at a refugee settlement near the border at Lakmaras, and by the end of 1976 the Indonesian Catholic Church was estimating that as many as 100 000 may have perished.[60]

The philosophy advanced by the Fraser government to explain its foreign policy was proclaimed in 1976 as 'an active and enlightened realism'. Perhaps it was framed in an attempt to resolve the contradictions posed by its policies on East Timor, or to cloak a baseline *Realpolitik* in a liberal gloss; in neither case was it an honest description of the structural challenges the government was seeking to manage. Perhaps the government hoped its acceptance of a *fait accompli* in East Timor could be explained by Fraser's argument that foreign policy must be based on assessments that are 'free from self-deception, self-delusion. We must be prepared to accept the world as it is, and not as we would like it to be.' It was classic Morgenthau, justifying a refusal to moralise by appeal to an epistemic realism – obscuring the ways in which Australian policy constantly sought to intervene in, shape and cheer on the very realities about which it claimed to be so stubborn.[61]

It was not as if the Fraser government was unaware of the principles at stake – in 1979 and 1980 it repeatedly stated its strident opposition to the Vietnamese invasion of Cambodia and the Soviet invasion of Afghanistan. Even though he admitted in 1979 that 'Pol Pot's regime horrified the world', Fraser said that 'Vietnam's invasion of Kampuchea cannot be condoned' and called for an immediate withdrawal. At the end of the year, when receiving the Soviet Ambassador at the Prime Minister's property at Nareen, Fraser rejected his explanation for the invasion of Afghanistan. At stake, he told the Ambassador, was the principle that 'The Australian Government and people could not accept that there should be military interference by one power in the affairs of a neighbouring state. It was morally wrong and totally contrary to the accepted norms of international society. In this particular case it could only have a destabilising effect on an area which already had its fair share of problems.'[62]

Transposed to the case of East Timor, his statement could not have been more apt. Yet by this time the government could only say that 'although it remains critical of the means by which integration was brought about it would be unrealistic to continue to refuse to recognise . . . that East Timor is a part of Indonesia'.[63] Perhaps words like 'hypocrisy' are overused, but it barely begins to capture the appalling double standards advanced in this case. Worse, opposition to the Soviets and Vietnam would become a rallying cry for Fraser's vision of international reality. The Afghanistan situation, he said, was 'the most dangerous international crisis since World War II' and had substantially changed 'for the worse the strategic order underpinning Australia's security'. To that he added a domino-like link with the Vietnamese invasion of Cambodia: 'both events are related within some larger strategic purpose . . . each carries implications for the other. Certainly the leaders of the ASEAN countries perceive linkages and are deeply concerned.'[64]

This neither showed understanding of what may have motivated Vietnam's action – the attacks by Khmer Rouge forces on its territory between 1975 and 1979 – nor took into account the genocide it had halted. Obviously Vietnam's early withdrawal should have been sought, but from here on Australian policy merely chimed in with a cynical US strategy which prolonged a settlement for over a decade. Nor could the Soviet Union's brutal invasion of Afghanistan be condoned, yet the hypocrisy of Australia's response was underlined by Fraser's long list of retaliatory measures, which included a refusal to supply wheat to replace imports embargoed by the United States, the suspension of Soviet cruise ship operations, a suspension of diplomatic relations, and the infamous attempts to force Australia's Olympic team to boycott the Moscow Games.[65]

In contrast, Indonesia's invasion of East Timor was rewarded with increased levels of development and military aid, along with active support in the UN.[66] At the 1982 General Assembly, both Gough Whitlam (as a private petitioner) and the Australian Ambassador argued that East Timor should be removed from the UN agenda permanently. This, after a famine which had killed almost 100 000 people in 1978 and 1979, and a massive military operation in 1981 (Operation Security) which disrupted planting, saw thousands of Timorese forced to march on military operations ahead of Indonesian forces to flush out Fretilin, and hundreds massacred at the village of Lacluta.[67]

On Cambodia, the Fraser government's policy quickly began to mimic that of the Reagan administration. Australia tacitly endorsed a US strategy which saw China, Thailand and Britain giving military support and sanctuary to the Khmer Rouge, while they and the ASEAN countries ensured that the UN seat remained with the Royalist Coalition (effectively controlled by the Khmer Rouge). This action prevented any of the UN's humanitarian machinery being activated inside Cambodia. Like the US and other Western nations, Australia supplied aid to Cambodian refugees in Thailand, much of which in turn fed Khmer Rouge fighters. The aim of the US, wrote journalist John Pilger, was to 'bleed Vietnam white on the battlefield of Cambodia'.[68] The policy also provided a reassuringly stark model of identity, with the reversion to comforting images of Western alliance and commonality with the United States and a continuation, by proxy, of war against Vietnamese communism. In 1982 Foreign Minister Tony Street said that the USSR now 'combines both an expansionist ideology and military power on an unprecedented scale' and praised the Reagan administration's effort to increase US military power. Street also praised the US's new 'regional level assertiveness' in El Salvador, saying: 'The Australian Government fully understands the Administration's wish to cut off sources of disturbance and revolution there.'[69]

Hawke and Asia: The end of certainty II

When the Hawke Labor government took power in 1983 it was in a context of global recession, resurgent economic liberalism, a dangerous and unprecedented level of Cold War confrontation and a hyper-aggressive United States. It inherited a foreign policy which was building Australia's defence capabilities, and cheering on the US's new assertiveness and its brutal geopolitics in Indochina and Central America. War was still raging in East Timor, and ASEAN had turned into a cohesive political bloc which protected its members from criticism of their 'internal affairs', rigidly enforced outward solidarity and was putting up a (seemingly) united front against Vietnam. These contexts, with their implications for both international policy and domestic economic and cultural management, provided real challenges to Labor, which – at least in theory – was committed to employment growth, public welfare and a liberal foreign policy. The ALP platform, for example, expressed opposition to uranium mining and support for an act of self-determination in East Timor, and provided for the suspension of defence co-operation with Indonesia until it was carried out. The party was committed to Aboriginal land rights, multiculturalism and a non-discriminatory immigration policy. Its relations with the US – following the shadowplay of 1975 and the revelation of the CIA's role during the Christopher Boyce trial in 1977 – were marked by mutual suspicion.

Domestically Hawke's first two terms saw a bewildering array of policy and structural changes – including a formal 'Accord' with trade unions which delivered consistent falls in real wages through the next decade, the floating of the Australian dollar on international money markets, a dramatic reduction in industry protection, and cuts to federal budget deficits which saw surpluses being achieved by the mid-1990s. By that time centralised wage indexation under the Accord was beginning to yield to a push for wage bargaining at the enterprise level, paving the way for a systematic attack on workers' rights by the conservative Howard government after 1996.

The 'reforms' were quickly claimed, at least in elite rhetoric, to embody a systematic vision for a new Australian prosperity amid the ascendancy of monetarism and increasingly 'globalising' patterns of trade in goods, services, capital and labour. Free market economists and senior government ministers began to espouse an integrated approach which linked domestic economic management and reform (along with substantial cultural and attitudinal changes) with new priorities for diplomacy and regional economic integration – in short, a new combination of 'the political double-bind' and the strategic imagination.

Much of this thinking was collected in the 1989 report *Australia and the Northeast Asian Ascendancy*, written by Hawke's former adviser Ross Garnaut, although its detailed themes had been flagged by Foreign Minister Bill Hayden as early as October 1983. Such thinking influenced Hawke's and Keating's energetic promotion of the Asia-Pacific Economic Cooperation trade liberalisation forum (APEC), the development of secondary and tertiary education policy, and new rhetorics of national identity. By 1984 Hayden was arguing that 'Australia's long-term future is as a Eurasian country', while Hawke spoke of seeking to 'enmesh' Australia in Asia. Journalist Paul Kelly argued in 1992 that it is 'the rise of a massive and prosperous middle class in the Asia/Pacific which will trade, travel and live in Australia that is the ultimate guarantor of a new identity'.[70]

While boosters of Labor's reforms such as Kelly emphasise their courage and vision, they could also be portrayed as an accommodation to the imperatives of late-20th-century capitalism and corporate power. Within Australia Labor prevailed over a dramatic transfer of wealth from poor to rich, while internationally they accepted the hegemony of liberal ideas and Western economic domination, which exacerbated the same trends. The third world challenge to the international economic order now seemed a memory; Labor merely echoed the doctrines of the World Bank/IMF in urging the need for greater liberalisation of global trade and investment, with emphasis on commodities markets, while ignoring labour rights and environmental protection. In short, Labor would not recognise that the world economy was fundamentally characterised by unequal *power* relationships, both between and within nations.[71]

There was also continuity in strategic policy. Strong support for ANZUS was an axiom of Hawke's and an early point of friction within the party. In 1985, when ANZUS co-operation was faltering, Hawke stated that he would not want to be Prime Minister 'if central elements of the alliance, such as port access for nuclear ships and Australia's hosting of the joint facilities, were repudiated'.[72] Not that this translated into the slavish devotion to US foreign policy that characterised the Fraser years. The government distanced itself from the Reagan administration's support for the Nicaraguan Contras and brutal regimes in Honduras and El Salvador, pressed hard for the negotiation of a comprehensive nuclear test ban treaty, criticised the space-based Strategic Defence Initiative and supported the South Pacific Nuclear Free Zone. However, Australia used its influence in the South Pacific Forum to preserve transit rights for nuclear-armed vessels – crucial to the Pentagon's aggressive naval strategy – and its disarmament initiatives were designed partly to pre-empt pressure from a rapidly growing anti-war movement, which saw huge Palm Sunday marches and the formation of the Nuclear Disarmament Party (which contested the 1984 federal election). Hayden later explained that he feared that if 'we [did not] move quickly to establish our ascendancy on peace and disarmament issues' the government would face pressures from the Left to close the US bases, refuse ship visits and withdraw from ANZUS.[73]

Of greater moment was Labor's break with the US on Cambodia. Here, in an initiative suggested by Hawke, Hayden pursued an active diplomacy with Vietnam, the Khmer Rouge-Royalist Coalition and ASEAN in pursuit of common ground which might lead to a settlement. In doing so Hayden clashed with Thailand and Singapore, and directly undermined declared US policy. On the other hand, Indonesia supported Australian initiatives strongly within ASEAN and pursued parallel diplomatic efforts. US officials attempted to undermine Australia's diplomacy in Asian capitals, and Secretary of State George Shultz tried to dissuade Hayden in 1983.[74]

In contrast with Fraser, Hayden was sanguine about the strategic implications of the Vietnamese invasion, saying that while Australia opposed it in principle, he understood why the Vietnamese had intervened and could not withdraw while there was a chance the Khmer Rouge could return to power. On the other hand, Hawke baulked at resuming aid to Vietnam.[75] *The Australian* declared in 1985 that Hayden's diplomacy was 'not the conduct of a worthwhile ally', and that Australian foreign policy was 'sliding into chaos'. Unfortunately, the worth of the initiative was marred by the cynicism with which Hawke conceived it – in his memoirs Hayden argues that 'Hawke had encouraged the Indochina initiative as a red herring to distract the party, especially the Left, from the vexatious and difficult to manage issue of East Timor.'[76]

In 1984 Hawke offered *de jure* recognition of Indonesian sovereignty over East Timor, and Hayden worked hard (and successfully) at the ALP's 1984 National Conference to remove support for East Timor's self-determination from the platform. With the New Order government reassured, negotiations over the Timor Gap could resume. While this capitulation preserved the friendly tenor of relations, at least until 1986, tensions remained. In September 1983 Hayden made a public statement of concern about the new military offensive in East Timor, but no stronger action was taken. Hayden would have been aware of the appointment of Benny Murdani as the new Indonesian armed forces (ABRI) commander, and of his cancellation of the ceasefire (and negotiations with Fretilin) which had been in place since March. Hayden would also have been aware that the International Committee of the Red Cross (ICRC) had suspended relief operations because of new restrictions on its activities. Launching the new offensive on Indonesia's independence day, 17 August, Murdani warned: 'We are going to hit them without mercy.'[77]

Later the Australian government would defend its East Timor policy by arguing that it was supplying humanitarian and development aid for East Timor – including through the ICRC – and that preservation of its political relationship with the New Order enabled it to take up human rights concerns. Yet the new military offensive made a mockery of this logic. Amnesty International reported that the operation initiated a new wave of repression, including hundreds of arrests, disappearances, summary executions and the massacre of 200 people at the village of Kraras.[78]

At the same time another crisis was brewing on the Papua New Guinea–Irian Jaya border. Following an abortive uprising by the Free Papua Movement (OPM) in and around the capital Jayapura in early 1984, Indonesian reprisals and security operations led to a flood of refugees into Papua New Guinea. By the end of the year 11 000 West Papuans were living in hastily erected camps near the border. Papua New Guinea policy, influenced by Indonesian pressure, was to repatriate them as quickly as possible. While Indonesia provided 22 000 kina (A\$33 000) to feed the refugees, after this ran out in June the Papua New Guinea government allowed supplies to dry up in an attempt to make camp life as unappealing as possible, and refused to allow the UN High Commissioner for Refugees (UNHCR) to become involved. Famine struck, killing over ninety people by August 1984. Only then were the UNHCR and ICRC asked for assistance.[79]

The refugee influx was accompanied by severe tensions between Papua New Guinea and Indonesia, which culminated in the deportation of Indonesia's defence attaché in protest at repeated Indonesian incursions. Loathe to buy into these tensions, the Australian government consistently maintained that the refugees were a bilateral matter for Indonesia and Papua New Guinea to resolve. Nor did they try to alter Papua New Guinea's declared intentions to repatriate them to Indonesia, or encourage them to involve the UNHCR. Only after the deaths by starvation did Australia push for UN involvement and provide $600 000 in relief funds.[80]

The Australian government also stepped up pressure on Papua New Guinea plans to police the OPM. The 1983 *Strategic Basis* argued that 'Australian policy should encourage Papua New Guinea wherever possible to suppress anti-Indonesian activity by Irian Jaya dissidents', and journalist Brian Toohey revealed in 1989 that the Australian SAS joint exercise with Papua New Guinea, 'Night Falcon', included scenarios in which OPM guerrillas were captured and interrogated by Papua New Guinea Defence Force units. Australia also provided $500 000 to map the Papua New Guinea border area and promised an army engineering contingent and four Iroquois helicopters for use there. Upon delivery, the helicopters were diverted to the war on Bougainville.[81]

Having turned a blind eye to the Indonesian killings, and accepted a *fait accompli* in East Timor, Australian policy now faced a situation in which any pretence to principle in its relations with Indonesia was continually thrown back in its face. While Hayden was arguing that a working relationship enabled Australia to make positive human interventions, Benny Murdani had begun a new military offensive in East Timor – over Australian protests – which equalled previous campaigns in its ferocity. He also initiated the Petrus campaign, endorsed by Soeharto, which saw the summary killings of over 5000 alleged criminals between 1983 and 1986. In 1984 Murdani ordered troops to fire on Muslim protesters in the Tanjung Priok area of Jakarta, killing fifty. This was followed by a series of arrests and trials. In 1989, provoked by protests during visits by the Pope and the US Ambassador to East Timor, Murdani warned a meeting of community leaders to abandon their dreams of freedom: 'There is no such thing as an [East Timor] nation, there is only an Indonesian nation . . . If you try to make your own state and the movement is strong, it will be crushed by ABRI. Don't start imagining things, don't start dreaming.'[82]

On the other hand, the economic payoffs for Australia's quiet diplomacy, while slow, were progressing well. By 1987 Indonesia was Australia's eighteenth-largest export market, with Australia enjoying a handsome trade surplus of $200 million in 1986–67.[83] The slow pace of this progress had little to do with political tensions (though they were never far from Australian minds) and more with limited complementarity between the two economies and an undeveloped foreign investment culture in Australia. This did not prevent a hundred Australian enterprises having investments in Indonesia, making Australian corporations Indonesia's ninth-largest foreign investor in 1987.[84]

Yet perhaps as testament to their frustration with the robust criticisms they were suffering in Australian public life, the New Order government chose the publication by the *Sydney Morning Herald* in 1986 of an article critical of Soeharto family corruption as an opportunity to strike back. Defence co-operation and high-level government-to-government contact were unilaterally suspended, talks on the Timor Gap postponed, journalists expelled and a planeload of tourists deported.[85] No matter that successive Australian governments had stood alone in providing *de jure* recognition of Indonesia's brutal incorporation of East Timor, and had defied the majority public opinion in doing so. It seemed that the price of having made Indonesia so critical to Australian security and being was increasing dramatically. Ironically, while seeking to restore relations as quickly as possible, Australian officials found themselves, for the first time, downplaying the significance of the relationship – Hawke said its importance had been 'exaggerated' and foreign affairs official John Holloway argued for 'greater pragmatism and reduced expectations'.[86] With one of its bricks so easily kicked away, the whole structure and promise of certitude sought so anxiously since 1969 was beginning to seem like an illusion.

After the Cold War: The politics of uncertainty

Policy-makers seemed genuinely shocked that a relationship they had elevated to a guarantee of certitude amid the change of the post-Guam period could be damaged so easily. In speech after speech they returned to the trope, already visible in 1969, which anguished over the disjunction between the 'common interests' shared by the two countries and the dissimilarity in culture, politics and historical experience. From the New Order's side, such rhetoric served as a warning against the too-zealous promotion of 'Western' democratic values; from Australia's, as an attempt to manage the same contradictions by acknowledging 'differences' while also emphasising the need for co-operation. Yet the rhetoric was hardly a call for the respect of difference – in any ethical sense – deriving as it did from an overdetermined drive for sameness on both sides.

As the Cold War ended and the Soviet Union dissolved into a federation of independent states, more questions were asked about the long reign of Soeharto and the inevitability of Indonesia's boundaries. Launching a campaign for dialogue over East Timor on behalf of resistance leader Xanana Gusmao, the Australian Council for Overseas Aid argued that the time for a just resolution of the issue had come. The geopolitical environment which surrounded Indonesia's 1975 invasion was gone, along with any rationale for its continued occupation. Likewise, the UN was now a more significant force in world affairs, especially in the area of conflict resolution and peacekeeping.[87] Indonesia's response to the crisis in sovereignty was the massacre of hundreds of independence demonstrators (many of them children) at the Santa Cruz cemetery in Dili in November 1991, and an intensified campaign of torture and intimidation in urban areas; Australia's was to press for a return to the pre-1986 status quo and to trust Soeharto to maintain 'stability' throughout Indonesia.

This approach appeared to bear fruit in 1989, when new Foreign Minister Gareth Evans, with Indonesian counterpart Ali Alatas, signed the Timor Gap Zone of Co-operation Agreement aboard a Garuda jet flying to Jakarta. The tensions of 1986 now seemed a memory, as Evans boasted that the agreement – effectively a combined act of theft from the Timorese – would add much-needed 'ballast' to the relationship and 'illustrate[d] eloquently how differences between the two systems can be overcome for our mutual benefit'.[88] Yet it only deepened the basic contradictions which had led to the rift of 1986. Australia had worsened the compromise of its own declared values, and provided Indonesia with both a potential economic windfall and renewed recognition of 'the sovereign reality' of its annexation, in continued defiance of Australian public opinion. Portugal, still recognised by the UN as the legitimate administering power in East Timor, vowed to prosecute Australia in the International Court of Justice.[89]

The Timor Gap agreement was symptomatic of a powerful tendency at this time: for Australian elites to seek predictable, Cartesian frameworks with which to manage a whole series of new challenges and uncertainties. The end of the Cold War was removing the visible landmarks which had guided policy-makers for decades; the strategic environment was changing; the question of the 'succession' in Indonesia was looming. Within Australia, Aboriginal claims were gaining prominence, in sober contrast to the populist celebrations of the Bicentenary, and 'multiculturalism' was moving further into the mainstream of domestic life – where it aroused considerable anxiety among some. A whole framework of political, cultural *and* ontological certitude was unravelling. As Gareth Evans later wrote:

> When I became Foreign Minister in 1988 . . . it was not very long before I had to confront the reality that the set of verities that had fixed the shape of the post-war world as we had known it, and within which we had defined and pursued our national interests, was rapidly crumbling. Trying to make sense of this avalanche of change, and not be overwhelmed by it, I found myself asking some very basic questions. Where did Australia now fit? How should we be reacting to the myriad of events and choices crowding in on us?[90]

However, the drive for Cartesian solutions to this uncertainty only stifled innovation. In 1989, Evans released the report *Australia's Regional Security*, which betrayed a faith that space and politics could be easily mapped and interpreted, and that on the basis of this interpretation it was possible to construct a coherent and systematic approach to policy which could harmonise all its instruments, clearly identify and rank Australia's 'interests' and control the environment in which it would intervene.[91]

At its core was a conventional neo-realism which assumed that 'the possession of military power will always be of major importance in international affairs'. Based on a view that the government's 1987 defence White Paper – which developed a regional strategy of 'defence-in-depth' based on substantial long-range strike capabilities – had 'liberated' Australian foreign policy, the statement bragged that 'Australia's military capabilities are, and are perceived to be, formidable in regional terms'. This in turn contributed to the 'strategic stability' of the Pacific and South-East Asia and provided 'the foundation for our capacity to contribute to a positive security environment through the exercise of what might be described as military diplomacy, or politico-military capability'. Thus Australia's military capability enhanced the nation's international status and, in combination with defence co-operation programs, 'strengthen[ed] our ability to exercise leverage across many fields'.[92] By the time Indonesian troops had utterly destroyed East Timor in 1999, in defiance of repeated Australian concerns, such claims were sounding rather hollow.

The statement was notable for laying out the broad outlines of Australian defence policy for the next ten years, and for articulating a vision of its seamless integration with broad areas of domestic and foreign policy – a vision in which military force and diplomacy could be an effective intervention into the future shape of the regional political, strategic and economic order. Superficially, Evans may have been right to argue its distinction from the Menzies-era 'forward defence' doctrine, but this was to obscure both the permanent escalation in Australian air force and naval deployments into the region, the projected growth in defence co-operation, and the endeavour – identical in its sweep and ambition with that of the 1950s and 1960s – to use military capability to influence change within the region.[93]

By 1994, when the Keating government issued a new defence White Paper, such ambitions would be bluntly stated:

Australia's future security – like our economic prosperity – is linked inextricably to the security and prosperity of Asia and the Pacific. Australia's strategic engagement with the region is an integral element of *our national effort to make our place* in the region. Our defence relationships underpin the development of closer links in other fields. Our ability to defend ourselves and contribute to regional security does much to ensure that we are respected and helps us engage in the region by giving confidence that we can manage uncertainty and assure our security.[94]

Visible here was a frank statement of the desire to control and manage uncertainty. Yet discernible also, two years after Paul Keating became Prime Minister, was a view of how defence policy was contributing to a transformation of Australian identity within an optimistic vision of economic and cultural progress. Drawing on concepts from Indonesian security doctrine, the 1993 *Strategic Review* had made a similar argument – that the Australian Defence Force (ADF), by 'contributing to regional resilience and security' could 'protect key trade and commercial interests, and thus our national way of life'.[95]

The full import of this drive for policy coherence and certainty, and its part in a larger ontological enterprise, would become most clear in the speeches and policy of Paul Keating. Taking his cues from the 'governmental' visions of Curtin and Whitlam, Keating sought to revision the Australian identity in a way that, while recognising pressures for change, preserved an essential continuity with the past. Keating called this his 'Big Picture'. Revolving around a repetition of three main themes – 'Mabo', 'the republic', and 'Asia' – it again invoked the 'political double-bind' in its vision of a future which might finally reconcile security, justice and progress.

In some ways the gesture was quite radical. Keating's Redfern Park speech was an historic landmark in the official recognition of the crimes committed against Aboriginal people during colonisation, and of a remaining series of debts to be discharged. In that speech, for the first time, an Australian Prime Minister acknowledged the violence of colonisation: 'It was we who did the dispossessing. We took the traditional lands and smashed the traditional way of life. We brought the diseases. The alcohol. We committed the murders. We took the children from their mothers . . . ' Keating seized particularly on the High Court's *Mabo* decision as an opportunity to legislate a limited form of native title in permanent recognition of prior Aboriginal settlement of the continent. The judgement, he said, 'establishes a fundamental truth and lays the basis for justice'.[96] If, as I have argued, a deep-seated version of the Australian identity was constituted in the decades-long struggle for the nation's very *interior* – in a simultaneously physical, economic and ontological sense – the disturbance represented by

Mabo and Labor's vocal support for it was quite profound. Similarly, Keating's public support for multiculturalism (following the dangerous public debates over immigration initiated by the Coalition parties in 1988) was a frank challenge to the silent matrix of attitudes which had underpinned the White Australia policy and which, despite three decades of public disavowal, still remained strong.

On the other hand, each of these themes possessed utility for a particularly significant element of the vision: 'Asia'. Keating's vision went beyond pragmatic calculations of economic interest, to the projection of a new national destiny in close partnership with Asia in ways which would both force and require significant cultural and attitudinal changes. Thus Aboriginal 'reconciliation' and growing cultural diversity would enhance Australia's reputation for tolerance and encourage acceptance from a region with enduring memories of the White Australia policy; republicanism would make Australia more politically coherent to Asians; and structural economic reform would serve as an example of the kind of neo-liberal changes the government sought in the regional political economy.

Like Whitlam before him, Keating saw the New Order as crucial to the realisation of this vision. This became clear soon after he became Prime Minister in early 1992, when he chose his first meeting with Soeharto as an opportunity to outline his vision of change. The anguished trope repeated since 1986 was at the forefront, with Keating saying at the banquet held in his honour that 'at a time of rapid economic and strategic change, Indonesia and Australia have more in common than our different histories and cultures suggest'. Here a common destiny – 'to participate fully in the rapid economic growth of the Asia–Pacific region' – required more than a rich endowment of natural resources. For Indonesia it required 'national resilience', and for Australia something he portrayed as its mirror image:

> We know that to reach our full potential we must work co-operatively, combine our talents and energy, harness our human and material strength, and make Australia more truly one nation . . . In the 1990s I believe you will see Australia face these realities as never before. I think

you will see us pursue our goals as never before – with an unparalleled sense of purpose and efficiency.[97]

A more frank statement of the liberal ontology, and of the economic bottom line for Keating's vision of the new Australian identity, would be hard to find. This he reinforced by outlining the changes he saw as necessary if Australians were to 'positively engage with the region in which we live': 'in the 1990s I believe the Australian identity is being reshaped in a way which is consistent with the multicultural reality of our society, and the final passing of the vestiges of our colonial past'.[98]

It was an extraordinary claim, a claim which showed little understanding of how his embrace of Soeharto may have been intimately connected with Australia's 'colonial past'. A clue was visible in his assertion that Australia and Indonesia shared 'fundamental interests in the stability and security of our region' and, as he said the following day, that Australia had benefited from Soeharto's achievement in 'establishing political stability and economic progress in Indonesia'. In asserting Australia's stake in 'national resilience' – the doctrine which had legitimated the Army's oppressive control of Indonesian life for twenty-five years – Keating illustrated how the two states shared common ontological assumptions and political technologies. These he would try to deepen through arguments about a common neo-liberal future and through increasing defence co-operation (which would increasingly double as a diplomatic and political channel to the New Order). In this vision of desired sameness, played out in a 'shared future', Keating saw a reconciliation of otherwise substantial differences: 'We are different – culturally, historically, politically – but *we can handle the difference* . . . The Asia–Pacific, as well as Indonesia, can achieve unity in diversity.'[99]

The stakes involved in this foreign policy enterprise were made clear by the occasion which shadowed his visit – the Santa Cruz massacre in East Timor, which had taken place only four months before and which formed the greatest challenge to the bilateral relationship since the original invasion in 1975. As many as 400 people may have died in the killings, which were secretly videotaped and subsequently broadcast around the globe. Australian-based journalists and aid workers witnessed the massacre, and a Malaysian-born activist living in Australia, Kamal Bamadhaj, was one of its first victims. Gareth Evans, at an APEC meeting in Seoul with Indonesia's Ali Alatas, said that 'everyone feels a little sick in the stomach about the news'. Hawke said the killings were 'an appalling tragedy' and demanded that the perpetrators be punished. A few days later, in an unprecedented development, he urged the Indonesians to negotiate a settlement with the East Timorese, including the resistance movement, although he ruled out UN involvement. He also said that Indonesia's policies had failed to win the 'hearts and minds' of the East Timorese, and that his planned February 1992 visit to Indonesia hinged on the results of the Indonesian government's investigation of the massacre. Other sections of the ALP were pressing for the suspension of the defence co-operation program and a sweeping review of the bilateral relationship should Indonesia's response to the killings be inadequate.[100]

In each of his speeches in Jakarta Keating devoted only one line to the 'tragic events' in Dili, and publicly stated that the government's response to the massacre – a military-dominated commission of enquiry which blamed the demonstrators for provoking the troops, and the replacement of the regional and provincial military commanders (in the latter case, with a far more hardline figure) – was 'credible'. Hawke's earlier call for an inclusive dialogue on East Timor's future was ignored. While Keating also privately appealed for the criminal trials of independence protesters to be abandoned, he was rebuffed. This was not to stand in the way of rebuilding a relationship he later described as Australia's most important: 'If we fail to get this relationship right, and nurture and develop it, the whole web of our foreign relations is incomplete.'[101]

Keating's crowning gesture came in December 1995, shortly before he lost office, when he announced the conclusion of the Agreement on Maintaining Security (AMS), which he had personally negotiated with Soeharto, in secret, over the previous eighteen months. The AMS provided for substantial future increases in defence co-operation – by then already at an all-time high – and for possible joint deployments with ABRI in the event of 'adverse challenges' to either nation's security. When questioned by the ABC's Kerry O'Brien about the wisdom of involving Australia so closely with a force that had such a poor human rights record, Keating replied: 'We are not going to hock the entire Indonesian relationship on Timor. A Prime Minister's duty, his first duty, is to the security of his country.'[102]

This was the crux of the rhetoric of sameness and common destiny: the AMS had been negotiated against the initial advice of his defence and foreign ministers, without consultation with the broader Cabinet, party or community, and was frankly premised on the refusal to risk relations with Indonesia – and by implication, the whole ontological project of the Australian subjectivity – by recognising the legitimate claims of the Timorese.[103] Yet again, and rarely so baldly, the future and wellbeing of the East Timorese had been sacrificed for Australia's own *security*. When speaking of Australia's engagement with Asia in 1992, Keating had assured his audience that 'Australia's democratic institutions and traditions are non-negotiable' – yet in this case they had been blatantly negotiated away. Instead Australians had to be satisfied with assurances that the AMS was 'about providing for Australia's future and creating greater *certainty* about that future' (emphasis added). As foreshadowed in *Australia's Regional Security* and in the 1987 defence White Paper, the AMS was the logical extension of a judgement that Soeharto's regime had been the 'most beneficial strategic development to affect Australia and its region in thirty years'.[104]

Conclusion: Security, justice and Asia

Its last years of government saw Labor, and with it the nation, trapped between a series of contradictory dreams – between realism and internationalism, past and future, justice and uncertainty. Such dreams shared much with those of the Whitlam, Chifley and Curtin governments, and have been the central spiritual and discursive dilemmas of the entire period after 1969. After all, even Fraser claimed to have achieved an 'enlightened' realism. Yet the real problem lay in Labor's view that such contradictions could be harmonised – that, in short, security could be reconciled with justice. Furthermore, 1990s Labor claimed to be able to do this in a way which went beyond an idealist synthesis of domestic and international policy to a reconciliation of some of the darkest features of the Australian historical experience. If there are doubts that these weren't all interlinked questions absolutely crucial to the survival – *and renewal* – of a unitary Australian subjectivity, they should be erased by Keating's remarkable Redfern Park speech in December 1992, made at the launch of the International Year for the World's Indigenous People, only thirteen months after the Dili massacre:

> This will be a year of great significance for Australia. It comes at a time when we have committed ourselves to succeeding in the test which so far we have always failed . . . a fundamental test of our social goals and our national will: our ability to say to ourselves and the rest of the world that Australia is a first-rate social democracy, that we are what we should be – truly the land of the fair go and the better chance. There is no more basic test of how seriously we mean these things. It is a test of our self-*knowledge*.[105]

They were eloquent, courageous, historic words – but when judged against the calculated indifference to the Timorese, horribly ironic. Consider another part of the same speech, which argued that the starting point in bringing justice to Australia's indigenous people must be an 'act of recognition' of the systematic crimes committed against them: 'With some noble exceptions, we failed to make the most basic human response and enter into their hearts and minds. We failed to ask, how would I feel if this were done to me? As a consequence, we failed to see that what we were doing degraded all of us.'[106] In vain may we wait for the day when an Australian prime minister makes the same gesture of recognition to Soeharto's many victims.

As wonderful as the speech was, its failure lies in its approach to the profound challenge of this moment – symbolised by the irreversible force of the *Mabo* decision – and in its attempt to close out one wound in the Australian identity while leaving others to fester; indeed, in its belief that such wounds can be ultimately closed out at all. At a time which called for a recognition of difference (on the other's terms and in ways which forced profound transformations of self), Keating's speech betrayed a continued quest for totality, for unity, for *one* Australian nation with one destiny and one path to realising it. While his praise for *Mabo* indicated a partial recognition of the need to destabilise identity, along with its historic

legacy, the reflex was towards the older certainty of being and the
spiritual integrity of the body politic. This is the subtext of his call,
in the Redfern Park speech, for 'the deepening of Australian social
democracy to include indigenous Australians':

> Where Aboriginal Australians have been included in the life of Australia
> they have made remarkable contributions. Economic contributions,
> particularly in the pastoral and agricultural industry. They are there in
> the frontier and exploration history of Australia. They are there in the
> wars. In sport, to an extraordinary degree. In literature and art and
> music. In all of these things they have shaped our knowledge of this
> continent and of ourselves. They have shaped our identity. They are
> there in the Australian legend. We should never forget – they have
> helped build this nation.[107]

*They have shaped our identity . . . they have helped build this
nation* – yes, in ways he hardly allows. What could be more basic
historical facts than that they have helped build 'this nation' by
being dispossessed, by dying and disappearing, by suffering eth-
nocide, by their exclusion from every act of law and sovereignty
and foundation? In the same speech that acknowledges the raw
fact of these crimes, their challenge to 'the Australian legend' is
wilfully forgotten; instead Keating seeks to assimilate indigenous
Australians into a new mythology of 'the Australian social democracy' in which their fundamental value is to nation-building and
production – the very forces which threatened their extinction. In
short, Keating's speech refused to acknowledge how this experience
of violence and dispossession burns an unbridgeable gap between
the economics of the liberal ontology and its moral claims to justice
and enlightenment. Some events, some wounds in the spirit of the
body politic, cannot be healed.

This part of the speech was symptomatic of a discourse which,
however remarkable the changes it advocated, still felt the need
to link up with mythical points of origin and lines of tradition –
such as Federation, the Pacific war and the development work of
the pioneers. This perhaps allowed 1990s Labor to reconcile its
compromises with its idealism – to call for a continued faith in
the ANZUS alliance and a US strategic and economic engagement
in Asia, to dispatch a naval force to the Persian Gulf following

Saddam Hussein's invasion of Kuwait and to support the Bush administration's appallingly violent solution to the impasse; and to seize on Soeharto's New Order as a Whitlamesque key to a (thirty years new) Australian identity. Even their most laudable foreign policy enterprise, the final achievement of a negotiated resolution of the war in Cambodia, in the face of resistance from the US, China and some ASEAN states, involved depressing compromises.

At the February 1993 session of the UN Commission on Human Rights in Geneva, Australian officials, at Evans' direction, helped scuttle a vote which would have provided for the appointment of a special rapporteur with wide powers to investigate and monitor human rights in Cambodia after UN forces left later that year. UN officials argued that Australia's lobbying contravened the spirit of the Paris Accords, which set out the terms of the peace settlement and the UN's mandate – but given the violence and instability which have marked Cambodian politics ever since, the rapporteur's appointment would have been a helpful move. Australian officials told the UN that Canberra's instructions warned: 'Don't provoke ASEAN [which feared the precedent of a country-specific monitor] on this.'[108] Such weak-kneed compromise, and the continuing deafness to the plight of the East Timorese, underlined the ultimate tragedy of the period. Whatever glimpses there were of an ethical future in talk of 'good international citizenship', the broad structure of stability and prosperity remained that which had been established over the blood-turned soil of Indonesia between 1966 and 1969.

Yet in the Cambodian solution, however problematic and flawed, were the seeds of a genuinely new vision of global community.[109] This was further pursued into Evans' 1993 'blue book' *Co-operating for Peace*, which sought to envisage a 'co-operative security' based on enhancing the UN's role in 'the prevention and resolution of all kinds of deadly conflict' in ways which emphasise 'reassurance rather than deterrence' and do not 'advance military solutions over non-military ones'. In a later article, 'Co-operative Security and Intrastate Conflict', Evans acknowledged that security should be 'as much about the protection of individuals as it is about the defence of the territorial integrity of states. "Human Security", thus understood, is at least as much prejudiced by major intrastate conflict as it is by interstate conflict.' Yet moves to involve the UN in a far-reaching dialogue on East Timor – surely the most pressing 'intrastate conflict' at Australia's shores – were not made, short of Evans' bizarre acknowledgement, late in Keating's term, that while the Timorese right to self-determination had never been expressed, this should occur within the framework of Indonesian sovereignty.[110] This was perhaps 1990s Labor's most intriguing legacy. In texts like these, we had glimpsed worlds they refused to give us.

5

Australia's Asian crisis 1996–2000

National identity develops in an organic way over time.

John Howard, 13 December 1995[1]

On 2 March 1996 the Liberal-National Coalition returned to government with a stunning forty-five-seat majority in the House of Representatives – the worst defeat for Labor since 1977. The new Prime Minister, John Howard, said that he would govern for all Australians. While the scale of the defeat had many commentators searching for some kind of sea change in Australian consciousness, the Coalition's near-total loss of the same majority in 1998 revealed a new and dramatic political volatility in the electorate, whose elements were more difficult to locate and analyse. One suggestion, encouraged by Howard himself, was the subject of an ironic cartoon carried in *The Australian*. It showed an artist's studio, in which Howard could be seen standing before an easel and a tiny canvas, painting a suburban idyll. Through a door at the back of his studio a forlorn Keating could be seen following an attendant as he wheeled out a massive, impressionistic work entitled 'The Big Picture'. On the wall of Howard's studio was a sign saying: 'Australia's Top Miniaturist. Quiet Please'.[2]

I read the text as directing the joke against Howard and those who elected his government, yet like all good satire, it also turned Keating's own hubris on him. An earlier version, printed two days before, had workmen carrying out Keating's canvas and asking a passer-by, 'Excuse me mate, where's the big shredder?' The cartoons captured the many layers of bitterness and confusion which seemed to make up the Australian dilemma at the end of the 1990s, given greater poignancy amid the ashes of defeat. The dilemma, of course, turned on the continued direction and viability of a unified Australian subject, and quickly took on some of the most profound elements of Australia's social cohesion and diversity – the fate of the mythical ideals of equality and opportunity amid globalisation, the capacity of Australians for tolerance and generosity, and their capacity to respond to the historical experience and contemporary political demands of Australia's indigenous people. The cartoons drew on a view, encouraged by the Liberals, that voters were reacting against the sweeping nation-building rhetoric of 1980s Labor, whose alienating slogans of reconciliation and a new Australian identity in Asia neglected their more grassroots concerns for personal advancement and security, and their roots in a historically Anglo-Celtic structure of identity. Indeed some commentators, including Howard himself, interpreted the victory as a blow against 'political correctness' in all its forms.[3]

Yet the text was also misleading, in its suggestion that Howard was not himself engaged in a totalising project. In this sense it was complicit in the Coalition's efforts to obscure its own social and economic engineering beneath the illusion of a politics which sought its roots in the 'autonomous' operations of 'the market' and the reproduction of modern domestic life.[4] As John Howard was to say later, simultaneously invoking the totalising and the individualising aspects of security, 'The success or failure of a nation essentially begins in the homes of its people.'[5] It was starkly clear that 'the political double-bind' retained its importance as an effort to link the production and management of individual subjectivity with that of national and transnational totalities.

Externally, the most visible and disturbing event of the period was the Asian political and economic crisis. Over a twelve-month period in 1997–98 the currencies of South Korea, Thailand, Malaysia, the Philippines and Indonesia plunged massively in value under sustained attack from speculators; this caused bankruptcies, a dramatic flight of foreign investment and tremendous falls in economic activity. By mid-1998 every Asian economy was in recession and some, such as Indonesia, were in deep depression.[6] This crisis was accompanied and exacerbated by the increasing protest and instability around the Soeharto regime – there was destructive rioting, violence and repression before he was finally forced to resign in May 1998. In its aftermath the army's war of counter-insurgency in Aceh intensified, religious pogroms flared up in Ambon and Kalimantan, and East Timor was plunged into its most serious political and humanitarian crisis since the Indonesian invasion of December 1975.

As I made clear in chapter 4, powerful images of a renewed and modernised Australian identity – which was simultaneously a renewed culture, polity and economy – were closely tied to the nation's ability to successfully integrate with Asia, particularly with New Order Indonesia. Thus it is right to assume that the Indonesian (and broader Asian) crisis held the potential to destabilise strong forms of Australian policy and being. After the fall of Soeharto many commentators took the opportunity to reassess Australia's policies towards his regime, asking how they reflected on our national character. The *Australian Financial Review*'s Peter Hartcher wrote that, in tolerating the 'ugliness' of the regime for thirty years, 'we became a little uglier ourselves'.[7]

Security and the loss of 'home': The Howard ideology

In this context, security has functioned, particularly in the rhetoric of the Howard governments, as a drive for historical, strategic, economic and ontological *certitude*. This has been manifest in the government's statements about Australian history and cultural tradition, about indigenous people, about the regional political economy, and about defence and foreign policy. Some of these took the form of combative interventions into public debate, while others, such as the 1997 foreign policy White Paper, were highly formalised statements of the real which were intended to frame and structure policy. While the Labor Party took many strongly oppositional stances – retaining its support for the Keating-era embrace of reconciliation and multiculturalism, and undertaking a courageous reassessment of its history on East Timor, for example – its own rhetoric of security also functioned to solidify an underlying elite consensus about Australia's integration with the global economy and basic forms of political and economic subjectivity.

It is thus unsurprising that the most visible appeals to security came in 1998, as an election campaign loomed, Indonesia boiled, and the long-term consequences of the Asian crisis remained unclear. Throughout that year Howard told Australians that his government had delivered them 'security, safety and stability', and that they should continue to place their faith in him to deliver 'safety and security' to the Australian economy.[8] In January, the ALP's national conference, under the leadership of Kim Beazley, adopted a new platform that declared the party's central values as 'security and opportunity' – elevating security to an overarching goal which linked, in a seamless continuum, the personal security of individuals and families to the security of the nation itself.[9] Announcing the election, Howard said the choice would be about which party could make Australia 'secure in a very turbulent and hostile environment'.[10]

Uncertainty seemed to be the only certainty there was, and the political desire to control and tame it was strong. But could this really be achieved so easily? The social theorist Zygmunt Bauman doesn't believe so. He sees uncertainty not as a transitory and easily controlled phenomenon, but as a 'permanent and irreducible' element of the postmodern condition: an uncertainty 'not limited to one's own luck and talents, but concerning as well the future shape of the world, the right way of living in it, and the criteria by which to judge the rights and wrongs of the way of living'. Images of identity in this condition are no longer stable, and reconstituting identity against uncertainty is no longer so easy – it is no longer a simple matter to 'arrest the floating and drifting self'.[11]

This is not entirely a negative idea. It tends to thwart the power of the 'political double-bind' even as it is put into operation, and raises important questions about how successful such efforts on the part of Howard (*or* Labor) could ever be. Even though such uncertainty can be corrosive of an open and tolerant cultural attitude, producing selfishness and xenophobia, it also holds the potential for more positive transformations because it puts existing understandings into question. Thus while Bauman often seems overawed by the negative features of our time – which *are* real enough – we can also focus on their optimistic and emancipatory potential. To ask what the world's 'future shape' will be is to create agency in making it; and to ask what is 'the right way of living' in the world to turn uncertainty around identity into a form of *ethical work* which asks about the alternative forms of being our previous ideas of identity have suppressed.[12]

For Bauman the symptoms of uncertainty included the increasing globalisation and deregulation of capitalism, the loss of social support networks and fellow-feeling, the loss of stable geopolitical references with the end of the Cold War, and the rise of the image industries which fracture identity into a series of fleeting and malleable modes of consumption.[13] Howard's own speeches in part echoed Bauman's diagnosis, with some important differences: he believed uncertainty could be controlled, and he sought to arrest the more positive transformations – such as the empowerment of Aboriginal people and history – that this condition of uncertainty might liberate. Profound dilemmas of justice and identity were instead reduced to a task of management: 'The task of modern government is to maintain the momentum for the changes which are necessary – whilst to the extent that it is possible, to cushion the personal and social consequences of that change.'[14] The challenge for us is to break this classic Hegelian double-bind, which seeks to release the revolutionary powers of market and technological modernity while stifling progressive social change beneath a suffocating social and political conservatism. In differing but interconnected ways, this struggle was the discursive subtext to the crises in both Indonesia *and* Australia.

Thus Howard chose to read the key events of this period as crises of identity – and as opportunities to intervene in and solidify those forms of identity he valued. The continuing globalisation of the economy and an (at least pragmatic) engagement with Asia were necessary, Howard thought, but they also had the power to destabilise traditional feelings of identity, security and 'home'. In 1997 he argued.

> Increasingly, modern government is about facing the challenges of very rapid change but also remembering that there are certain stabilisers in society that provide reassurance and support when a society is undergoing great change particularly of an economic character.[15]

Crucial to such stabilisation, Howard thought, was 'the Menzian concept of home', which provides a 'sense of security':

> I believe that the concept of home is a compelling notion in our psyche . . . The loss of security challenges traditional notions of home and people feel the need to react to alienation. Part of the job of a Prime Minister in these contemporary times is, whilst enthusiastically embracing change and globalisation, he or she must embrace what is secure, what people see as 'home' . . . I want to provide Australians with this security as we embrace, as we must and will, a new and vastly different future.[16]

It was security that protects us from the loss of home – as the cultural theorist Fiona Allon commented in her own meditation on the significance of home for Howard, a 'struggle over meanings and conceptions of "home" and "community", "family" and "nation" in Australian social and political history have found a significant juncture in the politics and policies of John Howard in the 1990s'. She argued that 'home, now more than ever, is seen as firmly connected to the world of politics and economics, as actively shaped and defined by the public sphere'.[17]

Howard's political concerns gestured ahead, to this 'vastly different' future, and backwards, towards the (illusory) unity of a tradition that might ensure stability through change. It was clear that in his mind security and identity were synonymous, and that he saw the manipulation of identity as an important political tool in ameliorating the resentments produced by his government's policies and the profound structural changes wrought by globalisation's 'different future': unemployment, the loss of services in rural and regional areas, the changing patterns of work and family life, an increasing gap between rich and poor, and reduced access to welfare, educational opportunities and health services.

The insecurity associated with the loss of home is also the loss of an (imagined) cultural homogeneity: a symptom both of the increasingly visible diversity of Australian society and of the enhanced political power and presence of the Other. Thus Howard's sense of 'loss' was not felt by all: for those who didn't share in his European nostalgia, a secure sense of home in Australia was yet to be found, and was in fact being destabilised by the new politics of 'home' – as Ghassan Hage ably demonstrates in his book *White Nation*.[18] This was particularly true of Australia's indigenous peoples, whose efforts to secure title and rights to their land – 'home' in its most profound and ancient sense – were actively thwarted by the government. This was the harder edge of the nostalgia for 'home': its deployment into a practice of continuing dispossession.

Howard's concern was not entirely cynical: he shared with other Australians a deep-seated anxiety about the transformations in identity which figures like Whitlam, Keating and journalist Paul Kelly had been arguing would inevitably come with accepting an 'Asian' future for Australia. As the government's 1997 foreign policy White Paper announced: 'closer engagement with Asia [does not] require reinventing Australia's identity or abandoning the traditions which define Australian society . . . Australia does not need to choose between its history and its geography.'[19] Similarly, one of Australia's most eminent poets, Les Murray, managed to rope together postmodernism, Keating-era diplomacy and multiculturalism into a bitter paean to the same anxiety:

> All of people's Australia, its churches and lore
> are gang-raped by satire self-righteous as war
> and, from trawling fresh victims to set on the poor
> our Mandarins now, in one more evasion
> of love and themselves, declare us Asian.
> Australians are like most who won't read this poem
> or any, since literature turned on them
> and bodiless jargons without reverie
> scorn their loves as illusion and biology,
> compared with bloody History, the opposite of home.[20]

Again there is the nostalgia for a lost sense of 'home', paired, however, with an anger at the hypocrisy of the 'mandarins' who, 'in one more evasion of love and themselves', offered an 'Asia' ruled by corrupt and repressive elites as the key to a new Australian destiny. While pandering to such anxieties about identity, Howard turned a deaf ear to the more salient critique of the Asianist amorality. Indeed, at a geopolitical level Howard sought to preserve the same structures of security and certitude that Labor had clung to: in the same breath that he distanced Australia from Asia he also reaffirmed Australia's closeness to the Soeharto regime and our need to develop ever closer defence and economic ties with Indonesia.[21]

Yet the crisis which would conclude two years later with Soeharto's resignation had already begun. Only two months before Howard's visit, in June 1996, Soeharto had ordered the Armed Forces (ABRI) to force the removal of the popular Megawati Soekarnoputri, Sukarno's daughter, from the leadership of the Indonesian Democratic Party (PDI); this provoked violent rioting in Jakarta and the occupation of her headquarters by supporters. The occupation was violently ended by the military on 27 July, leading to even more damaging riots, and some of her supporters were arrested and placed on trial. Other radical opponents of the regime, including the union leader Muchtar Pakpahan and activists from the People's Democratic Party (PRD) such as Dita Sari and Budiman Sudjatmiko, were also arrested at this time.[22] New foreign minister Alexander Downer's bold response to the attack on the PDI headquarters, in which five were killed and 170 seriously wounded, was to say, 'We don't conduct our affairs in Australia in the same way.'[23]

The depth of Howard's paranoia about identity was underlined by his insistence that Labor had been arguing Australia should seek to become Asian, when this was something Keating had persistently disavowed. In 1994 he said, 'We do not, and cannot, aim to be "Asian" or European or anything else but Australians.'[24] One suspects that the prospect of an 'Asian' Australia formed an emotive smokescreen for Howard's real anxiety about his ability to continue to define Australianness in ways which had political utility. Why else accuse Keating in 1995 of 'an attempted heist of Australian nationalism'? Howard instead portrayed national identity as a stable and unchanging set of traditions: 'it develops in an organic way over time'. Apart from effacing the enormous social and political conflict over identity throughout Australian history, this served to paper over a deeper anxiety that identity could never be fixed or made hegemonic: 'Constant debate about identity implies either that we don't already have one, or worse, that it is somehow inadequate.'[25]

What this points to is a profound ontological anxiety. It was thus especially ironic when *The Australian*'s Greg Sheridan praised the

Howard government's first Budget – with its drastic cuts to spending, increased tertiary education fees, cuts to childcare and bias towards nuclear families – for its good 'Asian values'.[26] Indeed, the political economist Richard Robison sees a broader attraction for Western conservatives in the Asian agenda: a new hybrid of conservatism and neo-liberalism that increasingly mimics an 'Asian' politics where 'the interest of economic growth is portrayed as the collective public interest and where the state smooths the way for the corporate or family agenda'.[27]

Political complacency and gathering storms

In attempting at the same time to accelerate economic change and retard cultural change, the Howard governments sought – as Labor had – to create overarching structures of Cartesian certitude within which more nuanced forms of governmentality could be deployed. Thus they sought to develop a strategy in which formations of national and individual identity, and domestic and international policy, could be brought into a cohesive and harmonic whole. This was clear in the 1997 foreign policy White Paper, *In the National Interest*, which argued for 'a whole-of-nation approach which emphasises the linkages between domestic policies and foreign and trade policies'.[28]

Through its own combination of the 'political double-bind' and the strategic imagination, the government sought to simultaneously transform and police individual subjectivities, 'reform' domestic policy frameworks and relations between market and state, while continuing previous lines of international policy in ways which might limit larger transformations in identity. In this sense the introduction of a consumption tax, the sale of Telstra, the inexorable tightening of eligibility for welfare, the restriction of workers' rights to strike and collectively bargain, the confrontation of waterside workers, the harassment of refugees and the aggressive pursuit of international trade liberalisation were part of a single totality. At the same time as rhetorics of the 'national interest' were deployed in an effort to universalise the interests of the (largely city-based) elites who benefited from the government's policies, a series of techniques were deployed for the differential control and production of subjectivity: discipline and surveillance targeted at welfare recipients, youth, workers and refugees; and desire and self-government used to develop self-interested and market-oriented subjectivities in citizens. These were then paired, where necessary, with more totalising deployments of legislative, police and bureaucratic power.[29]

At the national and transnational level, the government's rhetoric was characterised by hubris. In August 1997, at the onset of the Asian crisis and only eight months before the fall of Soeharto, the foreign policy White Paper declared that 'Australians should have confidence in Australia's capacity to shape its future' and that 'economic growth in industrialising East Asia will continue at relatively high levels over the next fifteen years'.[30] In order to preserve such certainties it would merely be necessary to strengthen Australia's alliance relationship with the United States, pursue regional security co-operation, economic integration and trade liberalisation as before, and strengthen key bilateral relationships with Indonesia, China and Japan.

The paper failed utterly to identify either the economic or political seeds of the Asian crisis – while it cited 'potentially serious factors' such as 'worsening current account deficits combined with high debt levels [and] institutional weaknesses', it did not see how the flight of massive amounts of short-term portfolio investment would combine with corruption and poor prudential supervision to precipitate, within eighteen months, the widespread collapse of regional economies.[31] This failure occurred even though, as the economist Jeffrey Winters argues, highly accurate warning signs were available in the analysis of regional think tanks like Jakarta's ECONIT.[32] About the looming flashpoints in Indonesia – the presidential succession and East Timor – all the paper had to say was that 'an improved human rights situation and a greater role in the administration of the Province for indigenous East Timorese would contribute to an overall resolution of the issue', and that the bilateral relationship would require 'careful management' through any leadership transition.[33] Yet in the wake of the July 1996 riots, regional media had already identified the broad-based resentments that would soon destroy Soeharto. *Asiaweek* quoted one Chinese businessman, who presciently said, 'If he wants to stay on, we will not be able to stop a social revolution. The poor will not differentiate . . . we will all come under attack.'[34]

Indeed, many others could see the coming storm. In September 1997 I warned in the *Jakarta Post* of 'the increasing despair over the current political stalemate in Indonesia', and of the fears of many that 'the myriad incidents of violence prior to and during the election campaign portend an explosion'.[35] In a similar vein the political scientists Jim George and Rodd McGibbon warned that 'Australia's support for the Soeharto regime is actually undermining, rather than enhancing, the long-term prospects for a stable, secure and prosperous regional environment.'[36] Yet it was inconceivable to the White Paper's authors that, within three years, East Timor would have voted for independence, Indonesia would be struggling to entrench democracy amid enormous social and political upheaval, and the bilateral relationship would be in deep crisis. Instead, the White Paper revealed a myopic and dangerous complacency. One of the most telling (and in retrospect ridiculous) boasts was John Howard's claim in May 1997, immediately before the Asian crisis, that his government's policies would 'contribute to our region's strategic resilience. They will help provide us and our neighbours with greater confidence that we can navigate safely a period of great economic, political and strategic change. They will help ensure that the economic progress of the past ten or twenty years is not disrupted.'[37]

One element of this complacency was the largely self-indulgent realism which the Howard government saw itself bringing to international policy. The White Paper repudiated Labor's (already limited) commitment to international citizenship and multilateralism, emphasising bilateral relationships over international structures and institutions. While the government emphasised multilateralism in trade, in crucial questions on conflict and diplomacy it chose bilateralism. Yet the later crisis in East Timor showed how this fed serious delusions about Australian influence with Indonesia, at the same time as it cruelled badly needed multilateral efforts to avert the looming disaster. Labor's spokesman on foreign affairs, Laurie Brereton, identified the hidden agenda in the White Paper's argument for a 'selective approach to the international agenda ... in areas where our national interests are closely engaged'[38] by pointing out: 'The issue of human rights, including labour standards and child labour exploitation, has been very significantly downgraded in our foreign policy priorities, with the Howard government withdrawing from active participation in the International Labour Organisation and openly arguing for a "softly, softly" human rights approach designed to give no offence to authoritarian regimes in our region.'[39]

This contrasted, Brereton said, with Downer's previous harsh criticisms of the Keating government's weak approach to human rights. When Brereton had wanted Australia to impose sanctions on the Burmese junta after its renewed crackdown on the democracy movement, Downer refused.[40] Also in contrast to the government's pragmatic response to the Indonesian Army's removal of Megawati and brutal crackdown, three weeks after the riots Brereton was urging the government to be 'more actively engaged in encouraging the exploration of peaceful solutions to the current unrest . . . Australia should not confuse any particular political group with a country as a whole. Nor should we assume a necessary congruence between the interests of any group, including the Soeharto government, with the interests of both Indonesia and Australia.'[41]

Divide and rule: The government of individuals

The Howard government's narrow interpretation of Australia's security and 'national interest' was not only dangerously complacent; it also had its corollary in the government's vision of individual and social subjectivity. In a whole range of areas the government sought to break and dissolve the bonds which linked individuals with broader social obligations and forms of collective social organisation, and put in their place a more selfish and atomised citizen-subjectivity, attuned to self-interest first and suspicious of the claims of others. With its introduction of individual workplace contracts the government sought to attack the power of trade unions; with cuts to foreign aid and a harsh approach to refugees it sought to weaken a sense of obligation to outsiders; with cuts to welfare and attacks on 'special interests' it sought to scapegoat the already disempowered against an illusory 'mainstream'; and with cuts to the Aboriginal and Torres Strait Islander Commission (ATSIC) and Human Rights and Equal Opportunity Commission (HREOC) budgets they sought to weaken the concept of minority rights, undermine a crucial vehicle of Aboriginal self-determination and drive a wedge between indigenous and non-indigenous Australians.

This was consistent with the founding liberalism of the 1791 *Declaration of the Rights of Man and Citizens*, which Marx criticised as merely 'the liberty of man as an isolated monad drawn into himself . . . None of these so-called rights of man [equality, liberty, security, property] goes beyond the *egoistic man*, beyond man as a member of civil society, as man separated from life in the community and withdrawn into himself, into his private interest and private arbitrary will.' This was, however, the essential meaning of *security*: 'Civil society does not rise above egoism through the concept of security. Security is rather the *guarantee* of its egoism.'[42]

'We are special individuals, not special interests', Howard liked to say.[43] Political scientist Carol Johnson argued that implicit in the government's politics was 'a dismantling of a version of [Labor's] neo-liberal project which reshapes and commodifies *group* identities'.[44]

Yet how does this mesh with the government's social conservatism and its vision of international relations? Here the 'political double-bind' is at work again. With its elevation of the concept of 'national interest' over internationalism, the government traced an image of the self-interested individual subject on to the self-interested *national* subject. While 'internationalist' co-operation and generosity were not ruled out, they would be subject to 'this basic test' of national interest.[45] At the same time, the government traced a movement back into individual subjectivity, with Howard's lecture to Australians : 'The success or failure of a nation essentially begins in the homes of its people . . . Each one of us is responsible for building our lives and the life of our nation. All of us [are] accountable to ourselves, to those around us, to the future itself.'[46] Crucial to this was his idea of the *family* as having 'a pivotal role in the fabric of the Australian nation':

> . . . it is the influence of the family that has the most direct effect
> on moulding the character of individuals. It is there that love, dignity,
> morality and character are crafted. It is there that we are taught faith
> and loyalty and conscience and integrity.[47]

This was a classic vision of liberal governmentality, in which individuals do the work of politics *on themselves*, and in which families can act as spaces of subjectification in ways that governments never could – not only relieving the public of responsibility for welfare, as many Howard government policies were increasingly forcing them to, but also inculcating values that, while portrayed as contributing to a universal 'national' good, would in fact work in ways which benefited the particular interests of his party and its corporate backers.

The philosophical roots of this form of governmentality lie in Rousseau's attempt to derive principles for the running of the state from the family – while in the Cameralists' idea of *police*, this also worked in the reverse direction, to direct familial and individual behaviour along the lines of an efficient state. This culminated in Hegel's view, in the *Philosophy of Right*, of the individual, the family and the corporation forming successively higher manifestations of the 'ethical whole' of the state.[48] If there is a psychological tension between the selfish consumer and the public-spirited citizen, as Toby Miller suggests there is, the Howard government sought to efface it completely, to merge consumer and citizen into a single mode of subjectivity – one that was at once pliable to political intervention and discourse, and self-governing in ways which enhanced corporate power at the expense of the welfare state.

Beyond the abstract loyalties to the state and political authority, the 'family' was to be one of the few legitimate sites of social belonging and obligation. Certainly not trade unions, Aboriginal corporations, or community groups based around a desire for justice or social change – these were instead to be vilified as 'special interests'. As Toby Miller argues, 'to be branded a "sectional interest" is utterly disabling under these circumstances', to have one's rights and claims subsumed beneath a 'white, male, heterosexual, polite capitalist norm'. This was another subtext to Howard's idea of home,

Menzies' 'homes spiritual': 'the brave acceptance of unclouded individual responsibility'. Disturbingly enough, Howard even sought to deny unwelcome social participants the status of humans: 'the point at which a person seeks moral refuge in the crowd is the point at which he or she ceases to be an individual human being'.[49]

The enemy within: Reviving *terra nullius*

Carol Johnson has, rather wittily, called the Howard government's wedge politics the 'revenge of the mainstream', citing Howard's argument that Keating had privileged the views of a few powerful interest groups at the expense of 'mainstream' Australians. As Howard claimed, 'Under us, the view of all particular interests will be assessed against the national interest and the sentiments of mainstream Australia.'[50] Yet as Fiona Allon emphasises, Howard's imagination of the mainstream, his 'appeals to family and home-centred individualism . . . are politically mobilised constructions'.[51] Just as I have sought to question the imagined unity of the Australian subject and the 'national interest', the 'mainstream' is just as pernicious an ontological fiction, a fiction which undermines the very possibility of the common community it pretends to imagine.

Rather than being a unifying gesture, Howard's rhetoric of identity was divisive: as Johnson says, he sought to 'define identity by excluding other identities'. The implications of Howard's views were an even more rigid imagination of national identity based upon (an exclusionary) sameness, which eschewed even Labor's problematic efforts to 'meld economic and social identities in a socially inclusive form'.[52] When the High Court ruled in *Wik* that native title could coexist with pastoral leases, the government, long an opponent of the High Court's *Mabo* decision, launched a systematic attempt to limit Aboriginal native title rights by amending the Native Title Act. The High Court's 1996 *Wik* judgement initiated a crisis, driven by the government, mining companies and conservative farmers' organisations, which extended for over two years and whose effects are still being felt.

In the aftermath of *Mabo*, visceral conflicts over land management and power merged into highly political debates over identity, history and responsibility – conflicts in which the basic discursive and ontological foundations of the nation were at stake. From the initial acts of colonisation from 1770 through to the 1840s, to the establishment of a constitutional structure at Federation, Australia had been founded on *terra nullius*, which simultaneously effaced Aboriginal sovereignty and possession of the land and effaced them as political subjects. While they were gradually restored to political subjectivity during the postwar decades, and the *Mabo* judgement recognised limited native title rights, the *terra nullius* mindset remained strong as pressing practical questions of Aboriginal power and sovereignty were fought out. In all its dealings with Aboriginal people the Howard government played out the very same anxiety which had animated the 19th-century colonialists: that of securing the ontological link between soil, sovereignty and identity against the threat from the Other, the 'enemy without and the enemy within'.[53]

Even before the *Wik* judgement was handed down in 1996 the government had proposed amendments to the Native Title Act which had the objective of dramatically winding back Aborigines' rights to negotiate with miners, particularly on pastoral leases. However, the *Wik* decision confirmed the *co-existence* of native title with pastoral leases, which allowed Aborigines rights of traditional access and a veto over dramatic changes in land use such as mining or commercial development. While the Prime Minister considered legislating to completely extinguish native title on pastoral leases – as the Queensland Premier and the National Party were demanding – this option was abandoned largely because of doubts about its constitutionality, its costs to the public in compensation and the political impossibility of forcing such a law through the Senate. Yet until then, as the Jesuit lawyer Frank Brennan acerbically observed, the '*terra nullius* option' had been very much alive.[54]

Instead Howard released a 'ten point plan' whose key clauses confirmed the suppression of native title by farming activity on pastoral leases, the foreclosure of native title claims over water, fisheries and airspace, and the removal of the right to negotiate over developments within town and city boundaries. A six-year sunset clause on native title claims would be introduced. The right to negotiate with miners on vacant Crown land would be cut back to a once-only right (which could be suspended in the 'national interest', and would be virtually extinguished on pastoral leases through provisions which allowed the states to override native title). Rights to negotiate over infrastructure projects were removed.[55] While less crude than full extinguishment, the result would be the effective extinguishment of key native title rights recognised by *Wik* and *Mabo*. Howard justified this approach on television with a map that purported to show 78 per cent of Australian land potentially subject to veto by Aborigines[56] – even though Aborigines would never be able to establish native title over a vast proportion of it.

Such a return to *terra nullius*, where politically feasible, was central to the government's vision of security amid postmodern uncertainty. In his address to the nation Howard emphasised 'how important the rural and mining industries are to the future of our country', while when unveiling the 'ten-point plan' he claimed that it delivered 'certainty and security to farmers and justice to the Aboriginal community'.[57] ATSIC Chairman Gatjil Djerrkura refuted him by insisting that the right to negotiate was crucial to the 'protection of significant cultural and spiritual areas'. Eventually a different set of amendments was passed in July 1998, after negotiations with the independent Tasmanian Senator Brian Harradine. While the sunset clause was abandoned, and Aboriginal rights strengthened in a number of areas, the core of the 'ten-point plan' was unmodified. In particular, the states retained the power to extinguish the right to negotiate with miners. Aboriginal leaders were bitterly disappointed, but Harradine was feeling the pressure of the government's threat to call a double dissolution election if the Bill was not passed, which he feared 'would have torn the fabric of our society and set race relations back forty or fifty years'.[58]

The practical importance of these issues was thrown into relief at Jabiluka, Energy Resources of Australia's (ERA) $6 billion uranium development on Mirrar–Gundjehmi lands in Kakadu National Park in the Northern Territory. While under a different legislative regime (the Northern Territory Land Rights Act), this was a case where ERA and the government rode roughshod over bitter landowner opposition. ERA's Ranger uranium mine, also on Mirrar lands, had been developed against Aboriginal wishes, and had been operating for fifteen years. Even though the father of the Senior Traditional Owner, Yvonne Margarula, had approved the Jabiluka project in 1982, she had decided that the destructive social and cultural effects of mining were unacceptable. She told a 1999 Senate inquiry into the mine: 'Look what came with all this development – the alcohol, all sorts of unhappiness. We stand to lose our sacred sites but get a lot of money.'[59]

After a radically changed proposal was submitted by ERA in 1991, both she and the Northern Land Council opposed the development and asked for new negotiations, which were refused. Given that the project threatened the cultural survival of local society and a chain of sacred sites, this was clearly an instance where rights to negotiate were crucial. This case arguably exposes the negotiating scraps saved by Harradine as next to useless when it comes to protecting indigenous cultural and human rights over an extended period, because his compromise failed to guarantee a right to negotiate with miners, raising the prospect of future Jabilukas in other states. The Jabiluka project attracted large demonstrations and intervention by UNESCO's World Heritage Committee, while the Senate inquiry found serious flaws in the original negotiations and the government approvals process, and recommended that the project be stopped. The dispute reached an extraordinary low in May 1998 when Margarula was prosecuted for trespassing on the mine site – that is, *on her own lands*.[60]

The *Wik* debate clearly showed that genuine Aboriginal sovereignty had no place in Howard's imagery of national security and sameness, and that what was at stake were historic formations of elite landowner and corporate power, groups which resented having to acknowledge the rights of those who in decades past had been conveniently invisible. In such a context, Howard's insistence throughout the *Wik* debate that indigenous people should not be granted special rights – rights different from those of others such as pastoralists – took on a chilling quality. Consider the extraordinary lecture he delivered (after being re-elected in October 1998), when asked at a press conference to explain his newly declared commitment to reconciliation:

> Reconciliation in my mind is . . . an acceptance first and foremost that we are all Australians together and that our national unity and identity as Australians is the starting point . . . It also involves a recognition that [indigenous people] were unjustly treated in the past . . . that they have a distinctive culture and identity which is in no way inconsistent with their identity as Australians . . . But equally it carries with it an obligation on their part to see themselves as part and parcel of a harmonious Australian community.[61]

Like Howard's paranoia about the supposedly radical identity transformation implied by engagement with Asia, this statement is revealing as a profound ontological *anxiety*. This was palpable when he said that he refused to refer to a reconciliation document as a *treaty*, 'because treaty implies two nations within one, which is something I have never accepted and will never accept'.[62]

While he paid lip service to the injustices of colonial history and the difference of indigenous culture, his basic starting point was the necessity for a broad essential sameness between indigenous and non-indigenous Australians. Howard's insistence that indigenous people think of themselves as Australians first contains a sinister echo of the ethnocidal model of citizenship, such as in Western Australia between 1901 and 1941, under which Aborigines would be made citizens if they first 'dissolve native and tribal association' and adopt 'the manner and habits of civilised life'.[63] There was a basic refusal to acknowledge that native title derives from an irrefutable link to the land, a link that precedes and perpetually disrupts the 'sovereignty' that provides the ground for his discourse. In short, the true force of this history was denied at the very moment it was incited.

In the government's view, sameness was not so much a condition of absolute likeness as an artificial common *ground* upon which Aboriginal claims were to be determined and limited. While difference could be accepted up to a point, it was to be confronted when it threatened to transform into real political power and autonomy. This is the lesson of Jabiluka and the politics of *Wik*. That Aboriginal sovereignty might be exercised to protect traditional culture and spirituality meant little in the face of the drive for certainty and security. Indigenous claims were perennially forced aside in favour of the view of Hugh Morgan, Chairman of Western Mining Corporation, that *Mabo* 'directly threatens the unity of Australia. It brings in a separate law for one group of Australians.' Yet others, such as lawyer Noel Pearson and philosopher Paul Patton, have critiqued the repressive politics inherent in this reduction of Aboriginal difference to a single, colonial model of identity. Patton dryly observes that 'the equal treatment of indigenous and non-indigenous people is a perpetuation of injustice'.[64]

Howard's was an essentially Hegelian view of the nation-building project, in which difference is always to be subordinated to identity, and was thus central to a modern politics of *security* which seeks to counter the loss of 'home' through the preservation of a harsh and exclusivist image of the Australian subject. Yet *Mabo* is now a legal fact, and is well on the way to becoming a cultural one. It is thus a profound (if partial) deconstruction of the images of security and identity we have inherited from founding fathers such as Deakin and Parkes.[65] Whatever the setbacks to Aboriginal people – and they are substantial – it is also worth saying that the government's politics was continually shadowed by its own failure.

Australia's Asian crisis: The region melts down

The drive to limit Aboriginal autonomy and power was one important strand of the politics which sought to limit postmodern uncertainty, to restore the security of 'home' and thus contain the challenge to the imaginary continuity of Australian history and identity. Working in parallel, and at a larger geostrategic level, the growing economic and political upheavals of the Asian crisis posed similar challenges. Beginning with the massive devaluations of the Thai baht in July 1997, by the end of that year the contagion had spread to South Korea, Malaysia, the Philippines and Indonesia, forcing a haemorrhage of foreign capital and massive falls in employment and economic activity. In the first four months of the crisis regional currencies lost between 30 and 50 per cent of their value, and companies and banks went into liquidation as fantastic rates of growth (between 5 and 10 per cent through the 1990s) came to a shuddering halt. By the beginning of 1998 most Asian economies had fallen into recession, and political crisis had enveloped Thailand and Malaysia. The four ASEAN economies *contracted* by an average of 9.5 per cent in 1998, and under the influence of the crisis world growth slowed to 2.5 per cent.[66]

In Indonesia, already embroiled in a simmering leadership crisis, the impact was catastrophic. Over six months the rupiah lost 80 per cent of its value, and in mid-2000 was still trading at 8000 to the dollar, in comparison with 2400 before the crisis. In just three days in January 1998 it lost 40 per cent of its value. At that level analysts calculated Indonesia's annual output was worth only US$33 billion, in contrast with a total foreign debt of $140 billion. Two hundred and sixty-six of its 288 listed firms were classed as technically insolvent.[67] In the first quarter of 1998 Indonesia's gross domestic product (GDP) fell by 8.5 per cent, and a full year fall of over 13 per cent was recorded. Inflation for 1998 was 50 per cent, and official unemployment 20 per cent, some 14 million people. The International Labor Organisation (ILO) estimated that, by 1999, 60 per cent of the population – 140 million people – had fallen below the poverty line.[68]

Alexander Downer called the crisis the 'largest challenge to economic prosperity in our region since the Second World War', and said it had 'the potential to affect the security of the region'. It 'accentuated the uncertainty and complexity of the regional strategic environment', he said:

> . . . in many countries in our region internal stability and order have been underpinned by economic growth. And as the economies of the region have grown and become more integrated, this has helped reduce the risk of conflict. Now this virtuous cycle has been challenged. A region in stress is less predictable and less stable. Manageable internal problems can become unmanageable and spill over borders.[69]

Downer's comments were made in August 1998, a year after the crisis began and two months after Indonesia erupted in devastating riots that ended in the forced resignation of Soeharto in favour of his Vice-President, B. J. Habibie. At the end of these riots over a thousand people were dead, many of them Chinese, who were targeted in a deliberate campaign of rape, killing and destruction.

Ugly sectarian hatreds had been unleashed amid a dangerous struggle for political ascendancy involving Soeharto's son-in-law Lieutenant General Prabowo Subianto and armed forces head General
Wiranto. Although resolved with the dismissal of Prabowo, this
battle portended only further violence and upheaval.[70] At this time
Habibie also signalled that he might allow a referendum in East
Timor, beginning a dangerous escalation of conflict there.

In such a context the internal impact of the crisis was of
greater importance than any subsequent 'spillover' (as Downer had
argued) – indeed, with its complex interpenetration of 'national'
and 'international' effects, the crisis had undermined the analytical value of distinctions between inside and outside. Events 'within'
Indonesia were more chaotic than 'manageable', and had already
been enormously destructive not only of the personal security of
individuals and families but also of the larger apparatus of 'security' which had marked the entire discursive and administrative
structure of the New Order. In the wake of its partial demise,
and amid the broader resentments generated by the regional crisis,
Indonesia's political and economic direction – and perhaps its very
unity – were at risk. Similarly, a powerful meaning of security had
been discredited. Political economists Mark Beeson and Richard
Robison saw how profound these effects could potentially be: 'What
was initially taken to be a relatively isolated shock', they wrote, 'has
intensified and generated increasingly widespread economic and
political effects which threaten to overturn the region's established
political and economic order.'[71]

Given that Australian governments had expended so much effort
in constructing that order, and invested so much in the form of
the government and culture Soeharto had brought to Indonesia,
the crisis was deeply unsettling: threatening, as with so many of the
century's geopolitical ruptures, to disturb the fine calibrations of
the strategic imagination – to expose its flows and arrangement of
bodies, space and resources as untenable and unjust.

The crisis exposed the key assumptions of many policy-makers as
gravely wanting – from the realist belief that authoritarian regimes
provided a long-term guarantee of stability and order, to the neo-
liberal view grafted on to it that this, combined with increasingly porous flows of trade and capital, would achieve a virtually

endless prosperity. Despite the warning signs provided by the massive increase in short-term foreign portfolio investment, over-borrowing and poor prudential supervision, no official actors – not the Australian government, the IMF or ratings agencies like Moodys and Standard & Poors – were able to predict the crisis.[72] Likewise the Australian government was caught unawares by the fall of Soeharto until a few weeks before his fall, despite the visible crisis since 1996 and the warnings of many that the inequality and repression inherent in his rule would soon cause an explosion. This 'power-politics neo-liberalism' had long attracted the ire of writers such as Jim George, who appealed for policy-makers to listen to the voices of the millions impoverished and dispossessed by the 'globalisation fairytale'.[73]

In short, the malign combination of *Realpolitik* and neo-liberalism pursued by the international community was as much responsible for the crisis as were the corruption and venality of regional elites. True to its 'realism', Australia gave significant economic, military and diplomatic support to authoritarians like Soeharto, even as his repression and corruption became ever more blatant; likewise, neo-liberal ideology led Westerners to praise the relaxation of foreign investment and capital controls in the 1990s in Thailand and Indonesia, even as prudential regulation was undeveloped or, where it existed, politically unenforceable. Soeharto's last-ditch attempts to protect the business interests of his children and cronies and shore up his own rule – by resisting IMF 'reforms' and refusing to step down – only brought violent upheaval, further pressure on the rupiah and a continued haemorrhage of capital.[74] Yet Soeharto's policies had only a few years before been acceptable to Indonesia's international friends – the irony was neatly captured by economist K. S. Jomo's comment that the 'business organisations, practices and norms that had previously been credited with the East Asian miracle were now condemned as the sources of the debacle'.[75]

As the crisis unfolded the Australian government sought to cling to older structures of security and certitude, while also limiting potentially more radical transformations that might undermine their neo-liberal vision of international economic order. The government's initial responses were painfully orthodox – even eleven months into the crisis, in May 1998, Alexander Downer was arguing that for a sustained regional recovery to occur, affected nations must adhere to the conditions of IMF assistance packages and maintain 'the momentum for economic reform and liberalisation.'[76] There was no recognition that the IMF medicine was grossly inappropriate, forcing interest rate increases and deep cuts to government spending, which then pushed economies into recession and millions into extreme poverty. Analysts like Jeffrey Sachs, Director of the Harvard Institute for International Development, were arguing as early as November 1997 that the IMF was pursuing the wrong course in Asia – encouraging deflation rather than supporting 'slightly expansionary monetary and fiscal policies to counterbalance the decline in foreign loans' – and would push otherwise healthy economies into far deeper recessions than they should have faced.[77]

Likewise, Downer's speech betrayed no intuition that foreign investors or capital markets bore any blame: 'it is clear that the development of [Asian financial] sectors failed to keep pace with the spectacular inflow of capital and resources which fuelled the East Asian "miracle".'[78] Yet even former Philippines President Fidel Ramos – who had himself presided over a punishing structural adjustment process during the 1990s – argued that 'the IMF must rethink its bail-out tactics' and that calls for internal reforms and liberal policies did nothing to curb 'the volatility of short-term capital movements'. Sachs concluded that the 'bail-out operations could end up helping a few dozen international banks to escape losses for risky loans by forcing Asian governments to cover the losses on private transactions that have gone bad'.[79]

It took until late 1998, after a chorus of complaints from the region and moves in Malaysia and Hong Kong to impose unilateral capital controls, for the Howard government to acknowledge that international capital markets had failed Asians.[80] By this time Australia was supporting international financial reform, under the auspices of the G22 group of industrialised nations, which might increase transparency, limit massive withdrawals of capital during crises, and increase flexibility over debt.[81] However, the overriding theme was a desire to limit change to a minimum – at the same time avoiding the overwhelming need to address how issues of justice and autonomy were compromised by the international economic system. Howard said that 'we do not want to constrain the natural workings of the market beyond what is necessary to ensure its stable operation', while Downer warned that 'we must confront reform challenges with caution' and avoid 'the illusory quick fixes of a re-imposition of trade barriers or excessive capital controls'.[82]

The government understood the profound political challenge the crisis represented – indeed, said Downer, 'nothing less than the liberal-market economic model is at stake in this debate'. Howard admitted that 'recent financial instability and the role of hedge funds and short-term money flows have revived fears of globalisation', but insisted that 'APEC must stand against that view'.[83] While the government's Task Force on International Reform conceded that 'for those countries which lack the macroeconomic and regulatory arrangements to deal with large flows of mobile capital, liberalisation will need to be gradual', the bottom line was a 'continuation of the movement towards open international capital markets'. Perhaps more could not be expected from a group that included the chief executives of the insurance giant AMP and the IBJ Australia, Commonwealth and Macquarie banks.[84]

Australia's response meshed with the ongoing struggle for ascendancy between Asian governments and foreign investors. Analyst Jagdish Bhagwati argues that IMF policy had the strong backing of 'Wall Street financial firms [who] have an obvious self-interest in a world of free capital mobility since it only enlarges the arena in which to make money'. US Secretary of Commerce Jeffrey Garten argued that at the end of the crisis 'there is going to be a significantly different Asia, in which American firms have achieved much greater market penetration, much greater access' – as political economist Richard Higgott argued, 'large sections of the economies of the Asian Newly Industrialising Economies' will 'end up in foreign control . . . devaluation offers knock-down bargains for cashed up foreign buyers'. Those countries hardest hit by the crisis, he wrote, 'have little alternative but to relax restrictions on foreign ownership in sectors traditionally difficult for outsiders to access, such as services, property and retailing'. In addition to the riots and protests provoked by IMF policies, especially cuts to subsidies on essentials such as energy and rice, analysts argued the IMF approach could create 'an enduring legacy of ill-will and resentment'.[85]

At an elite level, changes were occurring which it was feared might slowly estrange 'Caucasian' states like Australia from regional forums. During the crisis, many were arguing for the formation of an Asian monetary fund – which the US went to great pains to prevent – while a new regional economic grouping of the ten ASEAN countries plus China, Japan and South Korea (ASEAN+3) was formed. This group specifically excluded Australia and, suggested Paul Kelly, raised the spectre of APEC being supplanted: 'the central idea of Australian foreign policy for the past decade is at risk'. Australian journalists and business people have expressed fears that the creation of this new group portends a shift to a 'closed regionalism', led by Japan, which might halt the liberalisation the West craves.[86]

Earlier Paul Keating had worried that APEC's silence during the crisis would imperil its future: 'the whole direction in which the Asia Pacific has been moving – towards economic and political openness, towards a sense of Pacific community – is at risk. It is a perilous moment and there are real questions in my mind as to whether we and our institutions can meet it successfully.'[87] As the political economists Mark Beeson and Stephen Bell demonstrate, liberalisation through APEC *did* falter; Japan led resistance with a claim 'that it represented a view which was widely supported by other nations in East Asia who were reluctant to speak out for fear of US retaliation'. On the other hand, they argued, the United States now saw APEC 'as largely irrelevant to US interests – the IMF and aggressive bilateralism have proved far more effective mechanisms for prising open Asian economies'.[88]

Just as the crisis saw APEC weakened and an elite politics of resentment flourish, other profound shifts also occurred across the region. In Malaysia former ruling party Finance Minister Anwar Ibrahim was dismissed and gaoled after attacking cronyism and advocating a freer political system, generating large protests against the government on the streets of Kuala Lumpur.[89] In August 1998 a meeting of ASEAN split over a Thai–Filipino proposal that the hallowed policy of non-intervention in internal affairs – which for thirty years had allowed members to ignore the repression and mismanagement of their neighbours – be abandoned. ASEAN's membership has expanded to include authoritarian states such as Burma, Vietnam, Laos and Cambodia, further undermining its moral legitimacy and putting pressure on its much vaunted structure of consensus.[90]

An August 1998 *Asiaweek* editorial, musing on ASEAN's failure to respond to the Asian crisis, the terrible forest fires in Indonesia or the India–Pakistan nuclear tests, asked whether the organisation was becoming irrelevant. Most dramatically, the editorial called on ASEAN to present a strong front to the IMF, to develop regional economic initiatives to deal with the crisis, and to seriously consider 'what kind of governance and political culture it wants to aspire to' – member nations, said *Asiaweek*, should nail their colours firmly to the mast of 'openness, justice and freedom'. Since its formation in 1967 at the height of the Vietnam War and in the wake of the Indonesia–Malaysia Confrontation, successive Australian governments have looked to the organisation as a bastion of stability and common regional cause. It forms a crucial conduit for Australian diplomatic influence, and hosts the eighteen-member security dialogue (the ASEAN Regional Forum [ARF]), which forms a significant plank of Australia's regional defence policy. Yet *Asiaweek* charged the ARF (of which Australia is a member) with being too weakened by the demand for harmony and consensus to act decisively on security issues.[91]

The Asian crisis generated a complex mix of pressures – an elite politics of resentment based partly on nostalgia for older 'Asian' politico-economic structures, and a grassroots push for more fundamental change – which Australian policy was doubly ill-equipped to address. In fact, Australia's policies could be seen as an attempt to contain and confront both pressures. The deeper problem, as the economist Walden Bello reminds us, is that an *entire model of development* is under question – a model which suppressed domestic capital formation and industrialisation in favour of huge inflows of foreign capital, in the illusory belief that countries could 'leapfrog' the arduous course to developed country status.[92] Yet such policies merely increased third world dependence on export markets and foreign investment, weakened domestic markets and sources of supply, and suppressed welfare spending and people-centred development strategies which might have moderated hardship and unrest. At the same time as workers were striking in Korea and Indonesia over layoffs and conditions, Human Rights Watch (HRW) expressed concern about further violations of already weak labour rights. In an ironic contrast to the IMF's intrusive agenda on behalf of foreign investors, HRW argued that 'multilateral and bilateral assistance programs, other than humanitarian aid, should be contingent on the recipient governments upholding human rights, including internationally recognized core worker rights'.[93] With so many more disenfranchised, and the promise of easy prosperity banished, workers' rights and social justice must surely move closer to the forefront of Asia's new political agenda.

Bello also argued that development strategies based on foreign investment and 'easy exports of manufactures' are no longer viable because export strategies involve 'beggaring one's labour force' in a 'race to the bottom that benefits only international investors'.[94] Whatever the nominal recovery in GDP growth in 1999 and 2000, the crisis set back regional states dramatically in human terms, and entrenched a flawed development model that needs substantial reform.[95] Few regional voices were more important than that of H. S. Dillon, Chair of Jakarta's Center for Agricultural Policy Studies, who called for a strategy of 'development through justice' which 'would have as its basic premise a desire to create a more just, egalitarian civil society':

> A development paradigm which has the people's autonomy as its objective, a transformation of extractive institutions into representative institutions, land policies which favour local populations, an education system serving as a ladder to carry all the people together to higher plateaus, an industrialisation process ensuring that farmers and labourers obtained a fair share of the value added, and fiscal and monetary policies generating greater justice in all walks of life.[96]

The East Timor endgame

Security, certainty, and home – the Howard government's obsessions would have their terrible culmination in the endgame which was played out in Indonesia and East Timor at the decade's end, as Soeharto abdicated power amid enormous destruction and upheaval, and the Timorese eventually seized their freedom only to see their sacred land raped, smashed and burned. In some ways it was a case of 'the return of the repressed', as the myopic and morally corrupt policy frameworks of the past crashed into the realities they had so long denied: the essential brutality of the Indonesian military, the struggle of the East Timorese and Indonesians against Soeharto, the illusory 'stability' sustained by the New Order's repression. At its end much of Australia's modern foreign policy had been cast, willingly or not, to the winds.

In 1990 the Australian Ambassador to Indonesia had said that 'the institutional framework of the New Order' should persevere through the succession and that Australian policy on East Timor 'must be based on the reality of Indonesian sovereignty'.[97] The same assumptions were at work in the 1997 White Paper and were maintained even as unbearable pressure built on Soeharto through the first months of 1998. Yet as anti-Soeharto protests grew, many hundreds were killed and injured, and after December 1997 large numbers of political activists were 'disappeared', tortured and killed.[98] By the time Soeharto was forced to resign on 21 May, more than 1100 people had been killed in Jakarta alone, and much of the city had been destroyed by riots and fires lit and fanned by provocateurs. Chinese women and children were made the target of a systematic campaign of murder and rape, and protesting students at Jakarta's Trisakti University were shot at long range by soldiers. The abductions of activists were later revealed as the work of former Kopassus commander (and Soeharto's son-in-law) Lieutenant General Subianto, and there were also strong suspicions that the shopping-mall fires, riots and attacks on Chinese were also linked to him. One of the army's fastest-rising stars, Prabowo was also close to many Australian officers and was rumoured to have been preparing the ground for a coup either against Soeharto or against ABRI commander General Wiranto.[99]

The Australian government condemned none of these atrocities, and no moves were made to downgrade defence co-operation. Instead, they lobbied the IMF to relax some of the conditions of the reform package to prevent social unrest threatening the regime – at the same time lobbying other Western states to oppose Soeharto's proposal for a currency board to stabilise the rupiah. This apparently contradictory approach may be explained by the fact that a number of large Australian-based resource and mining companies – such as Western Mining Corporation, Normandy, Newcrest and North Ltd – were waiting for Soeharto to sign new contracts for work. Originally delayed until after the March presidential election, they were signed in February 1998.[100]

Only when Soeharto had himself announced that he would step down after new elections at some future date did Howard praise the decision as a 'clear, orderly and statesmanlike path for the transition of power in Indonesia in a way that is more guaranteed than any other alternative to avoid bloodshed, to preserve intact the constitutional processes of the Indonesian state, and also to give hope to those many people within Indonesia who are looking for a more open society'.[101] This was the first time the government had acknowledged the force and claims of the democracy movement, a movement which denounced Soeharto's announcement as a sham and continued with plans for massive protests which the military vowed to crush. Two days later Soeharto resigned.[102]

One of the earliest and most surprising gestures of his successor, former Vice-President B. J. Habibie, was his suggestion that he would allow the East Timorese 'genuine autonomy'. During his term Habibie also announced new parliamentary and presidential elections for June and November 1999, restructured the Cabinet, released political prisoners and repealed laws that discriminated against Chinese. However, the military shot students protesting outside the Parliament, and abuses continued in Aceh, Irian Jaya and Timor. The military remained a powerful background force and Wiranto remained as both Defence Minister and Commander of the Armed Forces (known now as the Tentara Nasional Indonesia, TNI). Appalled by the prospect of losing Timor, the TNI intensified its operations and began developing a strategy that would thwart independence. By October Australian intelligence was receiving reports of the formation of 'Timorese' militias armed, trained (and sometimes manned) by the Indonesian military; in November, reports were also received of a massacre of fifty people by TNI forces near the town of Alas.[103]

In January Habibie suddenly announced that the Timorese would be offered a referendum on autonomy after the 7 June elections for the new People's Consultative Assembly (MPR). He also said that if the Timorese rejected the offer of special autonomy, he would recommend to the Assembly that it vote to grant the Timorese independence. It was over two months before an international agreement setting out the arrangements for the ballot was signed. During that time the Indonesian Cabinet demanded time to rewrite the special autonomy offer, and the TNI stepped up the organisation and activities of the militias. In April as many as fifty-seven people were massacred in Liquica when militias, assisted by Indonesian police, attacked 2000 people sheltering in a church, and twenty-five people were killed in the capital, Dili, after a militia rampage.[104] Thousands of people had already been forced by militia violence to leave their homes, and militia leaders declared that they would start a civil war if the people voted for independence. At the end of May East Timor's TNI Commander, Colonel Tono Suratman, gave a chilling warning to an Australian TV program:

> If the pro-independents do win, it won't just be the Government of Indonesia that has to deal with what follows. The UN and Australia are also going to have to solve the problem . . . there will be no winners, everything is going to be destroyed. East Timor won't exist as it does now. It will be much worse than 23 years ago.[105]

On 5 May Portugal and Indonesia signed an agreement covering the terms and conditions for the ballot on autonomy, to be conducted on 30 August. In my view, this agreement should go down in history as one of the most notorious examples of how *not* to pursue the resolution of a long-running conflict. Firstly, the negotiations did not include the Timorese. The agreement represented a cynical effort by both Portugal and Indonesia to make an end-run around the other: Indonesia hoped it would result in a vote for autonomy and Timor's permanent removal from the UN agenda, while Portugal hoped the Timorese would vote for independence. Hence there was *no* agreement about the final outcome – a potent recipe for more conflict given that one side was bound to be bitterly disappointed. Secondly, there would be no international peacekeeping force – instead, the Indonesian military would remain in the territory and security would be the responsibility of the Indonesian police. They would provide 'security' during and after the ballot, even though the (TNI-backed) militias had already threatened to go to war if the people voted for independence. There would be a UN mission (called UNAMET) to monitor the situation and run the ballot, with a contingent of unarmed police and military observers drawn from a number of countries, including Australia.[106]

Even as it was concerned at the growing violence, the Australian government also sought to preserve its relationship with the New Order and its older structure of security. It maintained that it preferred a vote for autonomy, and repeatedly downplayed the need for an armed international peacekeeping force. In April a former militia leader warned Australian intelligence of a TNI plan to wipe out the independence movement and kill nuns and priests, warnings passed on in official briefings in May.[107] As early as February, Labor's foreign affairs spokesman, Laurie Brereton, had been calling for peacekeepers, a call he repeated many times in the ensuing months. I also called for an armed force in early May, in a *Canberra Times* article that largely predicted the appalling events to come, and provoked a defensive phone call from one of the foreign minister's staff.[108]

Only in late April did Howard press the Indonesians on peacekeepers, at a meeting in Bali attended by himself and Habibie, foreign ministers Alexander Downer and Ali Alatas, and defence ministers John Moore and General Wiranto. The suggestion was angrily rejected by Habibie, and was not raised again until after the killings had begun.[109] Worse, the Australian government went as far as withholding intelligence reporting from the US and blocked possible moves within the US military to prepare contingency plans. Instead, the Australian Defence Force (ADF) developed limited evacuation plans of its own, while the Department of Foreign Affairs maintained that 'adept diplomacy' with Indonesia would stay the hand of the militias.[110] The tragic result was that no potential diplomatic or military coalition was in place when the terrible violence of September began.

The killings began in earnest on 31 August, the day after the vote itself, and exploded when the result, an overwhelming 78 per cent in favour of independence, was announced on 4 September. In just a few days as many as 1500 people were murdered, towns and dwellings were burnt and 250 000 people were abducted and taken to West Timor and other Indonesian islands. At least 200 people were massacred in the church at Suai, and thousands of frightened Timorese fled to the hills and into the UN compound in Dili, which became subject to a wild state of siege. It was clear that this was an organised campaign, planned and directed by senior Indonesian generals, whose aim was to drive out the international presence so that the killing could intensify unobserved.[111]

While many nations, including Australia, were now trying to assemble a multinational force, Indonesia refused to give its consent, and the UN Security Council wasted valuable days sending a delegation to Dili and Jakarta. Australia's great friend Ali Alatas told the international community, via the media, that 'you will have to shoot your way in'. Only the threat of sanctions and the cancellation of IMF funds, made by President Clinton and underlined by phone calls from the Chairman of the Joint Chiefs of Staff General Shelton to Wiranto, brought Indonesian consent to the force.[112]

Once this consent came – on 14 September, after ten days of carnage – the Security Council voted to authorise a 7000-strong force led by Australian Major General Peter Cosgrove, under a Chapter 7 mandate with powers to use all necessary measures to ensure peace and security. Thailand's Major General Songkitti was Deputy Commander of the force (known as Interfet), which included troops from Australia, Thailand, New Zealand, the UK, Canada and the Philippines, with logistical support from the US and Singapore.[113] The deployment saw firefights with militias and Indonesian forces and hundreds of arrests. Other grim work included the excavation of mass gravesites and the slow attempts to encourage frightened refugees in West Timor to return. A year later, over 50 000 of them remained in West Timor, prey to food shortages and harassment by militias, only one of many signs of the lasting trauma which saw the new nation of Timor Leste born into ashes.

The disaster provoked a furious debate in Australia over the perceived failures of the Howard government and many previous governments in their approach to Indonesia and East Timor.[114] This was accompanied by a violent cooling in the previously intimate relationship between Australia and Indonesia: the Agreement on Maintaining Security was torn up by Indonesia, Australia's embassy in Jakarta was fired upon and bitter attacks on Australians were made in the Indonesian media. Just as in 1986, it seemed that the apparent intimacy in the relationship was built on unstable foundations – they crumbled once the violent forces underpinning the New Order were challenged. Having hoped it could avoid a break with Indonesia by downplaying the threat of widespread violence, the Howard government had been forced by public pressure and its own revulsion into overturning the strategic doctrine of the past twenty years – that the irreducible control by the armed forces of the Indonesian archipelago was the ultimate guarantee of Australia's security.

But now Soeharto had gone, and the destruction of Timor had finally exposed the moral callousness, and political and strategic stupidity, of the entire policy. With their foreign policy assumptions being shredded in the mainstream media, their defence forces stretched materially and financially in East Timor, and their confidence shaken by the initial reluctance of the US to become involved, many Australians found themselves stripped of the illusions which had underpinned their post-Vietnam images of security and being.[115] *The Australian* captured the mood in its bitter editorial of 11 September: 'We have no weight with Washington that would convince it to commit troops to a peacekeeping force; and . . . no special relationship with the Indonesian leadership that would convince it to change its course. What the events in East Timor have shown is that we are militarily weak, politically naive and strategically alone.'[116]

Conclusion: 'bloody History, the opposite of home'

History – the opposite of home? What an extraordinary thing to say. The bitter line that closes Les Murray's 1996 poem 'A Brief History' seems at first glance to defy logic, but, on reflection, seems the perfect sign of the cultural weirdness and anxiety of the time, an intriguing window into the imagination of Howard and other conservatives at the close of a tumultuous, violent and hope-scarred century. In Murray's poem history is portrayed as a threat to the existential security and comforts of 'home', identified instead with the 'bodiless jargons' of the Left, 'ethnics' and others – all those who have dared look backwards in shame as well as pride, in horror as well as curiosity and satisfaction.[117] Fittingly, perhaps, this was security's last battleground: history, the narrative armature of national identity, the ever malleable prose of being.

Even Timor, 'bloody History' at its most terrible, could not escape Howard's efforts to tame the past and put it to political use. In his address to the nation announcing Interfet's deployment, he said: 'Our soldiers go to East Timor as part of a great Australian military tradition, which has never sought to impose the will of this country on others, but only to defend what is right.'[118] Of course Interfet marched for what was right, but we could not say this so certainly of the troops who went to Vietnam and Malaya, to South Africa and the Sudan, or even of the thousands who were sacrificed on the altar of European *Realpolitik* during the Great War. Yet for Howard the occasion called for history to be smoothed out, for our soldiers to march at the head of a line unbroken by mendacity or shame – as if the crisis they were now being sent to control resulted from the caprice of the gods rather than an easily traceable line of decisions, of which many were his government's own.

It did not end there: in Parliament he used the crisis to repeat his mantra that Australia's links with the United States and Europe – the 'common heritage' of which Spender spoke fifty years before – were beneficial when dealing with 'Asia': 'these links in our history are not an embarrassment to be lived down . . . We have stopped worrying about whether we are Asian . . . We have got on with the job of being ourselves in the region.'[119] As always, it is important to separate the kernel of commonsense from Howard's darker cultural politics, politics which would turn a deep political disagreement with a group of Indonesians (by no means representative of their nation or society) into a mark of totalising cultural difference. In short, *we are not Asian* – and once again the death and suffering of the Other had been appropriated as part of a fiction of Australian security and being.

At other times when the recitation of 'bloody History' threatened his imagery of home, Howard's assault was more direct. How else should we understand the government's response to the publication of the Human Rights and Equal Opportunity Commission's report *Bringing Them Home*? This report uncovered the history of the removal of Aboriginal children from their communities, removal which had been carried out with the deliberate aim, as Bruce said in 1927, of ensuring that they 'would not know in later life they had Aboriginal blood'.[120] Although belatedly consenting to a parliamentary 'statement of regret' in 1999, Howard consistently refused to make an official apology to Aboriginal people, despite this being one of the report's key recommendations. Things sank to an all-time low in a government submission to a Senate inquiry into the practice, where they argued that 'There never was a "generation" of stolen children' and that 'the nature and intent of those events have been misrepresented . . . the treatment of separated Aboriginal children was essentially lawful and benign in intent'. This provoked a storm of hurt and outrage among Aboriginal people. Senator Aden Ridgeway said that the government's argument was 'like denying the Holocaust', while Carol Kendall, one of the stolen children, said the submission was another 'stab in the heart'.[121]

'Bloody History, the opposite of home', at least 'home' of a certain kind. Whereas Whitlam and Keating had sought to close out wounds in the national identity through their visions of a future that would leave the past in its wake, Howard saw no loss, no need for substantive cultural change. Instead there was a smooth and natural continuity: 'national identity develops in an organic way over time'. To argue for change, any change that would bring the ontological integrity of the body politic into question, was to disrespect the past, to tear aside the threads that linked 'Australians' with a set of essentially proud and noble origins. This is, of course, just another elaborate fiction, one that continues to cause much hurt and hardship if the voices of the stolen are any guide.

Howard was often scathing about what he termed the 'black armband view of history', in which 'people essentially see Australia's past in a negative, pejorative light . . . a negative, carping, mean-minded, mean-spirited view of what this country has achieved'. To new citizens he claimed that, whatever its 'failures and its apportion of shame . . . in the great balance sheet of history it has been a remarkably successful society.'[122] This phrase he took from Geoffrey Blainey's *Quadrant* essay 'Drawing up a balance sheet of our history', which tilted the balance towards the 'three cheers' view of history, on the basis of Australia's democratic traditions and

> the steepness of the mountain that had to be climbed. This was a tough country to colonise. I am sure the Aboriginal pioneers found it difficult and in many ways they succeeded. The British also found it difficult . . . Australia was probably the finest triumph of long-distance colonisation the world had so far seen.[123]

The vast gap in his account is obvious – the history of war and dispossession which directly enabled the 'triumphant' economic colonisation – one which he seeks to close out with an 18th-century ontology that could have been drawn direct from Locke, or later from Bentham and Hegel. Infuriatingly coy about the murder and violence that accompanied colonisation, he argues that in 1788 'Aboriginal Australia was a world almost as remote, as different as outer space':

> Such [an extravagant] form of land use was bound to be overthrown or undermined. The world's history has depended on the eclipse of this old and wasteful economic way of life – wasteful in terms of human potential though not wasteful in terms, modern terms, of the whole range of living things. There is no way it could be preserved . . . It is strange that the Australian version of land rights almost tries to restore this archaic and untenable way of life.[124]

This is the language of dispossession. Just as security required the clearing and extermination of Aboriginal people through the 19th century, it now seemed to require that its own past be brazenly denied. In the righteous fires of Blainey's modernist chauvinism, our moral qualms shrivel and burn – a pity that Aboriginal people like Yvonne Margarula were still fighting to preserve their 'archaic' traditions, spirituality and way of life in defiance of the greater national interests – nay, civilisational progress – that abandoning their lands to mines and agriculture and industry would apparently bring.

And thus on the eve of the centenary of Federation a terrible historical circle was closed, from *security* to *security*, as if the intervening century had brought no lessons, no suffering, and no words. What could be next?

6

The wages of terror 2001–07

If the *Tampa* enters Australian waters illegally it should be sunk.
Posting to *ABC News Online* forum, 29 August 2001

Australians have become targets because of the values we represent.
Australian Foreign and Trade Policy White Paper, 2003

Four hundred and thirty-three human beings, seekers of asylum, stranded far from home. A Norwegian container ship, its enormous red hull floating listlessly off Christmas Island. A nation losing its soul. Or was it baring it?

CNN compared the stranded vessel with the Voyage of the Damned – the tragic story of the refusal by Cuba and the United States to accept Jewish refugees fleeing Nazi Germany in 1939 – but the Australian government and most of its citizenry were bereft of sympathy. 'Sink the *Tampa*' – the heading of a chillingly honest posting to the ABC's online forum at the height of the crisis – may have seemed an extreme opinion, but it was not uncommon and perfectly symbolic of the moral callousness that defined the government's disturbingly popular policy. A later correspondent to the forum reminded the female author that the *Tampa* had, indeed, already entered Australian waters. Was she volunteering to press the button?[1]

It was the last week of August 2001 – a week of such hollow laughter, which crowned months of controversy, bitterness and division over Australia's increasingly harsh treatment of asylum seekers. In the event, there was no need to sink the *Tampa*. As the ship pushed into Australian territorial waters, citing a condition of distress, SAS troops stormed aboard at the orders of the Defence

Minister, Peter Reith. There could be no more explicit proof of the increasing 'securitisation' of Australian policy discourse and practice about refugees.[2] Now, none of the refugees would be able to leap overboard, nor could the ship attempt to dock at Christmas Island.

The refugees had been rescued from a sinking ferry four days before, MV *Tampa* responding to a request from Australian maritime authorities to go to their aid. After initially heading for Indonesia, the *Tampa*'s captain turned around under pressure from the refugees. The government, facing a week of hell in Parliament and only a few months from national elections, saw its chance.[3] John Howard began to talk tough, in a depressingly familiar language and ontology: 'Whilst this is a humanitarian, decent country, we are not a soft touch and we are not a nation whose sovereign rights in relation to who comes here are going to be trampled on.'[4]

Over the next four days the asylum seekers waited on the deck of the *Tampa*, sandwiched between towering stacks of containers, surrounded by heavily armed SAS troops. They had no change of clothes and little shelter from the sun and rain, and some were pregnant or ill. For a toilet they were forced to use buckets placed behind wooden partitions in an empty shipping container. They would be trapped there for a further four days, as the government first tried to persuade Indonesia, East Timor and Norway to take them, then brokered what it called a 'Pacific solution' under which they would be transported to the tiny, impoverished island of Nauru for processing.

By the middle of the week, the two major parties and much of the Australian community had reached a malign consensus on the fate of *Tampa* and its new cargo of distressed human beings. This was underlined by an AC Nielsen poll, published in the *Sydney Morning Herald* of 4 September, which said that 77 per cent of respondents supported the government's decision to refuse the asylum seekers entry to Australia. Seventy-one per cent agreed with the policy of keeping refugees in indefinite detention.[5]

Less than two weeks later, on 11 September, New York City and Washington were attacked by terrorists, in one of the most brazen and destructive operations of its kind. Young members of the Al-Qaeda network led by Ayman al-Zawahiri and Osama bin Laden boarded domestic passenger flights in Boston and Washington, hijacked them, and crashed two of the planes into the World Trade Center and another into the Pentagon, killing more than three thousand people. The Prime Minister was in Washington as the attacks occurred. Over the next five years he would ally Australia with an American response that changed the strategic, cultural, and moral landscape of the world forever.

The '9/11' attacks and the so-called '*Tampa* crisis' also triggered significant changes in the Australian cultural and policy landscape – changes that were, however, consistent with the century-long politics and ontology of security I have analysed in this book. In the next two years Howard committed Australian troops to US-led wars in Afghanistan and Iraq, Australians were killed in large numbers in terrorist bombings in Bali, radical new counter-terrorism laws were enacted, and intense controversy was raised by the detention of two Australians, Mamdouh Habib and David Hicks, at a US military-run prison at Guantanamo Bay, Cuba. In 2006, in a move related to right-wing anxieties about the possibility of Islam constituting a kind of terrorist fifth column within the body of the nation, the government also removed the term 'multiculturalism' from official public discourse – renaming the Department of Immigration, Multicultural and Indigenous Affairs (DIMIA) the Department of Immigration and Citizenship (DIAC).

The government's response continued and intensified an historic Australian security approach that was coercive, exclusivist, anti-democratic and beholden to great power allies, as an apparent panacea for a new set of uncertainties. Yet this was not merely a period of rigid and inappropriate responses to objective uncertainty – the theme that dominated the period after 1969 – but the *deliberate manufacture* of insecurity and uncertainty as the key to a new and dangerous kind of politics. This 'security politics' had its antecedents in the Menzies governments' use of the red scare against Labor during the 1950s and 1960s, along with the subtle forms of governmentality developed over the century, but Howard arguably raised it to the status of a malign new art.

Howard won the elections held in October 2001 handsomely, turning around polls earlier in the year that predicted a loss, and won a fourth term in 2004 that included – for the first time in decades – control over the Senate. Claims about the government's reliability and effectiveness in national security, especially 'border protection' and terrorism, were central to these victories. As a by-product, discourse and anxiety about security permeated public and individual consciousness in ways they had not done since the Cold War. The government's success in this area not only raised the problem of how to analyse and understand this social phenomenon but also begged a series of very important questions for policy-makers and Australian society more generally.

How meaningful and viable was the security that they claimed to be giving us? How serious were the threats, if they were threats at all? Were they represented in ways that were legitimate and rational, and responded to in ways that were comprehensive, effective and humane? Could our response undermine or destroy security, our own and that of the myriad others whom our actions and decisions affect? Could the preoccupation with injecting security into politics distort security policy, producing a bizarre postmodernism where security is relentlessly invoked and signified but its possibility in reality is perpetually deferred? This chapter argues that while terrorism did form a real threat to Australians, government responses were piecemeal, inappropriate and counter-productive – at worst, provoking the very thing they claimed to defend us from. At the same time, the government deliberately ignored or exacerbated greater long-term challenges like human-induced climate change or the erosion of the nuclear non-proliferation regime, along with crucial international norms about human rights and the use of force. These decisions caused enormous and immediate suffering and insecurity to many while eroding the prospect of a secure long-term future for all Australians.

Security was fear once more.

Securing ourselves against asylum

In 2000, less than a year after the East Timor intervention, the government published a White Paper on national security, *Defence 2000*. Those looking for signs of human-centred innovation to reflect the role played by the ADF in stabilising East Timor were to be disappointed. Instead some disturbing new thinking was present: the broadening of security threats to take in 'many non-military threats to our national life, such as cyber attack, organised crime, terrorism, illegal immigration, the drug trade, illegal fishing, piracy and quarantine infringement'. Overtly signalling a new strategic doctrine, the paper stated that the ADF has 'a major part to play in coastal surveillance and enforcement activities. Our patrol boats, maritime surveillance aircraft and intelligence capabilities are fully engaged in the day to day monitoring and policing of our maritime approaches, and their efforts are closely integrated with other agencies.' These statements appeared alongside views that 'the United Nations has been responding to a growing sense in the international community that crises causing avoidable human suffering cannot be ignored just because they happen within the borders of a sovereign state. The trend to a more active and effective UN security role', stated the document, is 'welcome'. In this way the government recognised 'new demands on the armed forces of many countries … for humanitarian relief, evacuations, peacekeeping and peace-enforcement' and accepted that 'this is an important and lasting trend with significant implications for our Defence Force'.[6] It is arguable that such a human-centric perspective influenced later ADF and Australian Federal Police (AFP) deployments to East Timor, Bougainville and the Solomon Islands, although concerns about the effect of unchecked instability and state failure on Australia's long-term national security was also a significant consideration.

In many ways the government's efforts to grapple with new security challenges and issues was commendable, but the confident pose of the document papered over some profound moral and conceptual contradictions. This writer was told by a senior defence department official associated with the drafting process that 'illegal immigration' appeared in the document only at the insistence of the Cabinet and Prime Minister. Its listing alongside other non-state challenges and humanitarian intervention begged important questions about who was to be secured and against what. Perhaps unwittingly, the East Timor intervention was a policy pursued to defend the *human* security and rights of a neighbouring community, and Australia's strategic interests were only obliquely engaged, if at all. As readers of this book will appreciate, this constituted a profound paradigm shift – however partial and short-lived – from an approach to security consistently purchased at the expense of the Other. Inspired by the United Nations Development Programme's 1994 *Human Development Report*, scholars and policy-makers had been promoting human security as a new paradigm that might eliminate this contradiction, but it was never to be adopted in Australia.[7] To make the security of refugees and asylum seekers the focus of national policy was anathema to a government committed to a rigid and exclusivist idea of the national community that could be manipulated for political purposes.

The White Paper's alarmist view reflected intellectual developments in security studies, with scholars such as the RAND Corporation's Peter Chalk stating in a 2000 book that 'unregulated people movements' (UPMs) have 'the potential to challenge the integrity of both sending and receiving states'.[8] In such a view, the human security of individuals is of little moment; it is the national security of states that is important. The University of Sydney strategic analyst Alan Dupont acknowledged this contradiction, admitting that accepting a link between UPMs and international security 'masks sharp differences of view over whose security is being threatened – that of the refugees . . . or that of the receiving countries who care and provide for them', but claimed that 'these are not mutually incompatible positions. UPMs are a measure of both human and national insecurity.'[9] He also claimed that 'sudden large influxes of people who are ethnically and religiously different from the indigenous inhabitants, strikes at the whole notion of nationhood'.[10]

The examples used by Chalk and Dupont – the Palestinian refugee camps in Lebanon from which armed PLO fighters became embroiled in the civil war and attacked Israel, or terrorists emerging from communities of Sikh refugees in Canada – were factual but also inflammatory, and showed a disregard for the security of the larger displaced communities from which they came. Likewise appeals to threats to 'nationhood' make sense only if the nation is thought in ways that cannot make room for racial, cultural and religious difference. This, however, was a major element of the response to the *Tampa*. Given the lack of concern in the Australian community about the thousands of Europeans who overstay their visas, it was right to assume that the perceived threat of the boat people really lay in their *difference* – Muslim, Coloured, Oriental – in their status as an unassimilable excess that the pure being of the Australian subject could not abide. As the journalist Paul Sheehan claimed, 'the unspoken story that has emerged from the *Tampa* saga is that the majority of Australians appear unimpressed by the way a large Muslim population has been brought into this country with barely a shred of consultation or consent'.[11] This was the dark imagination of a white Australia insinuating itself into a future that (we thought) had buried its name; proof that, as Ghassan Hage argued in his book *White Nation*, fantasies of white supremacy had not disappeared with the official discourse of multiculturalism, but were ever-present in brooding backlash and repressive tolerance.[12]

Operation Relex II, which began as the *Tampa* crisis subsided, and involved naval and air surveillance and interception of refugee boats off Australia's north-western coastline, demonstrated the formal militarisation of Australia's refugee policy that was presaged in the 2000 White Paper. Official statements described Relex as part of 'a whole of government program to detect, intercept and *deter* vessels transporting unauthorised arrivals from entering Australia', which included shady efforts by Australian agents in Indonesia to disrupt the activities of people smugglers and the deportation of asylum seekers to camps outside Australia on Christmas Island, Nauru and Manus Island (Papua New Guinea).[13] Hence *deterrence*, a concept developed during the Cold War to shape nuclear and conventional military strategy, was shaping Australian policy towards the plight of vulnerable human beings. Yet this went beyond the use of military force, which was disturbing enough. As the more sinister theories of deterrence during the Cold War stated, efforts to invoke psychological fears of pain and suffering were also central to the policy.[14] The mandatory detention of unauthorised asylum seekers lay at the core of this policy.

The suffering of asylum seekers in detention centres was widespread, and provoked many cases of suicide, depression and selfharm, including the practice of lip-sewing, as a form of protest.[15] The pathos of this was brought home to Australians a few weeks prior to the *Tampa* crisis when an ABC *Four Corners* program revealed that a six-year-old Iranian boy named Shayan, who had been imprisoned in Sydney's Villawood detention centre with his parents for seventeen months, was severely mentally and physically ill. His distress was described by Robert Manne:

> Shayan no longer talks or eats. During the days he sits listlessly; during the nights he barely sleeps. When he hears a disturbance at the centre, he curls up into a foetal position. Shayan is taken to hospital regularly for rehydration. While at the hospital his condition improves slightly. As soon as he returns to Villawood, however, he reverts. The hospital where he is treated has diagnosed him as suffering from acute and chronic post-traumatic stress disorder. Another way of describing his condition is to say that Shayan, once a happy boy, is dying from the wounds inflicted on his spirit since his family's arrival in Australia.[16]

Shayan's family had been refused asylum in Australia, and were under threat of imminent deportation to Iran when the *Four Corners* program was made. When given paper and pencils, he drew the same picture over and over: grid-wire fences; a stick figure, blood dripping from its wrist; him and his sisters, their mouths drawn in tragic downward curving lines, tears streaming to the ground. Yet Shayan was just one example of the trauma suffered by those in detention. His crisis had, in part, been brought on by witnessing instances of self-mutilation and of seeing guards using batons to quell a riot at the Woomera detention centre in the South Australian desert.[17]

The disturbing truth about Australia's detention policy was that psychological torture is seen as an acceptable by-product of the regime – a subtle tactic to demoralise and deter asylum seekers. According to clinical psychologist Dr Zachary Steel, 'within our detention centres are probably the most traumatised people on the face of the planet . . . Almost everybody within that detention environment is presenting with symptoms of clinical depression.'[18] In short, the harshness of the detention regime was deliberate – it was designed as a form of *deterrence* that would hopefully dissuade others from beginning the long journey to Australia. As the Immigration Minister Phillip Ruddock told *Four Corners*: 'We go out of our way to ensure the detention centres provide as much amenity as reasonably possible without making them holiday camps. Without making them an incentive for people to come in the first place.'[19] Once we cut through the doublespeak, it could not be more clear. The suffering and pain experienced by asylum seekers in detention is *necessary* – and thus the dark Orwellian paradox at the heart of our obsession with security is made real once more. War is Peace. Ignorance is Strength. Security is Fear.

Exceptional and extraordinary powers: Undermining democracy

Could such an approach to refugees and asylum seekers not only prejudice their human security but also have significant costs to the national community? This requires questioning the idea of achieving security for an abstract 'nation', and shifting to more concrete considerations of the negative effect on real institutions and people: on the rule of law, on our political culture, on the structure of tolerance and diversity in Australian society, on the rights and guarantees supposedly enjoyed by citizens, and on the security of those who live outside our borders. It also requires recognising that our national interests and security are becoming ever more dependent on the evolution of international norms and institutions. If we undermine these, are we not objectively less secure? And is the society, the 'national life' we are seeking to secure through coercion and exclusion, worth defending? As the corrosive impact of the widespread rule-breaking in refugee policy spread into our policies on counter-terrorism and Iraq, serious questions about the basic integrity and effectiveness of our national security policy were also posed. As I have argued at length elsewhere, this ought to be of concern to the most conservative and pragmatic of readers.[20]

The domestic and international rule of law was the first victim. Despite an acknowledged contradiction in the 1951 Convention and 1967 Protocol on Refugees that fails to oblige states to allow asylum seekers access to their territory to make asylum claims, there was a strong view internationally that Australia was morally obliged to do so. Australia's refusal to allow the *Tampa* refugees to land, for example, was condemned by Amnesty International, Human Rights Watch, the European Parliament and the UN High Commissioner for Human Rights, Mary Robinson. 'We are dealing with human rights here and it is unacceptable that these people remain stranded on the ship, even if medicines and food were supplied to them,' she said. 'There are clearly established international procedures that Australia should have followed. Australia is a signatory to international conventions.'[21]

The British Home Secretary Jack Straw at one point argued for a radical change to the conventions to allow asylum seekers to make claims from offshore.[22] However, the Howard government worked instead to preclude any possibility of asylum seekers triggering Australia's international legal obligations. In the midst of the *Tampa* crisis the government introduced legislation into the Australian Parliament – the Border Protection Bill – which aimed, retrospectively, to shore up the government's legal powers to expel the ship and any such vessels in future. Disturbingly, the Bill sought to preclude judicial review of any government decision and would even have empowered officials to eject unseaworthy vessels from Australian waters. As such, the Bill violated the principle of the separation of powers and was potentially unconstitutional.[23] On these two grounds only the ALP opposed the Bill; once those provisions were removed they voted to pass it into law.[24]

Since 1996 the Howard government has systematically compromised the fairness and independence of the refugee assessment process – placing political pressure on the Refugee Review Tribunal (RRT), failing to inform refugees of their legal rights, restricting access to legal aid, and shaping departmental reasoning so that the Federal Court cannot question the process by which decisions are made. The court can only overturn decisions if the tribunal erred in law – breaches of natural justice, unreasonableness, bias or unfair process are beyond the court's jurisdiction. But that was not enough, it seemed: by 2001 the government was seeking to quarantine RRT decisions from judicial scrutiny altogether by eliminating any recourse to the Federal Court. These measures were ruled unconstitutional by the High Court in February 2003.[25] All in the name of *security*, Australians seemed willing to accept a gross perversion of legal process that is not worthy of a country that calls itself a democracy.

Further efforts to evade public scrutiny, the rule of law and international human rights obligations came with repeated government efforts to excise large parts of offshore northern Australia from the legal 'migration zone'. Any asylum seekers picked up in this area would be detained outside Australia – on Nauru, Manus or Christmas Island – and have their claims assessed there, as occurred with the refugees from the *Tampa*. Under Section 494A of the Migration Act asylum seekers assessed under such circumstances have *no access* to the review processes available in Australia, such as the RRT and the courts. They would then either be returned to their country of origin or accepted by a third country – and, if not, face the prospect of indefinite detention. They would not be able to apply for any visa to come to Australia, and would instead be dependent entirely on ministerial discretion to do so.[26]

Christmas, Ashmore and Cartier islands were excised under legislation passed in 2001. Twice in 2002, and twice again in 2003, the government introduced legislation to excise some 4000 islands to the north of 23°S (almost half the nation's coastline), but each time the Bills were rejected by the Senate.[27] However, in 2005 they were successful in having the regulations passed.[28] Then in 2006, after an hysterical reaction by Indonesia to the granting of temporary protection visas to forty-three West Papuan asylum seekers, the government introduced a new Bill to force arrivals on the Australian *mainland* into the offshore processing regime, which at the time of writing had been withdrawn by the government pending a change in senators' voting intentions. However, asylum seekers landing on Australian islands will be subject to the offshore regime.[29]

Lawyers and human rights advocates gave telling evidence to a Senate inquiry reviewing the Bill, stating that reviving the offshore detention and processing system used for the *Tampa* group presented serious risks of wrongful decisions and deportations, violating the fundamental principle of non-refoulement of persons to situations of danger. Mary Crock pointed out that children were especially vulnerable, saying that 'the percentage of unaccompanied and separated children whose claims were rejected on Nauru was dramatically higher than in Australia':

> International Organisation for Migration statistics suggest that 32 of 55 unaccompanied children were returned to Afghanistan in 2002–2003. At least one of these was subsequently killed. Of 290 such children who made it to Australia, none were returned . . . A related problem with the proposed regime is that children [who, after enormous community outrage, are to be detained only as a 'last resort' under 2005 changes to the Migration Act] will be returned to immigration detention, and that children and vulnerable adults will be placed in a processing regime that involves infringements of their basic human rights.[30]

Concerns about the possibility of genuine refugees being denied protection, and subsequently being deported to situations of grave danger, were widely raised after 2001. The Edmund Rice Centre published a report in which they interviewed forty deportees to high-risk countries, finding that thirty-five of them 'were living in dangerous circumstances immediately on arrival at the point of deportation'.[31] Lawyer Savitri Taylor has criticised the use by DIMIA of forcible removal from Australia, and comments that 'there are many aspects of Australia's asylum seeker law, policy and procedures that raise legitimate concerns that among the asylum seekers whose claims we reject are many persons who are, in fact, very much in need of international protection'.[32] David Corlett, whose book *Following Them Home* tells the stories of a number of forcibly returned asylum seekers, argues that 'returning people who need protection to situations where their human rights may be violated undermines the reason for having a refugee protection system at all'.[33] In the light of these facts, and the evidence presented to it, the Senate Committee charged with reviewing the 2006 Bill unanimously recommended that the government withdraw the proposed law.[34]

Some Australians may have taken comfort in a belief that the dangerous and exceptional powers granted to government officials under border protection policy could never be turned upon Australian citizens. However, the 2005 revelations that two Australian citizens, Cornelia Rau and Vivien Alvarez Solon, had been swept up in the DIMIA dragnet, showed that no one was safe. Rau was a mentally ill woman who was detained on the suspicion that she was an unlawful non-citizen and held at the

Brisbane Women's Correctional Centre and South Australia's Baxter detention centre for ten months in 2004, while Solon had been wrongly deported to the Philippines in 2001. An official inquiry into the cases by Mick Palmer AO confirmed disturbing details of their treatment and numerous mistakes by officials, and made forty recommendations for changes to government detention, assessment and oversight policies.[35] At a press conference Ms Rau stated that she had 'been locked up like a caged animal' and that she 'wasn't aware that they normally do that type of thing . . . it's quite incredible'.[36] Still, sections of the community had little sympathy. Rau's sister Christine, who had been publicly critical of the government during the investigation, was sent faeces-smeared hate mail on the eve of the Palmer report's release.[37]

During the inquiry the Immigration Minister Amanda Vanstone referred approximately 200 other suspect detainee cases to Palmer, which were then passed to the Commonwealth Ombudsman (who now has a statutory role under Section 486O of the Migration Act to assess the situation of people detained for two years or more). However, there remains *no* formal process to review decisions made by the Department of Immigration and Citizenship to deny visas, deport persons, or detain them for under two years.[38] By May 2007, 137 of these reports had been completed, and more than sixty other cases were still under investigation. The Ombudsman's conclusions are arguably an indictment of the current system.[39] My own survey of the reports on people, some of whom have been detained as long as five to six years, shows that a large proportion suffered severe depression, post-traumatic stress disorder (PTSD) and other psychiatric illnesses. In 67 cases the Ombudsman recommended release from detention or alternative accommodation, and in twenty cases he recommended the grant of permanent visas (where people either remained in detention or had only been given temporary visas). In six cases he recommended that the Immigration Department either delay or not pursue deportations.[40] The most distressing cases echoed the experience of Cornelia Rau: a formerly homeless Turkish man in detention for three years suffering from a delusional disorder with impaired ability to make decisions, whom the minister declined to release following an earlier Ombudsman's report of May 2006; and a 35-year-old woman from China in detention for four years, who had a three-year-old daughter born in detention and who claimed to have been sexually assaulted over a six-month period in Villawood detention centre. Both mother and daughter suffered PTSD, depression and anxiety, and it was only upon completion of the Ombudsman's report that they were granted permanent visas.[41]

One of Palmer's most telling official findings, which has been doubly confirmed by the Ombudsman's investigations, was the following:

> DIMIA officers are authorised to exercise exceptional, even extraordinary, powers. That they should be permitted and expected to do so without adequate training, without proper management and oversight, with poor information systems, and with no genuine quality assurance and constraints on the exercise of these powers is of concern. The fact that this situation has been allowed to continue unchecked and unreviewed for several years is difficult to understand.[42]

Exceptional and extraordinary powers. What Palmer recognised was something that scholars have repeatedly said is especially sinister about the politics of security, especially when it is played out in liberal democracies. The Danish scholar Ole Wæver in fact argues that the 'securitisation' of issues such as migration signifies them as existential threats to survival, the 'special nature' of which 'justifies the use of extraordinary measures to handle them'.[43] The philosopher Giorgio Agamben argues that the exercise and defence of sovereignty all too often involves invoking what the Nazi intellectual Carl Schmitt called 'the state of [legal] exception' whereby the sovereign (in Australia, the Prime Minister and Cabinet) can suspend the rule of law and assume 'unlimited authority' to meet 'a danger to the existence of the state'.[44] Agamben suggests that the state of exception is often realised in 'camps' where human beings are detained, tortured or killed, their dignity and humanity denied and reduced to 'bare life'.[45]

In her powerful analysis of Australia's detention system, 'What is a camp?' Suvendrini Perera linked it to the new extra-legal norms developed as part of the war on terror. Drawing on an article by the novelist Bernard Cohen, she saw Australia's asylum seeker policy as a coercive system wherein one can be imprisoned by the nation but never fully included within it. Asylum seekers find themselves in a bizarre non-place, 'Not-Australia':

> The structure of the camp … is a space where the 'national' is placed in suspension: not-Australia. This space of the camp, where the category of 'citizen' is no longer operative, also is the space where the claims and limits of the 'human', what remains as a residue of the 'citizen', are tested and revealed in lethal form. The figure of the refugee or 'stateless' individual exposes the purchase of 'the human' and its rights once divested of the rights it bears as a citizen.[46]

She concluded that after 9/11 the threat of terrorism and refugees were merged into single image, with a diabolical purpose. 'Among the innocent victims of the 9/11 terror attacks', she wrote, 'are several thousand asylum seekers in the West, non-combatants painfully caught at the point where the "war on terrorism" meets the "war at home". Indeed, the "bodies of asylum seekers and refugees are the very media through which the "war on terror" is normalised into "the war at home"'.[47]

The strategy of 'values': Australia's war on terror

The occurrence of the *Tampa* crisis and the 9/11 attacks within the same month in 2001 created a diabolical convergence not just of events but also of policy paradigms and forms of political being. Illegal immigration and terrorism were collapsed into a single shapeless threat less to the direct physical security of Australians than to vast ideological abstractions: their national 'values' and 'way of life'. This had its historical echoes – the characterisations of threats from Japan and Asian communism in the speeches of Curtin and Spender that I discussed in chapters 2 and 3 – but very destructive effects in reality. As Perera and many others have pointed out, the wilful conflation of terrorism and refugees was central to a *domestic* politics of identity and intimidation designed to transform Western societies in ways that encourage xenophobia and consent for coercive and extra-legal policy approaches, gravely undermining the rule of law and the national structure of social tolerance. They have also had very negative impacts on defence and security policy, by distorting threat and intelligence assessments and overemphasising the utility of armed force. An obsession with identity, and the increasing influence of US-style neo-conservative ideology, repeatedly trumped a more rational and inclusive policy process. The Howard government's conceptual and policy approaches to the 'war on terror', and especially the US-led invasion and occupation of Iraq, have been especially corrosive in this regard.

As the hijacked aircraft crashed into the World Trade Center towers and the Pentagon on 11 September 2001 John Howard was on a visit to Washington, where he unilaterally invoked the ANZUS treaty, despite the fact that the attacks could in no way be interpreted as being in the 'Pacific area' as the treaty states. He declared that Australians were 'resolute in our solidarity with the Americans' and that 'now is the time for calm but lethal responses . . . now is the time for the civilised world to work out the most effective way of responding'.[48] His government's response was to combine a familiar preference for force with increased intelligence, policing and financial co-operation with allies and regional governments and, more controversially, radical new counter-terrorism laws and a campaign of advertising and public statements to keep the public at heightened levels of alert and anxiety.[49] The use of military force went further than joining coalition operations; it was part of a deeply problematic shift in Australia's defence policy that closely resembled the Cold War 'forward defence' concept, and mirrored the Menzies government's belief that cleaving closely to the side of the United States was the surest guarantee of national security.

Australian forces were dispatched to Afghanistan in December 2001 and to Iraq in February 2003, and force contingents were returned to southern Iraq and Afghanistan in 2005. As if to under-line the convergence of asylum seeker policy and the US alliance, it was subsequently revealed that the same SAS regiment that stormed the *Tampa* was dispatched to US Central Command (CentCom) in Florida prior to deployment to Afghanistan, and thence a joint service liaison team led by Brigadier Ken Gillespie was placed in CentCom. The government's National Security Committee of Cabinet secretly decided to send Gillespie's team back to Florida in August 2002 to participate in the planning for war against Iraq.[50] Neither the broader Cabinet, Coalition party room nor the Parliament were informed, and the Prime Minister publicly claimed that no decision to join the war was taken prior to March 2003.[51]

In December 2001 intelligence agencies uncovered plans by the Indonesian-based Jemaah Islamiyah (JI) organisation to attack the US, UK, Israeli and Australian missions and a range of other targets in Singapore, and arrested forty-one people. In October 2002 JI operatives detonated two large bombs in the nightclub district of Kuta Beach, Bali, killing 202 people, eighty-eight of them Australians, and wounding 209 others. By this stage it was clear that al-Qaeda terrorism was a serious threat to Australians and South-East Asians, requiring a serious and carefully weighted response. However, the government's characterisation of the threat, and the policy responses that derived from it, were deeply problematic.

Clues to the motives of the bombers were many. Indonesian Islamist cleric Abu Bakar Bashir, who had close links to JI members, gave an interview to an Indonesian newspaper in which he accused Australia of being a 'cocky trouble maker' whose real agenda was to dominate and destroy Islam. The senior JI operative, 'Imam' Samudra, in a website set up after the Bali bombings, used anti-Christian rhetoric that named the enemy 'the Coalition Army of the Cross . . . America, England, Australia, Germany, Belgium, Japan and almost all members of NATO and so on'.[52] Bin Laden himself issued a short statement on 12 November 2002, adding this comment to his familiar litany of complaints about the destructive impact of UN sanctions on Iraqis and Western support for the Israeli occupation of Palestine:

> We warned Australia beforehand not to take part in the war on Afghanistan, as well as its disgraceful attempts to separate East Timor, but it ignored the warning until it woke up to the sound of explosions in Bali. Its government then falsely contended its citizens had not been targeted . . . How long will fear, killing, destruction, displacement, orphaning and widowing be our sole destiny, while security, stability and happiness is yours?[53]

The overwhelming emphasis of Western counter-terrorist policy in the wake of 9/11 has been on degrading and hampering the *capabilities* of terrorists to organise and act: arresting and detaining individuals, breaking up financial networks, improving intelligence gathering and co-operation, and using military force to kill the members of terrorist organisations and destroy their bases. This was made clear in the two major statements of US policy in 2003 and 2006, and in the Australian White Paper, *Transnational Terrorism: The Threat to Australia*, published in 2004. Certainly capabilities ought to be an important focus, and much of Australia's policy effort has been appropriate. Yet reducing the threat of terrorism required careful attention to other important issues. As the Harvard University terrorism expert Louise Richardson argued in 2006: '. . . we cannot defeat terrorism by smashing every terrorist movement. An effort to do so will only generate more terrorists, as has happened repeatedly in the past.'[54] With regard to capabilities, there were difficult decisions about when and how to strike at terrorists, especially using means as destructive as armed force, and whether to widen the conflict and divert resources to a war against Iraq. And with regard to the primary issue of terrorists' rationale and motivations – especially for striking civilians – there were crucial (and highly political) decisions about how the threat was to understood and conceptualised, and what weight was to be given to terrorist arguments. On both levels Australia chose poorly.

The political scientist William Maley, an expert on Afghanistan, has argued that while there was a strong legal and strategic case for war against Afghanistan in 2001, neither was true for war against Iraq in 2003. 'The threat posed by al-Qaeda was not hypothetical or speculative,' he wrote. 'The Taliban [regime] had provided Osama bin Laden with a secure operating environment . . . and if al-Qaeda were left to fester, further attacks on the scale of 9/11 could be expected to materialize.'[55] This said, a legal and strategic case does not constitute a *security* case, which exists only if the actions are part of a policy and communication framework that is likely to reduce the threat over the long term and is committed to a holistic vision in which no one's security is sacrificed for policy ends. In this situation, normative judgements about both the legitimacy of terrorist violence and of Western policy are of equal, if not greater, importance than capabilities. Even the FBI estimated that the destruction of al-Qaeda's bases reduced its capacity to act by only 30 per cent, and the International Institute of Strategic Studies'

2002–03 *Strategic Survey* speculated that the war in Afghanistan 'perversely impelled an already highly decentralised and elusive transnational terrorist network to become even harder to identify and neutralise'.[56] The willing flow of recruits to the movement, and the deep well of Muslim and Arab anger they draw on, can be stemmed only by affecting their desire to do harm to the West and their conviction that innocent civilians are legitimate targets.

Bin Laden's statement in the month following the Bali attack clearly emphasised that a potent source for his followers' outrage was the overwhelming historical evidence that the West seeks 'security, stability and happiness' while condemning others to 'fear', 'displacement' and 'widowing'. In October 2004 he made the point more clearly: 'Security is one of the pillars of human life . . . We want to restore security to our [Muslim] *Umma*. Just as you violate our security, so we violate yours.'[57] It must be said that bin Laden and other al-Qaeda ideologues are often deeply misguided. They fail, for example, to acknowledge how the interventions in Bosnia, Kosovo, northern Iraq and East Timor were aimed directly at protecting Muslims or the security of vulnerable communities. Even the US, so often complicit with Israeli violence, sent troops to Lebanon in 1982 to protect Palestinians. Likewise bin Laden's conclusion that the West's failure to distinguish between civilians and combatants justified al-Qaeda's own violence against civilians was immoral and repugnant. Yet this is where the real policy challenge lies. Countering and discrediting this normative judgement – that our evil justifies theirs – must be a core focus of the war on terror, especially if we are to take seriously official policy pronouncements that argue, as the US *National Strategy for Combating Terrorism* did, that there is a need to 'de-legitimise terrorism', win 'the battle of ideas' and 'diminish the underlying conditions that terrorists seek to exploit'.[58]

Even the government's White Paper, which boasts that '3400 terrorist operatives and associates have been detained or killed' and '$285 million in terrorist assets have been frozen', admits that 'despite the attrition they have suffered, terrorist networks such as Jemaah Islamiyah are flexible and resourceful' and 'have a capacity to regenerate'. But the paper is utterly silent about the normative challenge central to the war on terror, and defensive about any suggestion that Western policy might be rethought in response to expressed terrorist grievances. This it portrays in highly ideological terms as 'buckling in the face of this new form of terror . . . it would validate terrorist violence and embolden the terrorists, giving them cause to think they can influence government policy and intimidate electorates'.[59] This statement was made in response to an 'offer' made by bin Laden after the Madrid bombings of a 'truce' to European countries if they withdrew their forces from 'Muslim lands' within three months. The war in Iraq was the obvious shadow behind the exchange.

The haste and secrecy with which the Prime Minister made the decision to commit Australian forces to the wars in Afghanistan and Iraq indicates that the government failed to make a thorough strategic analysis – drawing upon both public and governmental sources of analysis and debate – of how the conflicts would affect either Australian or global security against such an unconventional enemy. War in Afghanistan may have been legally and strategically defensible, but the US Air Force killed a very large number of civilians in 2001 and 2002 – much greater in number and proportion than during NATO's far larger air campaign against Yugoslavia in 1999 – and again in 2007 the *New York Times* revealed that the use of air power by coalition forces against the Taliban was killing very large numbers of civilians, stimulating new anti-American feeling and even provoking the ire of the Afghani President Hamid Karzai.[60] The *Times* stated: 'What angers Afghans are not just the bombings, but also the raids of homes, the shootings of civilians in the streets and at checkpoints, and the failure to address those issues over the five years of war. Afghan patience is wearing dangerously thin, officials warn.'[61]

The international community failed to make the needed commitments of aid and security to the rebuilding of Afghanistan, and in mid-2007 the Taliban and their al-Qaeda allies were making a dangerous resurgence in the south of the country and in northwest Pakistan.[62] Many analysts were recommending much more robust military action against the Taliban, but if it was accompanied by more civilian casualties its effectiveness would be gravely undermined.[63] As the US military analyst Anthony Cordesman wrote in a 2006 CSIS *Commentary* on the war on terror:

> Carelessly seeking immediate tactical advantage at the cost of major strategic risks and penalties is stupid and dangerous. Creating more enemies than you kill is self defeating; making it politically and ideologically impossible to end a war and [thus] spreading new levels of anger and hatred to other countries and/or factions.[64]

Australian forces of 150 SAS and 1400 other personnel were withdrawn from Afghanistan by 2004, primarily because of the government's desire to join the invasion of Iraq, and were returned only after an appeal from the new Afghani government in 2005. While being a small contingent, it served a valuable role as part of a Netherlands-led Reconstruction Task Force in the Oruzgan province, and was to be expanded to about a thousand personnel (including SAS combat troops) by 2008. In contrast, in 2007, 1575 personnel were assigned to Australia's force in Iraq, Operation Catalyst, and the 2003 invasion was supported by 2000 personnel, including an SAS battalion, and fourteen F/A18 Hornets, which conducted bombing missions.

If the mismanagement of the war in Afghanistan, which is acknowledged even by Howard government supporters,[65] undermined the struggle against terrorism in normative terms, the *decision* to wage war on Iraq was an even more serious mistake, one immeasurably worsened by its conduct and impact. US bombing and operations killed as many as 7000 civilians during the invasion and caused serious damage to crucial infrastructure such as electricity, a situation worsened by the failure to secure the country in the wake of the fighting and the looting of hospitals and ministries. The United Nations has estimated that in 2006 alone more than 34 000 civilians died violently and 36 000 were wounded.[66] While most of them were killed by insurgents and in sectarian attacks, reports of civilians dying at the hands of US forces – especially in major attacks such as the December 2004 offensive in Falluja – were all too common.[67] By 2007 the violence was causing a vast flow of fleeing humanity into Iran, Syria and Jordan, with the UNHCR estimating that 750 000 people had fled since February 2006 and 50 000 more were being displaced each month.[68]

Not only did the war grossly violate the lives and human security of Iraqis but also the Howard government's participation and diplomatic support for it undermined Australia's intelligence machinery, its national security (especially against Islamist terrorism), and the global security and non-proliferation regimes that are so essential to that security. Howard made patently false claims in Parliament about Iraq's weapons of mass destruction programs and capabilities, even when advice from Australian intelligence agencies failed to support them. The political interference in the intelligence process – which also occurred during the 1999 East Timor crisis and the 2001 *Tampa* crisis – alarmed many observers and stimulated a highly critical public inquiry in 2003.[69]

By 2005 the direct cost to Australia's security of involvement in Iraq was becoming clear: under interrogation a JI member involved in an October 2004 terrorist attack in Jakarta explained that 'the intention to bomb the Australian embassy was because the Australian Government is the American lackey most active in supporting American policies to slaughter Muslims in Iraq'.[70] His claim was confirmed later that year when, in the wake of the revelations of the systematic torture and abuse at the Abu Ghraib prison, it was revealed that Australian officials based in Iraq were aware of the abuse and had told Canberra, but the information was suppressed.[71] The effect was further worsened when Howard gave prominent support to Israel's deeply controversial attack on Lebanon in 2006, after which al-Qaeda second in command Ayman al-Zawahiri vowed that 'we cannot sit back in submission' to a war 'produced and financed by all the countries of the Crusader alliance'.[72] Given the increased visibility of Australia on al-Qaeda's radar, and numerous official statements that the Australian mainland would almost certainly face attack, it was a further indictment of the government that experts were saying as late as May 2007, only a few months ahead of the APEC summit in Sydney, that Australia's ability to respond medically to a major incident on its soil was woefully inadequate. The preparations simply had not been made.[73]

In the light of this discussion, the government's claims about the link between the Iraq conflict and the war on terror, and their broader understandings of terrorism and security, were surreal and dangerous. The White Paper on terrorism claimed that Iraq 'presents the international community with a crucial contest of will in the campaign against terrorism' – as if, by their actions, the allies had not unwittingly opened a vast new front in the war on terror and placed both their own citizens, and especially the people of Iraq, in enormous danger. It claimed that 'Australia's alliance with the United States is a key plank of our international counter-terrorism strategy' – as if the decisions and policies of a foreign power can be trusted blindly; and it also claimed that 'protecting ourselves against terrorism is a fundamental human right' and 'by preserving a society in which fundamental human rights and freedoms are exercised, our counter-terrorism strategy enhances human rights'.[74] Such claims about the sanctity of 'fundamental freedoms' rang hollow in the light of the government's opposition to a bill of rights, its treatment of asylum seekers, and its controversial counter-terrorism laws giving ministers and security agencies exceptional powers of surveillance, detention and censorship.[75] In reality the statement expressed the very Orwellian strategy this book has been at pains to unmask, in which we buy our security at the expense of others, and thereby deny it to ourselves. As the ever-growing toll of civilian dead in Iraq and Afghanistan and the chilling warnings of Osama bin Laden have shown, there is no security to be bought in such a way any more.

Prominent in such policy statements is a narcissistic performance of self in which 'Australia' is represented as pure and good, a subject possessing 'values' and a way of life that it shares with allies such as Britain and the US, but not with its neighbours or the religion of Islam. This was reflected in the statements of many conservative politicians during 2005 urging Australian Muslims to accept 'Australian values' or 'clear off' – a demand they saw as important for Australia's security – which arguably set the scene for the appalling mob attacks on Australian Arabs and Muslims in Cronulla in December of that year.[76] Here, as Brett Bowden has remarked, a claim to superior civilisation all too quickly veers into a 'clash of civilisations', within and beyond the nation. I have written about the sinister political function of such discourses of national purity elsewhere, but here I simply ask one question.[77] If the Howard government claimed that Australians had become targets because of the values we represent, was this not indeed true, for reasons the government could never admit or recognise?

Conclusion: Signs of a different future?

In mid-2007 the ALP opposition led by Kevin Rudd had a strong lead in opinion polls, suggesting the possibility of a change of government by early 2008. This opens up an opportunity to explore whether the most dominant alternative political forces possess the willingness to think and act differently. Rudd outlined his foreign policy vision in a February 2007 article in *The Diplomat*, where he marked out some clear alternatives to the Howard government's policy approach and its understanding of what the core challenges and threats are for Australia. Of particular interest was his claim that the government was hampered by a 'deep ideological conservatism that resists the need to build new regional and international structures in response to emerging pan-regional challenges ... and, most damaging of all, a consistent, crippling tendency to see foreign policy primarily as an extension of Australian domestic politics of the narrowest kind we saw in the response to Hansonism'.[78] He described the decision to support war in Iraq as 'our worst foreign and national security disaster since Vietnam' and the Bush administration's approach as 'a deeply flawed policy . . . with serious implications for the future stability of the wider Middle East'.[79] In contrast to Alexander Downer's overheated fear that opposing the invasion of Iraq would have created 'a great and historic breach with the United States' and left 'us as a country very vulnerable', Rudd calmly stated that 'Labor believes that the ... alliance is overwhelmingly in Australia's national interests' but that it 'does not believe [that it] mandates automatic compliance with every aspect of US foreign policy'. His view echoed a number of important scholarly analyses over previous years by writers such as Gary Brown, Jim George and Mark Beeson.[80]

Rudd also brought a different perspective on two core security concerns neglected or mismanaged by the government: climate change and the proliferation of weapons of mass destruction (WMD). He criticised the government's decision to reject the Kyoto Protocol to the United Nations Framework Convention on Climate Change, saying that 'climate change is the great moral challenge of our age'. He promised to ratify the protocol, cut national greenhouse emissions by 60 per cent by 2050, introduce a national system of emissions trading (to put a market price on pollution) and make Australia 'part of the global solution on climate change'.[81]

On proliferation, Rudd expressed concern about the nuclear tests by India, Pakistan and North Korea in recent years and plausibly argued that 'one of the most serious consequences of the Iraq war has been to reinforce Iran's growing determination to develop nuclear weapons'.[82] Rudd's concerns were well founded. It was no accident that proliferation crises in North Korea and Iran followed the US President's 2002 'State of the Union' speech in which he described these countries and Iraq as 'an axis of evil', and followed it up with a new doctrine of regime change and preventive war put into action in Iraq.[83] Since then the world has watched nervously as the US and North Korea play a dangerous game of bluff, with Bush consistently saying that the US 'reserves all options'.[84] Such concerns were revived with public revelations of advanced US war-planning for a major bombing campaign (including the possible use of small-yield nuclear weapons) against Iran if diplomatic pressure to cancel its uranium enrichment program failed.[85]

While the Howard government criticised the US for failing to support a treaty controlling the production of fissile materials (FMCT) and gently urged it to do more to meet its disarmament obligations under the 1969 treaty on the Non-Proliferation of Nuclear Weapons (NPT), it failed to question the Administration's nuclear weapons research or its withdrawal from the 1969 Anti-Ballistic Missile (ABM) treaty, and has even joined US research on the potentially destabilising National Missile Defense System.[86] Worse, by joining the war in Iraq and endorsing preventive action against WMD proliferators in its 2003 *Defence Update* paper, the government helped to fuel the concerns of such 'rogue states' about their own security, which are a major stimulus to their programs.[87] In contrast, Rudd indicated that he would 'establish a national diplomatic initiative to strengthen and restore the integrity of the NPT regime', which remains the best hope of restraining and reversing the proliferation of such destructive weapons. The potential importance of such an initiative could not be underestimated. The NPT system – which rests on a global bargain by which the rest of the world agrees not to develop nuclear weapons or spread the technology if the nuclear weapons states disarm – is in grave crisis, with its last five-year review conference in 2005 breaking up in acrimonious failure to reach agreement.

Rudd's article did have disturbing silences also. There was no discussion of asylum seekers and refugees, a policy area in which Labor has been very disappointing in recent years, yet is crucial to re-establishing Australia's credibility as a principled supporter of human rights and international law. The only signs of change here were resolutions passed at the 2007 National Conference to eliminate the temporary protection visa in favour of permanent residency, and to return many offshore islands (excluding Christmas and Cocos-Keeling islands and Ashmore Reef) to the migration zone.[88] Likewise there was no mention of Indonesia, where a welcome improvement in the relationship, and very positive political and security sector reform in Indonesia itself, have been accompanied by a disturbing reversion to older patterns of coercion and *Realpolitik*. Under the umbrella of the war on terror, training between the ADF and the feared Kopassus special forces resumed, and Indonesian President Susilo Bambang Yudhoyono supported the return of TNI troops to villages. A policy once crucial to enforcing Soeharto's repressive rule and military corruption is now portrayed as essential to defence against terrorism.[89]

Memories of Australia's uncritical policies over East Timor were evoked by the government's efforts to appease Indonesia by legislating to prevent future West Papuan asylum seekers coming to Australia and by the clauses in the 2006 bilateral security agreement – the first and most comprehensive since the AMS was ripped up by Indonesia in 1999 – which forbid either party to 'support or participate in activities by any person or entity which constitutes a threat to the stability, sovereignty or territorial integrity of the other Party, including by those who seek to use its territory for encouraging or committing such activities, including separatism, in the territory of the other Party'.[90] While supporting West Papuan independence from Indonesia would not be a constructive or effective option, even very pragmatic commentators argued that the government ought to urge Indonesia to implement the far-reaching autonomy agreement it made in 2001 with West Papuan leaders, only to promptly renege on its commitments.[91]

Rudd's hybrid of mainstream foreign policy traditions, which he termed 'multilateral realism', was consistent with the earlier Labor concept of 'good international citizenship' in which liberal principles were to be applied in the national interest. This, ultimately, is merely a modification – if a welcome one – of the fundamental ontology of security and identity that this book has sought to uncover and critique. Rudd declared that one of the fundamental objectives of Australian foreign policy was 'to protect our national security', rather than the security of the world or of human beings in general, and hence we may legitimately worry that – like many previous Labor leaders – he left the door open to coercive and exclusivist policy approaches that ultimately buy our security at the expense of others.

After two centuries of suffering and failure, there is a better way.

Conclusion: A cosmopolitan future

It is fear's repressive consequences, not just the personal suffering it inflicts, which make it a toxic force to be resisted . . . We need a moral dimension to the public realm. We need an answering vision of justice and optimism. We need to learn to manage our fears and face the realities of our complex world. The survival of our democracies depends not on the capacity to hit back at the terrorists, but on our capacity to think for ourselves.

Carmen Lawrence, 2006[1]

In this book I have told a grim and sometimes terrible story, but it is all true. Many may dispute my analysis or my conclusions, and they are welcome to. However, as a society existing on that part of the earth where South-East Asia and the South Pacific meet, colonised and coveted for its strategic location and its wealth, and still in its mind an anxious and threatened outpost of Europe, we must face some uncomfortable facts. Throughout two centuries of colonial history we have all too often purchased our security with the suffering, destruction and abandonment of others, and sometimes ourselves. We have constructed our identity in racist and exclusivist terms, terms exclusive of Aboriginal people, Asians, Muslims, communists and asylum seekers, people who could be named Other before they could be recognised as human. Even as we have sought to modify this historical legacy to create space for other traditions and cultures and structures of value, it has welled up again and again, an enduring possibility under the surface of our present. We have not questioned the meaning of the security we seek, or wondered at its costs, or thought how it might be made legitimate and universal and comforting for as many as can receive its gift. We have instead turned it into a dark system of politics, one used to divide and accuse, a weapon in an endless struggle over privilege and power and ideas. In doing so we have undermined our democracy, corroded the rule of law, divided our communities and cheapened the value of citizenship. Above all, we have damaged our nation. We have damaged what our nation could be.

What then is my answering vision? Once we think for ourselves, what might we think? I feel heavily the responsibility to offer a better path, but thousands of Australians – working in parliaments, churches, NGOs, community groups, political parties, the arts, media and universities – are already mapping it out with their words and actions daily. They come from every race, every faith and every region, and from across the political divide. I can only add my voice to theirs. As Matthew McDonald argues, they form an immanent possibility for change, a hope that 'while core themes exist no single security discourse ever completely captures the way a particular political community conceives of itself and the world around it'.[2] This conclusion maps out my thoughts about the future, but let me preface them with some comments about the challenge.

Challenges of the past and present

What some readers may find disconcerting about this book is its refusal to grant Australia a narrative of progress, a narrative of unblemished origins, unbroken traditions, social consensus or stable values, developing in an 'organic way over time'; a story that, by itself, might offer hope. I do sympathise with the desire of many for such narratives, but neither the historical record nor a credible political science supports them. The very meaning of Australianness – its inclusiveness, justice and scope – have been the subject of bitter political battles that are still underway. This need not make the idea or value of being Australian mean any less; but it suggests some important ethical and political responsibilities that come with it. It suggests that hope is something we have to make, not inherit.

We all bear the weight of our history and our political culture, which can be nurturing or lethal depending on the accidents of fate that place us here or there: safe in a suburban home, our bank accounts healthy and our children sleeping soundly; cold and fearful, as our boat takes on water racing for these shores; struggling to preserve our language and traditions against developers and governments busy legislating our rights away; walking miles barefoot to vote in a referendum that could expel our oppressors, only to have them take a terrible revenge; or shivering in muddy khaki on a far-off battlefield, desperate not to fail our mates. Such lives and experiences are vividly real, but they are hostage to complex political structures, discourses and intellectual abstractions that shape the world we live in and the possibilities we have to exist in and to change it. It is those abstractions, and the kind of lives they enable or deny, that are the real subject of this book. My narrative and analysis is sometimes sobering, but do not mistake it for pessimism. Its aim is to establish the necessity for a work of social and political change that would be very easy were it not for some frustrating obstacles.

Three key objections have often been made against the kind of analysis I have presented here. One, directed against the (broadly Foucauldian) understanding of individual and political subjectivity, discourse and power woven throughout this book, might accuse me of presenting many Australians as excessively gullible and pliable in the face of power, as lacking in agency or, if not agency, lacking a will to challenge authority and received wisdom or to think for themselves. As I will argue below, even if this is partly true, the problem is that in modern societies our thoughts are not always our own, and the burden of blame lies with those most capable of shaping the public agenda: journalists, experts, public officials and politicians. A second objection, as set out by the political historian Judith Brett, an incisive analyst of the Liberal Party, accuses critics of Howard as wrongly arguing that 'his election victories' show the Australian people to be 'racist, uncaring, reactionary and so on'.[3] She accuses the Left of being overly 'suspicious of nationalism' because of 'its power to harden boundaries between people and to make them hate and kill each other'. This blinds them to the fact that,

> in a relatively new country like Australia, nationalism has been partic-
> ularly important for binding people together . . . Nations can create
> experiences of community and commonality that people value greatly.
> Nations can also be used to exclude others. They can help people make
> sense of who they are and build reciprocal bonds between strangers –
> fellow citizens who will never know each other.[4]

Brett shares the moral concerns of Howard's critics, but directs a rebuke to Australian intellectuals whom she thinks 'have been unable to develop any effective or plausible counter-strategies for talking to their fellow Australians. If you regard any talk of "us" as illegitimate, it is not clear to me who you are going to talk to.'[5]

A third objection, a more belligerent version of Brett's, has come from the academic David Burchell, the author of a book about western Sydney. He argues that the 'leftish intelligentsia's' concerns with Iraq and asylum seekers exhibit 'an almost heroic incapacity to evince sympathy for the bleached backyards of Australia's suburbs and provinces, and the local, humdrum concerns of those who live there':

> Ever since the nineteenth century, it's been a defining trait of the higher
> professions to be preoccupied by questions of political conscience and
> morality ahead of those of interest and personal security, by the global
> at the expense of the local, by the grand vision rather than the reassuring
> gesture.[6]

It would perhaps be too easy to mock Burchell for 'evincing' a deeper affinity for the common person in language plucked from the most obscure reaches of the dictionary, but there is a serious objective to his rhetorical strategy. On one level Burchell's argument is quite incredible. He writes as if Australia's very existence as a settler colonial nation was not a function of international forces at all times in its history and as if foreign policy is some kind of abstraction from the concerns of real life or indeed the nation. However, his arguments also betray a sinister undertone: a desire to silence dissent by making it conceptually impossible. He reproduces an ideological construct of Howard's – that of the simple suburban and rural 'battler' – and mimics his strategy of imagining and reinforcing divisions, not only between communities but also

between people who think and those who allegedly don't, between
security and morality, between the local and the global, between
grand visions and ordinary lives. None of these distinctions holds
in reality, and to affirm a tradition that would suggest security is
opposed to morality is to remain hostage to a particularly crude
and myopic ideology of political realism. However, both Burchell
and Brett make me confront a challenge: to connect a better vision
of security and nationhood to the lives and concerns of individuals
within *and* beyond our borders. Brett puts it this way:

> One does not counter [Howard] by arguing that the centre is empty,
> or does not exist, and that he is really only ever policing the borders.
> One stands in the centre with him and argues about its meanings and
> responsibilities, and tells different stories to one's fellow Australians
> about their past and present and the bonds they share.[7]

So, some different stories. My first point is to say that the concerns of Australians for security and certainty are legitimate and
important. For the majority of us with little or no knowledge of
Islam and global conflict over the last few decades, the terrible
images of 9/11 must have seemed both horrifying and inexplica-
ble. Because of my training in the field of international relations
and security studies I could claim some expertise, but even I struggled for understanding. To make sense of these images one marshals
whatever resources one has, but most often turns to the most immediate and authoritative conduits of expertise, analysis and certainty
available: the media and government, who themselves scramble to
assimilate the events to pre-existing narratives of action, identity
and self. We trust our leaders and security managers to provide us
with the most credible and impartial analysis, to tell us honestly
what the events mean for us and, if necessary, to fix on a course of
action and take it. When our leaders are especially Machiavellian,
impulsive and cynical, and when they are imprudent and refuse to
look widely for advice, we are in trouble.

The Defence Minister and a coalition backbencher said after
9/11 that the *Tampa* refugees may contain terrorists among them,
and the Prime Minister deliberately evoked old fears of invasion
when he stated on 31 October 2001, less than two weeks prior to
the federal election, that if the government 'throws up its hands' it

will be a 'recipe' for 'I don't want to use the word invaded ... [but] the shores of this nation to be thick with asylum seeker boats, thick with asylum seeker boats [*sic*].'[8] Neither assertion had any basis in fact, but their psychological impact was profound. In such circumstances citizens look to their leaders for guidance and reassurance, and defer to their expertise and presumed authority. Such an effect is magnified when we consider that the historic political formation of the security state, the Hobbesian body politic, constructs a political community based on the alienation from and fear of outsiders and merges the identity of the citizen with that of the state. Invoking 'sovereignty' and 'border protection' as concepts entrenches such a political formation, and discredits the idea that a nation can happily contain many kinds of identities and values (indeed, many sovereignties) yet still be generally harmonious and ordered.

Against such a background, when citizens are told their security is at risk, they will acquiesce. While the public legitimisation of racist ideas may have been a factor in the response of many Australians to the *Tampa* crisis, in my view it was the deliberate securitisation of the issue that was most significant. As I have shown throughout this book, 'grand visions' and 'personal security' are utterly intertwined at such times, in ways that rob people of agency, choice and freedom. What is portrayed as a defence of autonomy and freedom is in fact the operation of a power that makes citizens into pliable and passive subjects. Achieving security, freedom and dignity then rests not in believing such cynical promises to make us safe – when they patently do not – but in finding ways to identify and resist such a power and linking them with more ethical and sustainable policy frameworks. This is to ask two things of citizens: that they exercise greater freedom of thought by being more sceptical of information, and to exercise greater personal responsibility by considering the ethical and political implications of their views; by considering how they will affect the lives of others.

Rethinking the idea of sovereignty is central to this effort. As a model for independent and self-governing communities (what is known in international law as 'self-determination') sovereignty is an important value, and needs to be preserved. Yet when turned inwards to suppress cultural and religious diversity within a society, to impose violent and coercive policies that produce deep suffering and hurt, or to deny our international responsibilities and connections, it can be a very dangerous thing.

Responsibility and sovereignty: Our global connections

To be meaningful and responsible, any discussion of the national and the local must acknowledge their unbreakable connection with a world beyond our borders: with a diverse international society of states, religions and cultures; with a globalised economy in which we have long been deeply integrated; and with global ecosystems – seas, forests, rivers and atmosphere – that respect no borders and are undergoing rapid human-induced change. These facts are often denied – or acknowledged selectively – by governments and commentators, but they are denied at our peril. They are facts in turn reflected in global and regional institutions that have been created for profound and honourable purposes: to help us solve problems that cannot be solved by one or two countries alone, to provide stability and order to international relations, to give hope and a voice to less powerful nations and communities, and to establish and defend universal principles that unite us in our humanity. Above all, they were established, after two terrible global wars and instances of genocide, to stand as a bulwark against the most terrifying powers discovered and exercised by modern man.

This is why the United Nations (with the close involvement of the Australian External Affairs Minister H. V. Evatt) adopted its Charter of 1945, which outlawed the use of force save in self-defence and aimed to 'save succeeding generations from the scourge of war, which twice in our lifetime has brought untold sorrow to mankind, and . . . to reaffirm faith in fundamental human rights, in the dignity and worth of the human person, in the equal rights of men and women and of nations large and small'.[9] It is why the Universal Declaration of Human Rights and numerous other rights instruments were adopted in the decades following, why the Convention on Refugees was adopted in 1951 and improved in 1967, why the Framework Convention on Climate Change and its Kyoto

Protocol were adopted in 1992 and 1998, and why at the United Nations' World Summit of 2005 – the most significant UN meeting since 1945 – its member states reaffirmed their 'faith in the United Nations and [their] commitment to the purposes and principles of the Charter and international law, which are indispensable foundations of a more peaceful, prosperous and just world'.[10] In a world in which all our fates – humans, animals, ecosystems – are bound together, there is no going it alone.

In this way the Howard government's rejection of the Kyoto Protocol and effective action on climate change, which so profoundly threatens the security of future generations, and its rejection of its responsibilities to refugees under international law and of the UN Security Council when it took the decision to join the invasion of Iraq, are so damaging. This is not an argument that these agreements (or the UN itself) are flawless or that collective action is simple or easy; it is that the government consistently acted as if it could be limited by the most narrow self-interest and turn its back on the burden of collective responsibility, not merely for trans-national problems but also for the consequences of those actions it chose to take.

Like genocide, terrorism or war, human-induced climate change is an example of the enormous creative power of modern humans to live and act in ways that have destructive and unpredictable consequences. Yet I worry that as a society, and as a world, we lack the moral and political capacities necessary to meet the challenges of climate change. Rising sea levels will potentially add millions of refugees and displaced people to the 21 million[11] that currently exist, and what will become of them if the current rejectionist approach of so many states continues?[12] Will we wall ourselves further into isolated islands of sovereignty, paying lip-service to international law, while terrible global problems are left to fester? Surely the earth's atmosphere, which we all breathe every few seconds, which protects us from lethal cosmic radiation, and which makes the earth habitable and is the engine of global climate, is the ultimate evidence of our common vulnerability? Action to reduce greenhouse emissions and forestall the worst effects will need to be taken by individuals, corporations and governments, but only at an international level can a genuinely fair and effective system, based on widely accepted principles, be agreed. This was the true value of Kyoto, whatever its flaws.

In such a context, sovereignty remains important, but it must be exercised *responsibly*, and collectively, when governments and various non-governmental organisations meet to debate their problems in international institutions with the duty to represent the interests both of their particular communities and of human beings in general. This is a broadly 'cosmopolitan' argument, which asserts that moral obligations flow from the common heritage and fate of humankind, in all its diversity. Nationalist politicians, and writers like Brett, promote a different line of argument towards the same goal: one that derives from national traditions and interests. For example, Gareth Evans maintained that the idealism in Australia's foreign policy derived from its convict experiences and its record of immigration, which saw 'a significant proportion' of the population made up of 'those fleeing persecution or seeking a better life'. As a result, 'at least part of the national psyche is profoundly committed to notions of reform or improvement. And being the size and weight we are, it is in Australia's national interest that the world should be governed by principles of justice, equality, talent and achievement, rather than status and power.'[13] There is much to agree with in Evans' argument, and it is possible for these two approaches – cosmopolitanism and progressive nationalism – to reinforce each other. However, Labor's sorry record on East Timor, and its failure to develop a principled policy towards asylum seekers, point to a deeper challenge.

Sovereignty contains not only the promise of representation, community and order but also the possibility of exclusion and violence. Like many indigenous peoples and national minorities, the refugee lives and suffers in the very space of this contradiction. As McKenzie Wark argued in 2001: 'It is the rule of the border in general that the refugee challenges . . . It is the justice of national sovereignty itself that the body of the asylum seeker refutes.' Lacking both rights of secure citizenship at home *and* abroad, they are doubly dehumanised within traditional ontologies of national security and identity – 'homeless' in a truly profound sense. Yet an 'international society' of sovereign states is singularly failing to provide them with hope. As Wark concluded: 'Only when the world is its own refuge will their limitless demand be met.'[14] The philosopher and historian Hannah Arendt, herself a former refugee, wrote in 1950 that in the face of the terrible 'homelessness' and 'rootlessness' of her time 'human dignity needs a new guarantee which can be found in a new political principle, in a new law on earth, whose validity this time must comprehend the whole of humanity while its power must remain strictly limited, rooted in and controlled by newly defined territorial entities'.[15]

One could also extrapolate from another of her observations – about how totalitarianism 'brought forth an entirely new form of government which as a potentiality and an ever-present danger is only too likely to stay with us' – to say that when any new political possibility is put into the world, be it death camps, indefinite detention, the torture of suspects or the routine suspension of the rule of law, it changes the fabric of reality and threatens to become a new norm.[16] From there, it is but a few fateful steps to dictatorship and terror. As a society, we are already peering down that terrible staircase. This is the danger that the war on terror and the abandonment of refugees brings us, built as it is on a tradition of security in which lives can be secured or sacrificed in the service of cruel political abstractions divorced from life as it is really lived. The asylum seekers are proof that our images of safety, community and being are built on a dangerously weak edifice. If their right to be means so little, how can ours mean any more? If their security is not protected, how, ultimately, can ours? What is to stop the violence turned on them from being turned on ourselves?

A cosmopolitan future is not merely a matter of states selectively choosing to participate in the solution of global problems, or altruistically bearing burdens that – in an ideal world – they would not have to. Our common fate and our common vulnerability are facts, as solid as the earth. We all breathe the same air, as John F. Kennedy said after an earlier period of profound collective peril in the Cuban missile crisis.[17] A cosmopolitan future is about domestic as much as international change: it requires that states transform themselves to embed universal principles like human rights in their political life, in their constitution, in their identity and *ethos*. It requires that political community no longer be based on images of claustrophobia and fear, of sameness within the borders and alienation beyond them.

In a cosmopolitan future our mode of being changes to one that Emmanuel Levinas calls a 'responsibility for the Other', a responsibility that overturns the selfish, insecure fictions of identity that rule us, that turns our gaze and our sympathies outward, to a world which craves our solace and our participation, a world upon which we are just as dependent for our existence. It is, says Levinas, 'as if I were devoted to the other man before being devoted to myself . . . as if I had to answer to the other's death even before *being*'.[18] In such a way of life sovereignty is not given up, or lost, it is *gained*, in a more just and enduring form that affirms global interdependence and community and provides the only hope of a secure life for all.

Notes

Introduction

1 Thomas Hobbes, *Leviathan* (London: Penguin, 1985), pp. 80–230.
2 Janine McDonald, 'Refugee crisis warning', *Age*, 18 November 1999, p. 1.
3 Alfred Deakin, Speech to the Australian Natives Association, March 1898, reproduced in Neville Meaney (ed.), *Australia and the World: A Documentary History from the 1870s to the 1980s* (Melbourne: Longman Cheshire, 1985), p. 34.
4 Carolyn Graydon, 'The heartless country', *Age*, 23 November 1999; ABC *7.30 Report* transcript, 15 November 1999, www.abc.net.au/7.30/stories.
5 John Howard and Philip Ruddock, Joint Press Conference, Sydney, 1 September 2001, www.pm.gov.au/media/Interview/2001/interview1206.cfm.
6 John Howard, interview with Phillip Clarke, Radio 2GB, 31 October 2001, www. pm.gov.au/media/Interview/2001/interview1430.cfm.
7 Jonathan King, 'At the beach', *Weekend Australian*, 8–9 September 2001, p. 3.
8 Richard Woolcott, 'The Perils of Freedom', *Weekend Australian*, 22–23 April 1995, p. 24.
9 These comments, made to journalist Kerry O'Brien on the ABC's *7.30 Report*, were cited in *Sydney Morning Herald*, 16 December 1995.
10 Paul Keating, 'Australia and Indonesia', in Mark Ryan (ed.), *Advancing Australia: The Speeches of Paul Keating, Prime Minister* (Sydney: Big Picture Publications, 1995), p. 201; Whitlam speech in *Australian Foreign Affairs Record*, 1973, p. 33; Paul Keating, 'Our common interest', speech to the Indonesian Foreign Policy Forum, Jakarta, 22 April 1992.
11 R. N. Berki, *Security and Society: Reflections on Law, Order and Politics* (London: J. M. Dent & Sons, 1986), pp. 32–3 (emphasis in original).

12 Quoted in Arnold S. Kohen, *From the Place of the Dead: Bishop Belo and the Struggle for East Timor* (Oxford: Lion Publishing, 1999), p. 192.

13 Ken Booth, 'Security and emancipation', *Review of International Studies*, Vol. 17, No. 4, 1991, p. 319; United Nations Development Programme, *Human Development Report*, 1994 (New York: UNDP, 1995); Anthony Burke, 'Caught between national and human security: Knowledge and power in post-crisis Asia', *Pacifica Review*, Vol. 13, No. 3, 2001, pp. 215–39.

14 Simon Dalby, 'Contesting an essential concept: Reading the dilemmas in contemporary security discourse', in Michael C. Williams and Keith Krause (eds), *Critical Security Studies* (Minneapolis: University of Minnesota Press, 1997), pp. 3–20.

15 Michael Dillon, *Politics of Security: Towards a Philosophy of Continental Thought* (London: Routledge, 1996), p. 16.

16 Foucault describes this as a 'multiform instrumentation' working across a range of institutions, and using a variety of coercive, educational and psychological techniques, to produce both economically *productive* and politically *docile* bodies. *Discipline and Punish: The Birth of the Prison* (London and New York: Penguin), 1991, p. 26.

17 Michel Foucault, 'Governmentality', in Graham Burchell, Colin Gordon and Peter Miller (eds), *The Foucault Effect: Studies in Governmentality* (London: Harvester Wheatsheaf, 1991).

18 Michel Foucault, 'The subject and power', in Hubert L. Dreyfus and Paul Rabinow, *Michel Foucault: Beyond Structuralism and Hermeneutics* (University of Chicago Press, 1983), p. 213.

19 Foucault, 'Governmentality'.

20 Hobbes, *Leviathan*, pp. 80–230; John Locke, *Two Treatises of Government* (Cambridge University Press, 1967), pp. 342–68.

21 Zygmunt Bauman, *Postmodernity and Its Discontents* (Cambridge: Polity Press, 1997), p. 20.

22 William E. Connolly, *The Ethos of Pluralization* (Minneapolis: University of Minnesota Press, 1995), p. xviii.

23 McKenzie Wark, *The Virtual Republic: Australia's Culture Wars of the 1990s* (Sydney: Allen & Unwin, 1997), p. 52.

1   Securing the Australian subject 1788–1918

1 Nicholas Jose, 'Cultural identity: "I think I'm something else" ', in Stephen Graubard (ed.), *Australia: The Daedalus Symposium* (Sydney: Angus & Robertson, 1985), p. 315.

2 Glyndwr Williams, 'New Holland to New South Wales: The English approaches', in Glyndwr Williams and Alan Frost (eds), *Terra Australis to Australia* (Melbourne: Oxford University Press, 1988), pp. 141–56.

3 Paul Carter, *The Road to Botany Bay* (London: Faber & Faber, 1987), p. 1.

4 Anthony Burke, *Beyond Security, Ethics and Violence: War Against the Other* (London and New York: Routledge, 2007), pp. 196–203.

5 Robert Hughes, *The Fatal Shore: A History of the Transportation of Convicts to Australia 1787–1868* (London: Harvill Press, 1996), pp. 163–74.

6 Hughes, *The Fatal Shore*, pp. 25–7, 167.

7 Hughes, *The Fatal Shore*, p. 66.

8 Alan Frost, *Convicts and Empire: A Naval Question 1776–1811* (Melbourne: Oxford University Press, 1980), p. xv.

9 Frost, *Convicts and Empire*, p. 135.

10 Hughes, *The Fatal Shore*, p. 42.

11 Hughes, *The Fatal Shore*, pp. 87, 120.

12 Hughes, *The Fatal Shore*, pp. 120–3; David Day, *Claiming a Continent: A History of Australia* (Sydney: Angus & Robertson, 1996), pp. 45–6.

13 Day, *Claiming a Continent*, p. 47.

14 Day, *Claiming a Continent*, pp. 61–5.

15 Day, *Claiming a Continent*, pp. 99–105.

16 Cited in Day, *Claiming a Continent*, p. 101; emphasis added.

17 Roger C. Thompson, *Australian Imperialism in the Pacific: The Expansionist Era 1820–1920* (Melbourne University Press, 1980), p. 13.

18 T. B. Millar, *Australia in Peace and War: External Relations 1788–1977* (Canberra: Australian National University Press, 1978), p. 57; Alan Dupont, *Australia's Threat Perceptions: A Search for Security* (Canberra: Strategic and Defence Studies Centre, Australian National University, 1991), pp. 2–3; Neville Meaney, *The Search for Security in the Pacific 1901–14* (Sydney University Press, 1976) pp. 15–16.

19 Meaney, *The Search for Security in the Pacific*, p. 16.

20 Meaney, *The Search for Security in the Pacific*, pp. 17–22; Humphrey McQueen, *Japan to the Rescue: Australian Security Around the Indonesian Archipelago During the American Century* (Melbourne: William Heinemann Australia, 1991), p. 13.

21 Ken Ross, *Regional Security in the South Pacific: The Quarter Century 1970–95* (Canberra: Strategic and Defence Studies Centre, ANU, 1993).

22 The figure of 60 000 is David Day's estimate; of the Aboriginal population in 1788 he writes that estimates 'vary from 300 000, which

was the accepted figure for many years, to the more recent estimates of between 750 000 and 1 500 000. To suggest that, of this dramatic drop in population, only 20 000 were killed by Europeans seems to stretch credulity to its limits. A more reasonable, even conservative, "guesstimate" would be somewhat more than 50 000 Aborigines killed during 150 years of sporadic conflict. This is taking the low estimate of ten Aborigines killed in retaliation for every white casualty. Such a figure would approach that of Australians killed in the First World War.' (Day, *Claiming a Continent*, p. 130.) Manning Clark, using estimates provided by F. Lancaster Jones in *The Structure and Growth of Australia's Aboriginal Population*, cites a fall from 251 000 to 67 000 between 1788 and 1888. Clark, *A History of Australia*, Vol. V, *The People Make Laws 1888–1915* (Melbourne University Press, 1981) p. 1.

23 Day, *Claiming a Continent*, p. 149.

24 Parkes' speech reproduced in Neville Meaney, *Australia and the World: A Documentary History from the 1870s to the 1890s* (Melbourne: Longman Cheshire, 1985), p. 100.

25 Meaney, *The Search for Security in the Pacific*, p. 28.

26 Reproduced in Meaney, *Australia and the World*, pp. 96–8.

27 Meaney, *Australia and the World*.

28 Meaney, *Australia and the World*, p. 105.

29 See Day, *Claiming a Continent*, pp. 220, 253, and William J. Lines, *Taming the Great South Land* (Sydney: Allen & Unwin, 1991), pp. 164–95.

30 Meaney comments that under ' "external affairs" the Australian founding fathers claimed powers for which there were no precedents in imperial constitutional history', and that the Pacific clause was 'a direct expression of the Australia's anxiety for security in its own geographical sphere' and 'derived directly from the colonies' diplomatic struggles with the British government in the 1870s and 1880s' (*The Search for Security in the Pacific*, p. 34).

31 Meaney, *The Search for Security in the Pacific*, p. 34.

32 Reproduced in Meaney, *Australia and the World*, p. 34.

33 Reproduced in Meaney, *Australia and the World*, p. 77; emphasis added.

34 Reproduced in Meaney, *Australia and the World*, p. 78.

35 This is a phrase Parkes himself used in his address to the 1890 Federal Conference, in which he declared that white Australians formed a unity on the basis of their British origins (Manning Clark, *A History of Australia* (Vol. V), p. 32).

36 Reproduced in Meaney, *Australia and the World*, p. 117.

37 Reproduced in Meaney, *Australia and the World*, p. 118.

38 John Docker, *The Nervous Nineties* (Melbourne: Oxford University Press, 1991).

39 Cited in Docker, *The Nervous Nineties*, p. 35.

40 Docker, *The Nervous Nineties*, p. 34; Humphrey McQueen, *A New Britannia* (Melbourne: Pelican, 1978), p. 36.

41 To balance the picture, Docker emphasised that Enlightenment sentiment also drove the *Bulletin*'s opposition to capital punishment, its criticism of church conservatism and missionary zeal, its push for greater democracy – whether in the election of politicians, JPs or judges – and its critique of British imperialism (*The Nervous Nineties*, pp. 40–5).

42 Clark, *A History of Australia* (Vol. V), pp. 263, 155.

43 Clark, *A History of Australia* (Vol. V), pp. 44–85.

44 Clark, *A History of Australia* (Vol. V), pp. 76–7.

45 Clark, *A History of Australia* (Vol. V), p. 67.

46 McQueen, *A New Britannia*, p. 31.

47 Clark, *A History of Australia* (Vol. V), pp. 167, 183. See also Peter Botsman, *The Great Constitutional Swindle* (Sydney: Pluto Press, 2000).

48 Clark, *A History of Australia* (Vol. V), pp. 240–56, 68.

49 Russel Ward, *A Nation for a Continent: The History of Australia 1901–1975* (Melbourne: Heinemann Educational Australia, 1977), p. 12.

50 Clark, *A History of Australia* (Vol. V), pp. 177–80, 201.

51 Clark, *A History of Australia* (Vol. V), pp. 213, 196.

52 Hugh Collins argues that the dominant legal structures and political ideologies in Australia derive from Benthamite utilitarianism, privileging the rational calculation of majority interests over an alternative enlightenment tradition of natural rights. Hugh Collins, 'Political ideology in Australia: the distinctiveness of a Benthamite society' in Stephen R. Graubard (ed.), *Australia: The Daedalus Symposium* (Sydney: Angus & Robertson, 1985), pp. 147–69.

53 J. La Nauze, *The Making of the Australian Constitution* (Melbourne University Press, 1972), p. 326; Clark, *A History of Australia* (Vol. V), pp. 217–18.

54 Meaney, *The Search for Security in the Pacific*, pp. 91–107.

55 Meaney, *The Search for Security in the Pacific*, pp. 43–68; Hutton's speech reproduced in Meaney, *Australia and the World*, pp. 130–1.

56 Reproduced in Meaney, *Australia and the World*, p. 52.

57 Meaney, *The Search for Security in the Pacific*, p. 214.

58 Meaney, *The Search for Security in the Pacific*, p. 52.

59 Reproduced in Meaney, *Australia and the World*, p. 12.

60 Meaney, *The Search for Security in the Pacific*, p. 241; emphasis added.

61 Cited in Dupont, *Australia's Threat Perceptions*, p. 14.

62 Humphrey McQueen, *Japan to the Rescue: Australian Security Around the Indonesian Archipelago during the American Century* (Melbourne: William Heinemann Australia, 1991), p. 27.

63 Meaney, *The Search for Security in the Pacific*, pp. 146–95, 225, 248; Dupont, *Australia's Threat Perceptions*, p. 18.

64 Ernest Scott, *Australia during the War*, Vol. XI, *The Official History of Australia in the War of 1914–18* (Sydney: Angus & Robertson, 1943), p. 858.

65 Scott, *Australia during the War*, pp. 22–4; Clark, *A History of Australia* (Vol. V), pp. 374–5.

66 Scott, *Australia during the War*, p. vii; emphasis added.

67 Clark, *A History of Australia* (Vol. V), p. 380, and *A History of Australia* (Vol. VI), *The Old Dead Tree and the Young Tree Green 1916–1935* (Melbourne University Press, 1987), p. 16.

68 Alistair Thompson, 'Passing shots at the Anzac legend', in Verity Burgmann and Jenny Lee (eds), *A Most Valuable Acquisition: A People's History of Australia Since 1788* (Ringwood: Penguin, 1988).

69 C. E. W. Bean, *Anzac to Amiens: A Shorter History of the Australian Fighting Services in the First World War* (Canberra: Australian War Memorial, 1948), p. 157; Clark, *A History of Australia* (Vol. V), p. 484.

70 Clark, *A History of Australia* (Vol. V), pp. 26–7.

71 Clark, *A History of Australia* (Vol. V), pp. 24–7; Scott, *Australia during the War*, p. 874.

72 The October 1916 result was Yes: 1 087 332, No: 1 151 881 (64 549 majority for No) and the December 1917 result Yes: 568 670, No: 718 465 (149 795 majority for No). After the first referendum Hughes and his followers were expelled from the Labor Party; he then formed a coalition government with Cook's Liberals under the rubric of the 'National Party'. At the May 1917 election the Nationalists won a decisive victory over Labor. Two days before the Australians had fought a second battle at Bullecourt, losing 7482 men. Clark, *A History of Australia* (Vol. VI), *The Old Dead Tree and the Young Tree Green 1916–1935* (Melbourne University Press, 1987), pp. 40, 77, 57.

73 Between 1914 and 1919 annual steel production rose from 130 000 tons to nearly a million, almost all of it by the already giant BHP. During the war it established the steelworks at Newcastle and began to integrate it with its Australia-wide network of mining, smelting and shipbuilding facilities. Ward, *A Nation for a Continent*, p. 110; Clark, *A History of Australia* (Vol. V), pp. 371, 380.

74 Clark, *A History of Australia* (Vol. VI), pp. 34–9, 53; Patricia Grimshaw, Marilyn Lake, Ann McGrath and Marian Quartly, *Creating A Nation 1788–1900* (Ringwood: Penguin, 1996), p. 213.

75 Scott, *Australia during the War*, pp. 105, 689, 679.

76 L. F. Fitzhardinge, *William Morris Hughes: A Political Biography*, Vol. II, *The Little Digger 1914–1952* (Sydney: Angus & Robertson, 1979), p. 456.

77 Day, *Claiming a Continent*, p. 240.

78 Bean, *Anzac to Amiens*, p. 535.

79 Bean, *Anzac to Amiens*, p. 534; emphasis added.

80 Bean, *Anzac to Amiens*, p. 539; emphasis added.

81 Clark, *A History of Australia* (Vol. V), p. 426.

82 Paul Keating, 'Anzac Day' (Speech at Ela Beach, Port Moresby), in Mark Ryan (ed.), *Advancing Australia* (Sydney: Big Picture Publications, 1995), p. 279, and *Speech to the Official Banquet Given by President Suharto*, Istana Negara, Jakarta, 21 April 1992, p. 4.

83 Michael Gordon and Patrick Walters, 'Howard embraces Indonesia: PM backs closer economic and security links', *Australian*, 17 September 1996, p. 1.

84 Ann Curthoys and John Docker, *Is History Fiction?* (Sydney: UNSW Press, 2005).

2 Dreams of Pacific security 1919–45

1 Reproduced in Neville Meaney (ed.), *Australia and the World: A Documentary History from the 1870s to the 1980s* (Melbourne: Longman Cheshire, 1985), p. 236.

2 The exchange had taken place during the arguments over Australia's desire to annex New Guinea and Samoa, which Wilson opposed – he asked Hughes 'whether he would set the five million people he represented against the twelve hundred million represented at the conference'. Fitzhardinge, *William Morris Hughes: A Political Biography*, Vol. II, p. 396.

3 Fitzhardinge, *William Morris Hughes*, Vol. II, p. 396; Stuart Macintyre, *The Oxford History of Australia*, Vol. 4, *1901–1942 The Succeeding Age* (Melbourne: Oxford University Press, 1986), p. 242.

4 Fitzhardinge, *William Morris Hughes*, Vol. II, pp. 389, 372, 399; Macintyre, *The Oxford History of Australia*, Vol. 4, p. 178; Greg Fry (ed.), *Australia's Regional Security* (Sydney: Allen & Unwin, 1991), p. 3.

5 Macintyre, *The Oxford History of Australia*, Vol. 4, pp. 181–91; Manning Clark, *A History of Australia* (Vol. VI), *The Old Dead Tree and the Young Tree Green 1916–1935* (Melbourne University Press, 1987), p. 171.

6 Clark, *A History of Australia* (Vol. VI), p. 120; Macintyre, *The Oxford History of Australia*, Vol. 4, p. 183.

7 Commonwealth Parliamentary Debates, *House of Representatives*, 10 September 1919, p. 12179.

8 Clark, *A History of Australia* (Vol. VI), p. 68; Macintyre, *The Oxford History of Australia*, Vol. 4, pp. 184, 194.

9 Commonwealth Parliamentary Debates, *House of Representatives*, 1 March 1923, pp. 81–3.

10 Commonwealth Parliamentary Debates, *House of Representatives*, 1 March 1923, pp. 81–3; Clark, *A History of Australia* (Vol. VI), p. 217.

11 William J. Lines, *Taming the Great South Land* (Sydney: Allen & Unwin, 1991), p. 168.

12 Clark, *A History of Australia* (Vol. VI), p. 225; Lines, *Taming the Great South Land*, p. 170.

13 Peter Cochrane, *Industrialisation and Dependence: Australia's Road to Economic Development 1870–1939* (St Lucia: University of Queensland Press, 1980), pp. 37–41; Macintyre, *The Oxford History of Australia*, Vol. 4, pp. 235, 219.

14 Clark, *A History of Australia* (Vol. VI), p. 245.

15 Commonwealth Parliamentary Debates, *House of Representatives*, 31 July 1923, p. 1878.

16 Commonwealth Parliamentary Debates, *House of Representatives*, 31 July 1923, p. 1879.

17 Commonwealth Parliamentary Debates, *House of Representatives*, 31 July 1923, p. 1879–80.

18 Commonwealth Parliamentary Debates, *House of Representatives*, 24 July 1923, pp. 1480–7, 31 July 1923, p. 1882; Macintyre, *The Oxford History of Australia*, Vol. 4, p. 205.

19 Reproduced in Meaney, *Australia and the World*, pp. 293–9, 348–51.

20 Clark, *A History of Australia* (Vol. VI), p. 158.

21 C. D. Rowley, *Outcasts in White Australia: Aboriginal Policy and Practice*, Vol. II (Canberra: Australian National University Press, 1971), p. 4.

22 Clark, *A History of Australia* (Vol. VI), pp. 299, 427; David Day, *Claiming a Continent: A History of Australia* (Sydney: Angus & Robertson, 1996), p. 266.

23 Clark, *A History of Australia* (Vol. VI), p. 285.

24 Commonwealth Parliamentary Debates, *House of Representatives*, 25 June 1925, pp. 460–1.

25 Commonwealth Parliamentary Debates, *House of Representatives*, 25 June 1925, p. 460.

26 Clark, *A History of Australia* (Vol. VI), p. 242.

27 Commonwealth Parliamentary Debates, *House of Representatives*, 28 January 1926, p. 467–8.

28 Macintyre, *The Oxford History of Australia*, Vol. 4, p. 245–50; Clark, *A History of Australia* (Vol. VI), p. 315.

29 Macintyre, *The Oxford History of Australia*, Vol. 4, pp. 253–4.

30 Macintyre, *The Oxford History of Australia*, Vol. 4, pp. 270–80; Clark, *A History of Australia* (Vol. VI), p. 333.

31 Cited in Lionel Wigmore, *The Japanese Thrust: Official History of Australia in the War of 1939–45*, Series I, Vol. IV (Canberra: Australian War Memorial, 1957), pp. 1–2.

32 Reproduced in Meaney, *Australia and the World*, p. 400.

33 Wigmore, *The Japanese Thrust*, pp. 5–6.

34 T. B. Millar, *Australia in Peace and War: External Relations 1788–1977* (Canberra: Australian National University Press, 1978), pp. 99–100; Meaney, *Australia and the World*, p. 397.

35 Reproduced in Meaney, *Australia and the World*, pp. 455, 438.

36 Millar, *Australia in Peace and War*, pp. 137–40; Humphrey McQueen, *Japan to the Rescue: Australian Security Around the Indonesian Archipelago during the American Century* (Melbourne: William Heinemann, 1991), pp. 40–4.

37 McQueen, *Japan to the Rescue*, p. 139.

38 Reproduced in Meaney, *Australia and the World*, p. 459.

39 Lloyd Ross, *John Curtin: A Biography* (South Melbourne: Macmillan, 1977), p. 184.

40 Ross, *John Curtin: A Biography*, p. 184.

41 Ross, *John Curtin: A Biography*, p. 186.

42 Paul Hasluck, *The Government and the People 1939–41, Official History: Australia in the War of 1939–45*, Series IV, Vol. I (Canberra: Australian War Memorial, 1952), p. 1.

43 Hasluck, *The Government and the People 1939–41*, pp. 6–7.

44 Hasluck, *The Government and the People 1939–41*, pp. 5–6.

45 Wigmore, *The Japanese Thrust*, p. 382; Paul Hasluck, *The Government and the People 1942–45, Official History: Australia in the War of 1939–45*, Series IV, Vol. II (Canberra: Australian War Memorial, 1970), pp. 13, 71, 102.

46 James Dunn, *Timor: A People Betrayed* (Milton, Qld: Jacaranda Press, 1983), pp. 22–4; Gavin Long, *The Six Years War: A Concise History of Australia in the 1939–45 War* (Canberra: Australian War Memorial, 1973), p. 223.

47 An Australian Chiefs of Staff analysis, dated 29 January 1942, stated: 'Timor and Ambon guard the eastern approaches to Darwin, an important naval and air operating base, and the eastern terminal of the Malay barrier. With the encirclement of the Philippines, Ambon is now virtually in the front line, while the threat to Timor is no less direct though perhaps further removed in point of time.' Hasluck, *The Government and the People 1942–45*, pp. 37, 102; Dunn, *Timor: A People Betrayed*, p. 22.

48 Cited in Hasluck, *The Government and the People 1942–45*, p. 39.

49 Hasluck, *The Government and the People 1942–45*, pp. 44–53.

50 Hasluck, *The Government and the People 1942–45*, p. 55.

51 Hasluck, *The Government and the People 1942–45*, p. 55.

52 Richard White, *Inventing Australia* (Sydney: Allen & Unwin, 1981), p. 158.

53 Hasluck, *The Government and the People 1942–45*, p. 71; McQueen, *Japan to the Rescue*, pp. 285–6.

54 Hasluck, *The Government and the People 1942–45*, p. 162; David Horner, *High Command: Australia and Allied Strategy 1939–45* (Canberra: Australian War Memorial, 1982), p. 183.

55 Hasluck, *The Government and the People 1942–45*, p. 164.

56 Hasluck, *The Government and the People 1942–45*, p. 168.

57 Herbert Vere Evatt, 'Charter Address at the University of California', *Current Notes on International Affairs* (Canberra: Department of External Affairs, 1945), Vol. 16, p. 118; McQueen, *Japan to the Rescue*, pp. 285–91.

58 Cited in Alan Watt, *The Evolution of Australian Foreign Policy 1938–65* (Cambridge University Press, 1967), p. 68.

59 Lex McAulay, *Blood and Iron: The Battle for Kokoda 1942* (Sydney: Hutchison, 1991), p. 1.

60 David Horner, *High Command*, p. 46, and *The Battles that Shaped Australia* (Sydney: Allen & Unwin, 1994), p. 161.

61 The image formed part of a sequence in Parer's Academy Award winning film *Kokoda Front Line*, discussed by Peter Luck in the historical popularisation (TV series and book) *This Fabulous Century*, p. 142.

62 Humphrey McQueen, *From Gallipoli to Petrov* (Sydney: Allen & Unwin, 1984), p. 4.

63 Roger Bell, *Unequal Allies: Australian–American Relations and the Pacific War* (Melbourne University Press, 1977), p. 181.

64 Coral Bell, *Dependent Ally: A Study of Australia's Relations with the United States and the United Kingdom Since the Fall of Singapore* (Sydney: Allen & Unwin, 1988), p. 26.

65 Roger Bell, *Unequal Allies*, p. 183; Millar, *Australia in Peace and War*, p. 153.

66 Roger Bell, *Unequal Allies*, p. 183; Millar, *Australia in Peace and War*, p. 153.

67 Watt, *The Evolution of Australian Foreign Policy*, p. 74; Millar, *Australia in Peace and War*, pp. 444–5.

68 Greg Fry (ed.), *Australia's Regional Security* (Sydney: Allen & Unwin, 1991), p. 3.

69 Horner, *High Command*, p. 413; Roger Bell, *Unequal Allies*, p. 191.

70 Watt, *The Evolution of Australian Foreign Policy*, p. 83.

71 Horner, *High Command*, p. 424; Roger Bell, *Unequal Allies*, p. 185.

72 Watt, *The Evolution of Australian Foreign Policy*, pp. 87–92; Hasluck, *The Government and the People 1942–45*, p. 635.

73 Ross, *John Curtin: A Biography*, p. 386.

74 Day, *Claiming a Continent*, pp. 302–3.

75 Hasluck, *The Government and the People 1942–45*, p. 449.

3   Cold War against the Other 1946–69

1 Cited in Gregory Pemberton, *All the Way: Australia's Road to Vietnam* (Sydney: Allen & Unwin, 1997), p. 162.

2 Louis L. Snyder, *The War: A Concise History 1939–45* (London: Robert Hale, 1962), pp. 519–24; Clive Ponting, *Armageddon: The Second World War* (London: Sinclair Stevenson, 1995), p. 294; Gar Alperovitz, *The Decision to use the Atomic Bomb and the Architecture of an American Myth* (New York: Alfred A. Knopf, 1995), p. 430.

3 Henry R. Luce, 'The American Century', *Life*, 17 February 1941, pp. 61–5; Snyder, *The War: A Concise History*, p. 513.

4 Department of Foreign Affairs and Trade, *Documents on Australian Foreign Policy 1937–49*, Vol. X, *July–December 1946* (Canberra: AGPS, 1993), p. 83.

5 Herbert Vere Evatt, 'Charter Address at the University of California', *Current Notes on International Affairs* (Canberra: Department of External Affairs), Vol. 16, 1945, p. 120.

6 Snyder, *The War: A Concise History*, pp. 196–7; Herbert Vere Evatt, *Foreign Policy of Australia: Speeches* (Sydney: Angus & Robertson, 1945), pp. 114–15.

7 Michael Schaller, *The American Occupation of Japan: The Origins of the Cold War in Asia* (Oxford and New York: Oxford University Press, 1995), pp. 11–15; Alperovitz, *The Decision to use the Atomic Bomb*, pp. 15–35.

8 Alperovitz, *The Decision to use the Atomic Bomb*, pp. 427–32; Herbert Feis, *The Atomic Bomb and the End of World War II* (Princeton, NJ: Princeton University Press, 1966), p. 101.

9 William S. Borden, *The Pacific Alliance: United States Foreign Economic Policy and Japanese Trade Recovery 1947–1955* (Wisconsin: University of Wisconsin Press, 1984), p. 4; Schaller, *The American Occupation of Japan*, p. ix.

10 David Lee, *Search for Security: The Political Economy of Australia's Postwar Foreign and Defence Policy* (Sydney: Allen & Unwin, 1995), p. 12; Carol Johnson, *The Labor Legacy* (Sydney: Allen & Unwin, 1989), p. 16.

11 David Day, *Claiming a Continent: A History of Australia* (Sydney: Angus & Robertson, 1996), p. 338.

12 Geoffrey Bolton, *The Oxford History of Australia*, Vol. 5, 1942–88, *The Middle Way* (Melbourne: Oxford University Press, 1990), pp. 53–8; Day, *Claiming a Continent*, p. 341.

13 Lee, *Search for Security*, pp. 18–22.

14 Lee, *Search for Security*, pp. 18–26, 67, 161.

15 Schaller, *The American Occupation of Japan*, pp. 122–40.

16 Schaller, *The American Occupation of Japan*, p. 136; Department of Foreign Affairs and Trade, *Australia and The Postwar World*, Vol. XII, *Documents 1947* (Canberra: AGPS, 1995), pp. 417–18, 543; R. N. Rosecrance, *Australian Diplomacy and Japan, 1945–1951* (Melbourne University Press, 1962), p. 123.

17 Department of Foreign Affairs and Trade, *Australia and the Postwar World*, pp. 413–15.

18 Department of Foreign Affairs and Trade, *Documents on Australian Foreign Policy 1937–49*, Vol. XI, *Indonesia 1947* (Canberra: AGPS, 1994), p. 106.

19 Department of Foreign Affairs and Trade, *Australia and the Postwar World*, p. 135.

20 See a 15 September cable from Evatt, and others from Tom Critchley, in Department of Foreign Affairs and Trade, *Australia and the Postwar World*, pp. 296–312; Margaret George, *Australia and the Indonesian Revolution* (Melbourne University Press, 1980), pp. 125, 149.

21 Lee, *Search for Security*, p. 87.

22 Lee, *Search for Security*, pp. 76–8.

23 Department of Foreign Affairs and Trade, *Australia and the Postwar World*, p. 292.

24 Department of Foreign Affairs and Trade, *Australia and the Postwar World*, p. 280 (emphasis added).

25 Peter Edwards and Gregory Pemberton, *Crises and Commitments: The Politics and Diplomacy of Australia's Involvement in Southeast Asian Conflicts 1948–1965* (Sydney: Allen & Unwin), 1992, pp. 54–5; Lee, *Search for Security*, p. 97.

26 Edwards and Pemberton, *Crises and Commitments*, p. 33–49.

27 Department of Foreign Affairs and Trade, *Australia and the Postwar World*, p. 295.

28 Lee, *Search for Security*, pp. 91–3.

29 Commonwealth House of Representatives, *Hansard*, 21 June 1949, pp. 1221–3.

30 Paul Hasluck, *Official History: Australia in the War of 1939–45*, Series IV, Vol. I, *The Government and the People 1939–41* (Canberra: Australian War Memorial, 1952), p. 88.

31 Borden, *The Pacific Alliance*, pp. 103–42.

32 Bolton, *The Middle Way*, pp. 75–7; Commonwealth House of Representatives, *Hansard*, 9 May 1950, p. 2273; Neville Meaney, *Australia and the World: A Documentary History from the 1870s to the 1890s* (Melbourne: Longman Cheshire, 1985), pp. 544–5.

33 Manning Clark, *A History of Australia* (Vol. V), *The People Make Laws 1888–1915* (Melbourne University Press, 1981), p. 68.

34 Commonwealth House of Representatives, *Hansard*, 27 April 1950, p. 1995.

35 Commonwealth House of Representatives, *Hansard*, 27 April 1950, p. 1995; Meaney, *Australia and the World*, p. 597.

36 Bolton, *The Middle Way*, p. 81.

37 Percy Spender, *Exercises in Diplomacy: The ANZUS Treaty and the Colombo Plan* (Sydney University Press, 1969), p. 195.

38 Meaney, *Australia and the World*, pp. 557, 681.

39 Meaney, *Australia and the World*, p. 557.

40 Meaney, *Australia and the World*, pp. 557–8.

41 Meaney, *Australia and the World*, pp. 558–9.

42 Meaney, *Australia and the World*, p. 560.

43 Gregory Pemberton, *All the Way: Australia's Road to Vietnam* (Sydney: Allen & Unwin, 1997), p. 12.

44 Meaney, *Australia and the World*, p. 560.

45 Pemberton, *All the Way*, p. 14.

46 Spender, *Exercises in Diplomacy*, p. 199.

47 Meaney, *Australia and the World*, pp. 564–5; *Current Affairs Bulletin* quoted in Nicholas Brown, *Governing Prosperity: Social Change and Social Analysis in the 1950s* (Melbourne: Cambridge University Press), p. 16.

48 Edwards and Pemberton, *Crises and Commitments*, pp. 101, 163–8; Lee, *Search for Security*, pp. 131–6.

49 Robert O'Neill, *Australia in the Korean War 1950–53*, Vol. I: *Strategy and Diplomacy* (Canberra: AGPS, 1981), p. 102.

50 O'Neill, *Australia in the Korean War*, pp. 12–20.

51 O'Neill, *Australia in the Korean War*, pp. 140, 147.

52 Edwards and Pemberton, *Crises and Commitments*, p. 169.

53 Pemberton, *All the Way*, p. 162; Meaney, *Australia and the World*, p. 236.

54 Pemberton, *All the Way*, p. 27; Meaney, *Australia and the World*, p. 587.

55 Meaney, *Australia and the World*, p. 586.

56 Pemberton, *All the Way*, pp. 20, 62.

57 Edwards and Pemberton, *Crises and Commitments*, pp. 146–9.

58 Edwards and Pemberton, *Crises and Commitments*, pp. 146–9.

59 Edwards and Pemberton, *Crises and Commitments*, p. 245; Neil Sheehan, *A Bright Shining Lie* (New York: Picador, 1990), p. 371.

60 Sheehan, *A Bright Shining Lie*, p. 188; Edwards and Pemberton, *Crises and Commitments*, pp. 195–201.

61 Edwards and Pemberton, *Crises and Commitments*, pp. 195–201.

62 Edwards and Pemberton, *Crises and Commitments*, pp. 195–201, 245.

63 Edwards and Pemberton, *Crises and Commitments*, p. 154.

64 Reproduced in Meaney, *Australia and the World*, pp. 612–13.

65 Kennan cited in David Campbell, *Writing Security: United States Foreign Policy and the Politics of Identity* (Manchester: Manchester University Press, 1992), p. 28.

66 Humphrey McQueen, *Japan to the Rescue: Australian Security Around the Indonesian Archipelago during the American Century* (Melbourne: William Heinemann, 1991), p. 68; Norman Harpur, 'Australia and the United States (with special reference to South-East Asia)', in Gordon Greenwood and Norman Harpur (eds), *Australia in World Affairs 1956–1960* (Melbourne: Cheshire, 1962), p. 175.

67 Harpur, 'Australia and the United States', pp. 178–81.

68 By the mid-1960s there were 85 Australian companies with investments in the territories, having grown from $US5.8 million in 1948–49 to $US32.8 million in 1964–65. The greatest presence was in tin. Pemberton, *All the Way*, p. 167.

69 Pemberton, *All the Way*, pp. 166–9.

70 Pemberton, *All the Way*, pp. 167, 246; Edwards and Pemberton, *Crises and Commitments*, p. 246; David Lee, 'Australia's commitment to the defence of Malaysia' (unpublished paper, 1997).

71 Edwards and Pemberton, *Crises and Commitments*, pp. 242–8.

72 Edwards and Pemberton, *Crises and Commitments*, pp. 271–300.

73 Edwards and Pemberton, *Crises and Commitments*, pp. 313–14.

74 Edwards and Pemberton, *Crises and Commitments*, pp. 313–14.

75 Pemberton, *All the Way*, p. 272.

76 Edwards and Pemberton, *Crises and Commitments*, pp. 364–61.

77 Reproduced in Meaney, *Australia and the World*, pp. 680–6.

78 Reproduced in Meaney, *Australia and the World*, p. 686.

79 Reproduced in Meaney, *Australia and the World*, p. 686.

80 Reproduced in Meaney, *Australia and the World*, p. 686.

81 Pemberton, *All the Way*, pp. 306–8.

82 Pemberton, *All the Way*, p. 306; David Hackworth and Julie Sherman, *About Face* (Sydney: Pan, 1989), pp. 494–5.

83 Fraser's comments were provoked by the publication of Robert McNamara's self-critical memoir, *In Retrospect*. See *Sydney Morning Herald* of 15 April 1995.

84 Stanley Karnow, *Vietnam: A History* (New York: Penguin, 1983), p. 11; Sheehan, *A Bright Shining Lie*, pp. 617, 687; Ben Kiernan, *How Pol Pot Came to Power* (London: Verso, 1985), p. xii.

85 See Anthony Burke, 'Violence and reason on the shoals of Vietnam', *Postmodern Culture*, Vol. 9, No. 3, May 1999, http://jefferson.village. virginia.edu/pmc/text.only/issue.599/9.3 burke.txt.

86 McQueen, *Japan to the Rescue*, pp. 68–9; Pemberton, *All the Way*, pp. 72–6.

87 Department of External Affairs, *Current Notes on International Affairs*, 1950, pp. 592–3; Pemberton, *All the Way*, pp. 70–106.

88 Pemberton, *All the Way*, pp. 182–245.

89 In May 1998 crucial information about Soeharto's role emerged. A close friend of Soeharto, Colonel Abdul Latief, told journalist Patrick Walters from Jakarta's Cipinang prison that he had known of the Untung strike in advance, had warned Soeharto of it weeks before and, in particular, had told him on 30 September that it would take place that night! Soeharto did not warn Jani or Nasution that they were in danger. Latief was close to Soeharto from their days together in Central Java's Diponegoro division in the 1950s, but was sentenced to death in 1972 and spent 11 years in solitary confinement because of his knowledge. The interview took place a few days after Soeharto's resignation as President. Latief said Soeharto 'should be tried for what

has happened to me'. Patrick Walters, 'Suharto's secret role in coup', *Australian*, 25 May 1998, p. 1.

90 Humphrey McQueen, 'How Suharto won power', *Independent Monthly*, September 1990, p. 29.

91 Gabriel Kolko, *Confronting the Third World: United States Foreign Policy 1945–80* (New York: Pantheon, 1988), pp. 180–3; McQueen, *Japan to the Rescue*, p. 75.

92 This account is based on files held in the Australian Archives. See CRS 1838/280 3034/2/1/8 Parts 2 and 3, 'Indonesia: 30 September 1965 Coup Attempt'. See also Karim Najjarine and Drew Cottle, 'The Department of External Affairs, the ABC and Reporting of the Indonesian Crisis 1965–1969', *Australian Journal of Politics and History*, Vol. 49, No. 1, pp. 48–60.

93 Holt cited in Noam Chomsky and Edward Herman, *The Washington Connection and Third World Fascism* (Montreal: Black Rose Books, 1979), p. 217; Gough Whitlam, *The Whitlam Government 1972–75* (Ringwood: Penguin, 1985), p. 102; Brian Toohey and William Pinwill, *Oyster: The Story of the Australian Secret Intelligence Service* (Sydney: Mandarin, 1991), pp. 106–7; see also Robert Cribb (ed.), *The Indonesian Killings: Studies from Java and Bali* (Clayton: Monash University Centre for Southeast Asian Studies, 1991).

94 Jim Green, 'Maralinga: Old test sites never die', *Green Left Weekly*, 10 May 2000, p. 15.

95 Chomsky and Herman, *The Washington Connection*, p. 217.

96 See David Jenkins, 'Lessons from the scars', *Sydney Morning Herald*, 29 April 1995, p. 23; Greg Sheridan, 'Why the Vietnam War was just and winnable', *Australian*, 19 April 1995.

97 P. G. Edwards, *A Nation at War: Australian Politics, Society and Diplomacy during the Vietnam War 1965–75* (Sydney and Canberra: Allen & Unwin/Australian War Memorial, 1997), p. 145; *Current Notes*, September 1969, pp. 525–7.

98 H. W. Ardnt, Coral Bell, Jim Cairns, Gregory Clark, Kenneth Gee, Frank Knopfelmacher, F. P. Serong, John Wheeldon, 'The Vietnam Debate Revisited', *Quadrant*, No 260, October 1989, p. 7; Meaney, *Australia and the World*, p. 705; Edwards, *A Nation at War*, p. 145.

4   *Realpolitik* beyond the Cold War 1970–95

1 Graham Freudenberg, *A Certain Grandeur: Gough Whitlam in Politics* (Melbourne: Macmillan, 1977), p. 200.

2 Freudenberg, *A Certain Grandeur*, pp. 189–91.

3 Cited in W. J. Hudson (ed.), *Australia in World Affairs 1971–75* (Sydney: Allen & Unwin, 1980), p. 347.

4 Robert O'Neill, 'Defence Policy', in Hudson (ed.), *Australia in World Affairs*, pp. 21–2; Gabriel Kolko, *Confronting the Third World: United States Foreign Policy 1945–80* (New York: Pantheon, 1988), p. 208.

5 Hudson (ed.), *Australia in World Affairs*, p. 173; Freudenberg, *A Certain Grandeur*, pp. 208–9.

6 Bell, *Dependent Ally*, pp. 96–7.

7 O'Neill, 'Defence policy', p. 14.

8 This modifies a broadly held view, expressed for example by Desmond Ball, that the decline of 'forward defence' and the Guam doctrine provoked a 'period of *radical* transformation in the basic elements of Australia's national security policy'. Desmond Ball, *The Politics of Defence Decision-making in Australia* (Canberra: ANU Strategic and Defence Studies Centre, 1979), p. 2.

9 Department of External Affairs, *Current Notes on International Affairs*, 1967, p. 327.

10 Kathryn E. Young, *The Guam Doctrine: Elements of Implementation – Key State Relations*, Australia and Indonesia (McLean, VA: Research Analysis Corporation, 1970), pp. 15–16.

11 This quote appears in a briefing paper written for the Australian delegation to a December 1965 meeting of the Western powers in London on the Indonesian situation. Australian Archives, CRS 1838/280 3034/2/1/8 Pt 2, 'Quadripartite discussions on Indonesia: Brief for Australian delegation'.

12 The major donors were Japan and the USA – Australia provided A$5.2 million of the US$200 million first annual grant. The Australian government provided A$500 000 emergency aid in 1966, with a further A$200 000 in February 1967. In 1967–68 bilateral aid was A$6.9 million, the amount doubling to A$12.7 million in 1968–69, making Indonesia Australia's largest aid recipient outside Papua New Guinea. By 1969–70 Indonesia was Australia's largest aid recipient, with A$16.8 million – 31 per cent of total bilateral aid. In 1970 aid was further increased with an undertaking of A$53.8 million over three years. At the conclusion of his visit to Indonesia in June 1972 Prime Minister McMahon announced a further three-year aid program for Indonesia (to June 1976) of A$69 million, an increase of A$16 million over the previous three years. *Current Notes*, 1967, p. 76; 1968, p. 105; 1970, p. 441; 1972, p. 291.

13 *Current Notes*, 1972, p. 17; Harold Crouch, *The Army and Politics in Indonesia* (Ithaca, NY, and London: Cornell University Press, 1988),

pp. 178–220; Adam Schwarz, *A Nation in Waiting: Indonesia in the 1990s* (Sydney: Allen & Unwin, 1994), p. 32.

14 *Current Notes*, 1972, pp. 35–6.

15 *Current Notes*, 1972, pp. 31–9.

16 Alan Dupont, *Australia's Threat Perceptions: A Search for Security* (Canberra: ANU Strategic and Defence Studies Centre, 1991), p. 69; *Current Notes*, 1972, p. 31.

17 Freudenberg, *A Certain Grandeur*, p. 230.

18 See Whitlam's account of his government's policy-making, *The Whitlam Government* (Penguin: Ringwood, 1985), and David Lee and Christopher Waters (eds), *From Evatt to Evans: The Labor Tradition in Foreign Policy* (Sydney: Allen & Unwin, 1997).

19 Whitlam, *The Whitlam Government*, pp. 19–22; Freudenberg, *A Certain Grandeur*, p. 234.

20 Freudenberg, *A Certain Grandeur*, p. 230.

21 Freudenberg, *A Certain Grandeur*, p. 235.

22 Department of Foreign Affairs, *Australian Foreign Affairs Review*, 1973, p. 97.

23 This figure is an Amnesty International estimate for the *minimum* number still held in 1974 – though they also commented there were 'probably as many as 100 000' prisoners still in detention. Harold Crouch suggests that the number held hovered between 200 000 and 300 000 between 1966 and 1969, and that a total of 540 000 may have been held during the period. Greg Fealy, *The Release of Indonesia's Political Prisoners: Domestic Versus Foreign Policy, 1975–1979* (Melbourne: Monash Centre of Southeast Asian Studies, 1995), p. 1; Crouch, *The Army and Politics in Indonesia*, pp. 225–6.

24 *Australian Foreign Affairs Review*, 1973, p. 33.

25 Robin Osborne, *Indonesia's Secret War: The Guerilla Struggle in Irian Jaya* (Sydney: Allen & Unwin, 1985), pp. 46–7.

26 Eighty-four states voted for integration, and thirty abstained. Australia, along with the USA, France and Holland, actively lobbied for Indonesia. Estimated Papuan deaths from 1963 to 1969 range from journalist Peter Hastings' figure of 3000 to former Governor Eliza Bonay's 1981 claim of 30 000. The ALP platform contained support for a fair act of self-determination. Osborne, *Indonesia's Secret War*, pp. 46–7; *Australian Foreign Affairs Review*, 1973, pp. 30, 43, 90, 101.

27 *Current Notes*, 1972, pp. 226–72; *Australian Foreign Affairs Review*, 1974, pp. 51, 653; Gregory Pemberton, 'Whitlam and the Labor

tradition', in David Lee and Christopher Waters (eds), *Evatt to Evans*, p. 158.

28 Whitlam, *The Whitlam Government*, p. 30.

29 The text of Whitlam's letter is reproduced in *The Whitlam Government*, pp. 42–3.

30 Neville Meaney, 'The United States', in W. J. Hudson (ed.), *Australia in World Affairs*, p. 183; Meaney, *Australia and the World*, p. 737.

31 Desmond Ball, *A Suitable Piece of Real Estate: American Installations in Australia* (Sydney: Allen & Unwin, 1980), pp. 20, 52–7, 91; Meaney, 'The United States', pp. 192–202.

32 Brian Toohey and Marian Wilkinson, *The Book of Leaks* (Sydney: Angus & Robertson, 1987), pp. 97–8; John Pilger, *A Secret Country* (London: Vintage, 1990), p. 217; Pemberton, 'Whitlam and the Labor tradition', p. 140.

33 Anthony Campagna, *The Economic Consequences of the Vietnam War* (New York: Praeger, 1991), pp. 83, 118.

34 Kolko, *Confronting the Third World*, p. 230; David Denoon (ed.), *The New International Economic Order: A U. S. Response* (New York University Press, 1979), p. 4; Robert K. Olsen, *U. S. Foreign Policy and the New International Economic Order* (Boulder, Colo.: Westview Press, 1981), p. 10.

35 Denoon (ed.), *The New International Economic Order*, pp. 5–18; Kolko, *Confronting the Third World*, p. 231.

36 Lindsay Barrett, 'The Prime Minister's Christmas Card: Modernism and Politics in the Whitlam Era' (University of Technology, Sydney: PhD thesis, 1995), pp. 177–82.

37 Barry Hughes, *Exit Full Employment* (London: Angus & Robertson, 1980), pp. 115–17; Whitlam, *The Whitlam Government*, p. 184.

38 Hughes, *Exit Full Employment*, pp. 115–17; Barrett, 'The Prime Minister's Christmas Card', p. 243.

39 James Dunn, *Timor: A People Betrayed* (Milton, Qld: Jacaranda Press, 1983), pp. 66, 85; Alan Renouf, *The Frightened Country* (Melbourne: Macmillan, 1979), p. 442; Nancy Viviani, 'Australians and the Timor issue', *Australian Outlook*, Vol. 30, August 1976, p. 199. Another excellent history is John G. Taylor, *East Timor: The Price of Freedom* (Sydney: Pluto Press, 1999). For the brief prepared for Whitlam prior to his visit to Indonesia and the official record of this meeting, see Department of Foreign Affairs and Trade, *Australia and the Indonesian Incorporation of East Timor 1974–1976* (Melbourne University Press, 2000), pp. 90–100.

40 *Sydney Morning Herald*, 16 September 1974.

41 Department of Foreign Affairs and Trade, *Australia and the Indonesian Incorporation of East Timor*, Document 26, pp. 95–6.

42 *National Times*, 11 November 1974.

43 Renouf, *The Frightened Country*, p. 445.

44 Dunn, *Timor: A People Betrayed*, p. 151; Renouf, *The Frightened Country*, p. 445; Commonwealth, *Parliamentary Debates*, House of Representatives, 26 August 1975, pp. 493, 509; 28 August 1975, p. 688; Hamish McDonald, *Suharto's Indonesia* (Sydney: Fontana Books, 1981), pp. 197, 207.

45 McDonald, *Suharto's Indonesia*, pp. 197, 207; DFAT, *Australia and the Indonesian Incorporation of East Timor* (Melbourne University Press, 2000), Document 190, p. 345, Document 188, p. 343.

46 Toohey and Wilkinson, *The Book of Leaks*, pp. 177–8.

47 Toohey and Wilkinson, *The Book of Leaks*, pp. 178–9.

48 Toohey and Wilkinson, *The Book of Leaks*, pp. 179–80.

49 Hamish McDonald, 'Revealed: How the Balibo murders were covered up', *Sydney Morning Herald*, 24 August 1998; *Herald Sun*, 27 November 1991. See also Desmond Ball and Hamish McDonald, *Death in Balibo, Lies in Canberra* (Sydney: Allen & Unwin, 2000), and for the briefings of Jakarta embassy officials by Indonesian intelligence, see Documents 160, 166–7, 210, 258, 262 and 265 of Department of Foreign Affairs and Trade, *Australia and the Indonesian Incorporation of East Timor*.

50 Documents 166 and 171 of Department of Foreign Affairs and Trade, *Australia and the Indonesian Incorporation of East Timor*, pp. 309, 317.

51 *Age*, 1 December 1975; Dunn, *Timor: A People Betrayed*, pp. 273–7; *Sydney Morning Herald*, 6 December 1975; *Australian*, 5 December 1975.

52 The cable was read into *Hansard* by Andrew Peacock and passed to the Department of Foreign Affairs. Commonwealth, *Parliamentary Debates*, House of Representatives, 25 February 1975, p. 641; Jose Ramos-Horta, *Funu: The Unfinished Saga of East Timor* (Trenton, NJ: Red Sea Press, 1987), p. 66.

53 Whitlam, *The Whitlam Government*, p. 112; Richard Woolcott, 'The perils of freedom', *Weekend Australian*, 22–23 April 1995, p. 24.

54 Toohey and Wilkinson, *The Book of Leaks*, pp. 166–7.

55 Amnesty International, *East Timor: Violations of Human Rights 1975–1984* (London, 1985), pp. 24–9; Dunn, *Timor: A People Betrayed*, pp. 282–5; McDonald, *Suharto's Indonesia*, p. 212.

56 Dunn, *Timor: A People Betrayed*, pp. 283–6; Carmel Budiardjo and Liem Soei Liong, *The War Against East Timor* (London: Zed Books, 1984), p. 23.

57 Claire Clark (1980), 'The United Nations', in W. J. Hudson (ed.), *Australia in World Affairs*, p. 148.

58 Dunn, *Timor: A People Betrayed*, p. 342; *Australian Foreign Affairs Review*, 1976, pp. 42–4.

59 Interview with author, Jakarta, 21 November 1996.

60 Dunn, *Timor: A People Betrayed*, pp. 342–5, 274; *Australian Foreign Affairs Review*, 1978, p. 46, 1979, p. 305.

61 *Australian Foreign Affairs Review*, 1976, p. 300, 1981, p. 242.

62 *Australian Foreign Affairs Review*, 1979, p. 96.

63 *Australian Foreign Affairs Review*, 1978, p. 47.

64 Coral Bell, *Dependent Ally: A Study in Australian Foreign Policy* (Sydney: Allen & Unwin, 1988), p. 135; *Australian Foreign Affairs Review*, 1980, pp. 16–24.

65 *Australian Foreign Affairs Review*, 1980, p. 24.

66 Development aid was increased to $86 million over three years, from the previous three-year total of $69 million, perhaps in response to the Pertamina crisis. The $20 million program announced by Whitlam in 1975 was also continued – it included patrol boats, field radios and officer training (including combat skills) in Australia. Ten Nomad 'Searchmaster' aircraft were donated, along with the use of RAAF aircraft for the aerial mapping of Irian Jaya, itself the focus of a war of counter-insurgency. The Nomads were provided ostensibly for maritime surveillance, but the ALP's Ken Fry argued that they were being used in East Timor to search for guerrillas. Twelve Bell 'Sioux' helicopters were also donated from 1977 along with training for Indonesian pilots and mechanics. *Australian Foreign Affairs Review*, 1976, pp. 129, 213; 1979, pp. 229, 236; Budiardjo and Liong, *The War Against East Timor*, p. 30.

67 *Australian Foreign Affairs Review*, 1982, p. 737–44; Dunn, *Timor: A People Betrayed*, pp. 322–46.

68 A 1982 press release from Foreign Minister Tony Street boasted that Australia had supplied $23 million to the relief operation on the Thai–Cambodia border, which compared with a paltry shipment of 862 tonnes of rice to Phnom Penh. *Australian Foreign Affairs Review*, 1982, p. 484; John Pilger, *Heroes* (London: Pan, 1989), p. 448.

69 *Australian Foreign Affairs Review*, 1982, pp. 240–1.

70 Ross Garnaut, *Australia and the Northeast Asian Ascendancy* (Canberra: AGPS, 1989); *Australian Foreign Affairs Review*, 1983, pp. 580–8, 1984, p. 10; Paul Kelly, *The End of Certainty: The Story of the 1980s* (Sydney: Allen & Unwin, 1992), pp. 2–4.

71 *Australian Foreign Affairs Review*, 1986, p. 895; 1987, p. 486.

72 *Australian*, 7 March 1985, p. 1.

73 *Australian Foreign Affairs Review*, 1986, p. 894; Bill Hayden, *Hayden: An Autobiography* (Sydney: Angus & Robertson, 1996), p. 392.

74 Peter Hastings, 'The Jakarta connection', *Sydney Morning Herald*, 5 March 1984; *Australian*, 8 March 1985, p. 1; Hayden, *Hayden: An Autobiography*, p. 382.

75 While US pressure to prevent a resumption of bilateral aid to Vietnam worked, Labor did provide $7.8 million between 1984 and 1986 through UN programs. *Australian Foreign Affairs Review*, 1985, p. 757.

76 *Australian*, 11 March 1985, p. 1, 12 March 1985; Peter Hastings, 'Thach's visit will clear the air', *Sydney Morning Herald*, 5 March 1985; Hayden, *Hayden: An Autobiography*, p. 382.

77 Budiardjo and Liong, *The War Against East Timor*, p. 48; *Australian Foreign Affairs Review*, 1983, p. 518; Taylor, *East Timor: The Price of Freedom*, p. 142.

78 Amnesty International, *East Timor: Violations of Human Rights* (London, 1985), pp. 18, 52.

79 Stephen V. Harris and Colin Brown, *Indonesia, Australia and Papua New Guinea: The Irian Jaya Problem of 1984* (Brisbane: Griffith University Centre for the Study of Australian–Asian Relations, 1985), pp. 1–44.

80 Osborne, *Indonesia's Secret War*, pp. 182; *Australian Foreign Affairs Review*, 1984, p. 711; Harris and Brown, *The Irian Jaya Problem*, p. 37.

81 Toohey and Wilkinson, *The Book of Leaks*, p. 258; Brian Toohey, 'Night Falcon', *Eye*, October–November 1990, p. 7; *Sydney Morning Herald*, 7 November 1985; Nic Maclellan, *Inside the Triangle: Strategic Relations between Australia, Indonesia and Papua New Guinea* (Melbourne: Australia West Papua Association, 1990), p. 5.

82 Amnesty International, *Power and Impunity: Human Rights under the New Order* (London, 1994), p. 64; Murdani's speech reproduced in *Inside Indonesia*, June 1990, p. 14.

83 The $790 million in two-way trade between Australia and Indonesia in 1984–85, for instance, was well behind the figures for Australia's largest Asian trading partners: China ($1.4 billion), Korea ($1.6 billion), Singapore ($1.7 billion) and Japan ($14.8 billion). Australian direct investment figures of $70 million contrasted with those in Singapore of $235 million. *Australian Foreign Affairs Review*, 1986, p. 791.

84 *Australian Foreign Affairs Review*, 1987, p. 485, 1986, p. 154.

85 A special issue of *Australian Outlook*, Vol. 30, No. 3, July 1987, was devoted to these events. See especially the articles by David Jenkins, H. C. McMichael, Richard Robison and Budiono Kusumohamidjojo.

86 *Australian Foreign Affairs Review*, 1986, pp. 421, 790.

87 David Scott, Herb Feith and Pat Walsh, *East Timor: Towards a Just Peace in the 1990s* (Melbourne: Australian Council for Overseas Aid, 1991).

88 Gareth Evans and Bruce Grant, *Australia's Foreign Relations in the World of the 1990s* (Melbourne University Press, 1995), p. 200.

89 Pat Walsh, 'Timor Gap: Oil poured on bloodied waters', *Arena*, No. 90, 1990, p. 14.

90 Gareth Evans, 'The Labor tradition: A view from the 1990s', in Lee and Waters (eds), *Evatt to Evans*, p. 17.

91 Greg Fry (ed.), *Australia's Regional Security* (Sydney: Allen & Unwin, 1991), p. 170.

92 Evans, 'The Labor tradition', p. 16; Fry (ed.), *Australia's Regional Security*, pp. 187–8.

93 Australian deployments of P3C Orions over the South China Sea from Butterworth assisted the USA in surveillance of Soviet naval movements from Cam Ranh Bay; a Western strategic presence also enabled the isolation of the communist New People's Army in the Philippines, which the 1987 White Paper said threatened 'the long-term prospects for reforming governments and also raises the possibility that unwelcome external powers could become involved'. Likewise the gift of Nomad aircraft and patrol boats to Indonesia helped ABRI to seal off Fretilin from sources of outside support. Department of Defence, *The Defence of Australia: Defence White Paper 1987* (Canberra: Australian Government Publishing Service, 1987), pp. 14–16.

94 Department of Defence, *Defending Australia: Defence White Paper 1994*, Canberra: Australian Government Publishing Service, 1994), p. 3; emphasis added.

95 Desmond Ball and Pauline Kerr, *Presumptive Engagement: Australia's Asia–Pacific Security Policy in the 1990s* (Sydney: Allen & Unwin, 1996), p. 121.

96 Paul Keating, 'The Redfern Park Speech', Sydney, 10 December 1992, in Mark Ryan (ed.), *Advancing Australia: The Speeches of Paul Keating, Prime Minister* (Sydney: Big Picture Publications, 1995), p. 228.

97 Paul Keating, *Speech to the Official Banquet Given by President Suharto*, Istana Negara, Jakarta, 21 April 1992, p. 2.

98 Keating, *Speech to the Official Banquet Given by President Suharto*, 21 April 1992, p. 4.

99 Paul Keating, *Our Common Interest: Speech to the Indonesian Foreign Policy Forum*, Jakarta, 22 April 1992, p. 5; emphasis added.

100 Tony Parkinson, 'Punish Timor killers, Hawke urges Suharto', *Australian*, 14 November 1991; Tony Parkinson, 'Hawke to be tougher

on Indonesia', *Australian,* 26 November 1991; Mark Metherall, 'PM deplores killings', *Age,* 14 November 1991; Mark Metherall, 'PM urges Indonesia to talk', *Age,* 15 November 1991; Greg Austin, 'Threaten Jakarta with sanctions, say Labor MPs', *Sydney Morning Herald,* 26 November 1991.

101 Peter Hartcher, 'Polite Keating keeps quiet about Dili', *Sydney Morning Herald,* 22 April 1992, p. 1; Paul Keating, *Our Common Interest,* p. 8; Adam Schwarz, 'Burden of blame', *Far Eastern Economic Review,* 9 January 1992, pp. 8–9; Mark Ryan (ed.), *Advancing Australia,* p. 201.

102 These comments, made to journalist Kerry O'Brien on the ABC's *7.30 Report,* were cited in *Sydney Morning Herald,* 16 December 1995.

103 Peter Hartcher, 'How the enemy became an ally', *Australian Financial Review,* 4 July 1996, p. 1; Peter Hartcher, 'The Indonesian deal – an act of faith', *Australian Financial Review,* 5 July 1996, p. 26.

104 Canberra Press Conference, 14 December 1995; Ryan (ed.), *Advancing Australia,* pp. 190–201.

105 Ryan (ed.), *Advancing Australia,* pp. 227–8; emphasis added.

106 Ryan (ed.), *Advancing Australia,* p. 228.

107 Ryan (ed.), *Advancing Australia,* p. 230.

108 Lindsay Murdoch, 'Australia draws fire on Cambodian rights', *Sydney Morning Herald,* 4 March 1993, p. 8.

109 Critics have focused on the failure to disarm the Khmer Rouge, the effects of the huge UN contingent (costing US$2 billion) on the stability of the Cambodian economy and the growth in prostitution, and on the poorly planned and corrupt pattern of development initiated by the return of Western loans, aid and investment to Cambodia. Lindsay Murdoch, 'The spoils of peace', *Good Weekend,* 15 May 1993, p. 41.

110 Evans and Grant, *Australia's Foreign Relations,* p. 102; Gareth Evans, 'Co-operative security and intrastate conflict', *Foreign Affairs,* No. 96, Fall 1994, p. 9; Jim George, 'Quo vadis Australia? Framing the defence and security debate beyond the Cold War', in Graeme Cheeseman and Robert Bruce (eds), *Discourses of Danger and Dread Frontiers: Australian Defence and Security Thinking After the Cold War* (Sydney: Allen & Unwin, 1996), p. 15.

5   Australia's Asian crisis 1996–2000

1 John Howard, 'Politics and Patriotism: A Reflection on the National Identity Debate', Grand Hyatt Hotel, Melbourne, 13 December 1995.

2 *Weekend Australian*, 9–10 March 1996, p. 18.

3 Deborah Hope, 'Poll suggests rejection of political correctness', *Weekend Australian*, 9–10 March 1996, p. 10; Donald Horne, 'Paul Keating's fatal abstraction', *Weekend Australian*, 9–10 March 1996, p. 21; Lindsay Tanner, 'How change fatigue lost the vote for Labor', *Weekend Australian*, 7 March 1996, p. 12; John Howard, 'Australia and Asia: An enduring engagement', Address to the Australia-Asia Society, 8 May 1997, p. 2.

4 See Howard's address, 'Politics and Patriotism: A Reflection on the National Identity Debate', 13 December 1995.

5 John Howard, 'The Australian Way', Federation Address presented to the Queensland Chamber of Commerce and Industry, Brisbane, 28 January 1999, p. 1.

6 International Monetary Fund, *World Economic Outlook*, April 2000, p. 23.

7 Peter Hartcher, 'Soeharto's regime can no longer be tolerated', *Australian Financial Review*, 16–17 May 1998, p. 9.

8 John Howard, Prime Television telecast, 25 May 1998.

9 Australian Labor Party, *41st National Conference Draft Platform*, Canberra, 1998.

10 *Australian*, 31 August 1998.

11 Zygmunt Bauman, *Postmodernity and its Discontents* (Cambridge: Polity Press, 1997), p. 21.

12 See Julia Kristeva, 'Strangers to ourselves' in Kelly Oliver (ed.), *The Portable Kristeva* (New York: Columbia University Press, 1997), pp. 264–94.

13 Kristeva, 'Strangers to ourselves', pp. 23–5.

14 John Howard, 'Australia and Asia: An enduring engagement', p. 1.

15 John Howard, 'The Inaugural Prime Ministers on Prime Ministers Lecture', Old Parliament House, Canberra, 3 September 1997.

16 Howard, 'The Inaugural Prime Ministers on Prime Ministers Lecture'.

17 Fiona Allon, 'Home as cultural translation: John Howard's Earlwood', *Communal/Plural*, No. 5, 1997, p. 2.

18 Ghassan Hage, *White Nation: Fantasies of White Supremacy in a Multicultural Society* (Sydney: Pluto Press, 1998).

19 Department of Foreign Affairs and Trade, *In the National Interest: Australia's Foreign and Trade Policy White Paper* (Canberra: AGPS, 1997).

20 Les A. Murray, 'A Brief History', *Subhuman Redneck Poems* (Potts Point, NSW: Duffy & Snellgrove, 1996), pp. 11–12.

21 Michael Gordon and Patrick Walters, 'Howard embraces Indonesia: PM backs closer economic and security links', *Australian*, 17 September 1996, p. 1.

22 Louise Williams, 'Shoot on sight: Cracks show in Soeharto's rule', *Sydney Morning Herald*, 3 August 1996, p. 25; Lewa Pardomuan, 'Leftist charged over riot', *Sydney Morning Herald*, 3 August 1996, p. 19; Patrick Walters, 'Army cracks down on "subversion" ', *Australian*, 1 August 1996.

23 'Press silent on Army response', *Australian*, 30 July 1996, p. 8.

24 Paul Keating, address to the Australia-Asia Institute, Brisbane, 26 October 1994, in Mark Ryan (ed.), *Advancing Australia: The Speeches of Paul Keating* (Sydney: Big Picture Publications, 1995), p. 217.

25 Howard, 'Politics and patriotism: A reflection on the national identity debate', pp. 2–3.

26 Greg Sheridan, 'Asian tigers link growth to values', *Australian*, 28 August 1996, p. 13.

27 Richard Robison, 'Introduction' and 'Looking north: Myths and strategies', in Richard Robison (ed.), *Pathways to Asia: The Politics of Engagement* (Sydney: Allen & Unwin, 1996), pp. xii, 10.

28 Department of Foreign Affairs and Trade, *In the National Interest*, p. vii.

29 Adele Horin, 'Trying a bit of stick: The most vulnerable may be hit by tough new welfare rules', *Sydney Morning Herald*, 18 March 2000, p. 44; Toni O'Loughlin, 'Making welfare work', *Sydney Morning Herald*, 28 March 2000; Virginia Trioli, 'The unwelcome mat', *Bulletin*, 14 December 1999, pp. 34–6; Chris Sidoti, 'Unlucky voyagers to the Lucky Country', *Age*, 28 May 1998.

30 Department of Foreign Affairs and Trade, *In the National Interest*, pp. iv–v.

31 Department of Foreign Affairs and Trade, *In the National Interest*, p. 25.

32 Jeffrey A. Winters, 'The financial crisis in Southeast Asia', in Richard Robison, Mark Beeson, Kanishka Jayasuriya and Hyuk-Rae Kim (eds), *Politics and Markets in the Wake of the Asian Crisis* (London: Routledge, 2000), p. 41.

33 Department of Foreign Affairs and Trade, *In the National Interest*, p. 61.

34 Susan Berfield and Keith Loveard, 'Suharto Under Fire', *Asiaweek*, 9 August 1996.

35 Anthony Burke, 'White paper sets off alarm bells', *Jakarta Post*, 25 September 1997, p. 4.

36 Jim George and Rodd McGibbon, 'Dangerous liaisons: Neoliberal foreign policy and Australia's regional engagement', *Australian Journal of Political Science*, Vol. 33, No. 3, 1998, p. 411.

37 Howard, 'Australia and Asia: An enduring engagement', p. 2.

38 Department of Foreign Affairs and Trade, *In the National Interest*, p. iii.

39 Laurie Brereton, 'Foreign policy under the Coalition: Confused not confident, often just plain dumb', Speech to Australian Institute of International Affairs, Queensland, 22 February 1997, pp. 8–9.

40 Brereton, 'Foreign policy under the Coalition'.

41 Laurie Brereton, 'Australia and Indonesia: A Labor perspective', Speech to the Second Indonesian Students Conference, ANU, Canberra, 21 August 1996, p. 11.

42 Karl Marx, 'On the Jewish question', in Eugene Kamenka, *The Portable Karl Marx* (London: Penguin, 1983), pp. 108–9.

43 John Howard, Prime Ministers on Prime Ministers lecture, p. 3.

44 Carol Johnson, 'John Howard and the revenge of the mainstream', Paper given to the Political Science Program, RSSS, ANU, 7 May 1997, p. 7.

45 Department of Foreign Affairs and Trade, *In the National Interest*, p. iii.

46 Howard, 'The Australian Way', p. 1.

47 Howard, 'Prime Ministers on Prime Ministers lecture', p. 3.

48 Michel Foucault, 'Governmentality', in Graham Burchell, Colin Gordon and Peter Miller (ed.), *The Foucault Effect: Studies in Governmentality* (London: Harvester Wheatsheaf, 1991), pp. 90–2; G. W. F. Hegel, *Philosophy of Right* (London: Oxford University Press, 1967), pp. 148–55.

49 Toby Miller, *The Well-tempered Self: Citizenship, Culture and the Postmodern Subject* (Baltimore and London: Johns Hopkins University Press, 1993), p. 221; Howard, 'Prime Ministers on Prime Ministers lecture', p. 7.

50 Johnson, 'The revenge of the mainstream', pp. 8–9.

51 Allon, 'Home as cultural translation', p. 12.

52 Johnson, 'The revenge of the mainstream', pp. 8–9.

53 Manning Clark, *A History of Australia* (Vol. V), *The People Make Laws 1888–1915* (Melbourne University Press, 1981), p. 68.

54 Frank Brennan, *The Wik Debate* (Sydney: UNSW Press, 1998), pp. 41–54.

55 Brennan, *The Wik Debate*, p. 60.

56 Brennan, *The Wik Debate*, p. 61.

57 John Howard, 'Wik Statement – Address to the Nation', ABC Television, 30 November 1997; Brennan, *The Wik Debate*, p. 54.

58 Brennan, *The Wik Debate*, pp. 82–91.

59 Senate Environment, Communications, Information Technology and the Arts References Committee, *Jabiluka: The Undermining of Process*, June 1999, p. 48.

60 Senate Environment, Communications, Information Technology and the Arts References Committee, *Jabiluka: The Undermining of Process*, pp. 88–93, xxii, 50.

61 John Howard, Press Conference, Prime Minister's Courtyard, Parliament House, 14 October 1998.

62 John Howard, Press Conference, Prime Minister's Courtyard, Parliament House, 14 October 1998. See also Henry Reynolds' thought-provoking book *Aboriginal Sovereignty* (Sydney: Allen & Unwin, 1996), which does argue for 'three nations, one Australia'.

63 Peter Botsman, *The Great Constitutional Swindle: A Citizen's View of the Australian Constitution* (Sydney: Pluto Press, 2000), p. 130.

64 Morgan and Pearson cited in Paul Patton, 'Justice and difference: The *Mabo* case', in Paul Patton and Diane Austin-Broos (eds), *Transformations in Australian Society* (Sydney: Research Institute for Humanities and Social Sciences, 1997), pp. 84, 91.

65 See Paul Patton's discussion in '*Mabo*, Freedom and the Politics of Difference', *Australian Journal of Political Science*, Vol. 30, 1995, pp. 112–13.

66 The four economies are Indonesia, Thailand, the Philippines and Malaysia. See International Monetary Fund, *World Economic Outlook*, April 2000, p. 2.

67 *Australian Financial Review*, 25 January 1998, pp. 1–3; *Sydney Morning Herald*, 3 June 1998, p. 1.

68 Richard Robison and Andrew Rosser, 'Surviving the meltdown: Liberal reform and political oligarchy in Indonesia', in Robison et al. (eds), *Politics and Markets in the Wake of the Asian Crisis*, pp. 171–2. Associated Press, 'UN report predicts 66 per cent poverty rate in Indonesia in 1999', *South China Morning Post*, 31 August 1998.

69 Alexander Downer, 'Australia and Asia: After the crisis', Asia Research Centre, Perth, 6 August 1998.

70 Susan Berfield and Dewi Loveard, 'Ten days that shook Indonesia', *Asiaweek*, 24 July 1998.

71 Mark Beeson and Richard Robison, 'Introduction' in Robison et al. (eds), *Politics and Markets in the Wake of the Asian Crisis*, p. 3.

72 Jeffrey Winters, 'The financial crisis in Southeast Asia', in Robison et al. (eds), *Politics and Markets in the Wake of the Asian Crisis*, p. 41.

73 See Jim George and Rodd McGibbon, 'Dangerous liaisons: Neoliberal foreign policy and Australia's regional engagement'.

74 Robison and Rosser, 'Surviving the meltdown: Liberal reform and political oligarchy in Indonesia', pp. 179–84.

75 See Winters, 'The financial crisis in Southeast Asia', p. 45; K. S. Jomo, 'Crisis and the Developmental State in East Asia', in Robison et al. (eds), *Politics and Markets in the Wake of the Asian Crisis*, pp. 25–33.

76 Alexander Downer, 'Australia's future in the Asia-Pacific: Cooperation, economic reform and liberalisation', Melbourne Institute Conference, University of Melbourne, 8 May 1998, p. 1.

77 Jeffrey D. Sachs, 'The wrong medicine for Asia', *New York Times*, 3 November 1997.

78 Downer, 'Australia's future in the Asia–Pacific: Cooperation, economic reform and liberalisation', p. 1.

79 Ramos cited in *Philippine Daily Inquirer*, 16 September 1998, www.inquirer.net; Filipino structural adjustment described in Walden Bello, 'The Philippines: The making of a neo-classical tragedy' in Robison et al. (eds), *Politics and Markets in the Wake of the Asian Crisis*, pp. 238–57; Jeffrey D. Sachs, 'IMF is a power unto itself', *Financial Times*, 11 December 1997.

80 Peter Hartcher, 'Australians fiddle as world burns', *Australian Financial Review*, 16 September 1998; Genevieve Ku and May Sin-Mi Hon, 'Tung defends crisis powers over exchange', *South China Morning Post*, 9 September 1998; Glenda Korporaal, 'Exchange Controls: Long-term damage to image feared', *Sydney Morning Herald*, 4 September 1998.

81 For a list of the Australian proposals see John Howard, 'Returning the region to sustainable growth', *Address to the 10th International Conference of Banking Supervisers*, Sydney, 22 October 1998.

82 Alexander Downer, 'Responding to the Asia crisis: Charting the way forward', Speech to the Sydney Meeting on Development Cooperation. Responding to the Asia Crisis, Customs House, Sydney, 4 March 1999, p. 2; Howard, 'Returning the region to sustainable growth', p. 4.

83 Ibid.

84 Task Force on International Financial Reform, *Key Findings* (Canberra: AGPS, December 1998), p. 1.

85 Bhagwati and Garten cited in Richard Higgott, 'The international relations of the Asian economic crisis: A study in the politics of resentment', in Robison et al. (eds), *Politics and Markets in the Wake of the Asian Crisis*, pp. 272, 266; Mark Beeson and Stephen Bell,

'Australia in the shadow of the Asian crisis', in Robison et al. (eds), p. 307.

86 Paul Kelly, 'United States of East Asia', *Weekend Australian*, 29–30 April 2000, p. 22.

87 Paul Keating, 'Australia and the Asian crisis', University of New South Wales, 25 March 1998; www.keating.org.au.

88 Mark Beeson and Stephen Bell, 'Australia in the shadow of the Asian crisis', in Robison et. al., pp. 304–7.

89 *Australian*, 21 September 1998.

90 Editorial, 'Divided we fall: ASEAN must take a firm stand on regional matters', *Asiaweek*, 7 August 1998.

91 Ibid.

92 Walden Bello, 'Asia–Europe relations in the light of the Southeast Asian financial crisis', Address to Transnational Institute Seminar, Amsterdam, 31 October 1997.

93 Louse Williams, 'Flashpoint fear as workers hit the streets', *Sydney Morning Herald*, 5 July 1998; Human Rights Watch Report, *Bearing the Brunt of the Asian Economic Crisis: The Impact on Labor Rights and Migrant Workers in Asia*, March 1998, www.hrw.org.

94 Bello, 'Asia–Europe relations in the light of the Southeast Asian financial crisis'.

95 Between 1998 and 1999 GDP growth figures changed from −13 to 0 per cent in Indonesia, −10 to 4.5 per cent in Thailand, −7 to 5 per cent in Malaysia, and −6 to 10 per cent in South Korea. International Monetary Fund, *World Economic Outlook*, April 2000.

96 H. S. Dillon, 'A people-driven approach to strategy', *Jakarta Post*, 10 April 2000.

97 Philip Flood, 'Australia and Indonesia: An investment for tomorrow', Address to the National Press Club, Canberra, 14 April 1990, *Monthly Record* (Canberra: Department of Foreign Affairs and Trade, April 1990), pp. 206–13.

98 Louise Williams, 'How opposition to Soeharto is being made to disappear', *Sydney Morning Herald*, 13 April 1998, p. 1.

99 Susan Berfield and Dewi Loveard, 'Ten days that shook Indonesia', *Asiaweek*, 24 July 1998.

100 Don Greenlees, 'Howard to lobby IMF for Suharto', *Weekend Australian*, 21–22 February 1998, p. 1; Don Greenlees, 'Food aid bid to quell riots in Indonesia', *Australian*, 23 February 1998, p. 1; Damon Frith, 'Indonesia signs away contract uncertainty', *Australian*, 4 February 1998.

101 John Howard, Press Conference Transcript, Parliament House, Canberra, 19 May 1998.

102 David Jenkins, 'How Soeharto fell on his sword', *Sydney Morning Herald*, 23 May 1998, p. 29.

103 Bernard Lagan, Lindsay Murdoch and John Martinkus, 'Alas inquiry labelled a PR exercise', *Sydney Morning Herald*, 9 January 1999, p. 14.

104 Amnesty International Report, *East Timor: Paramilitary Attacks Jeopardise East Timor's Future*, ASA 21/26/99, 16 April 1999.

105 Cited in Commonwealth, *Hansard*, House of Representatives, 20 September 1999, p. 7459.

106 *Agreement between the Republic of Indonesia and the Portuguese Republic on the Question of East Timor*, New York, 5 May 1999, www.thejakartapost.com:8890/et_doc_6.htm; *Agreement Regarding the Modalities for the Popular Consultation of the East Timorese through a Direct Ballot*, New York, 5 May 1999, www. thejakartapost.com:8890/et_doc_5.htm; *Agreement Between the United Nations, the Republic of Indonesia and the Portuguese Republic Regarding Security*, New York, 5 May 1999, www.thejakartapost.com:8890/et_doc_4.htm; I. Williams, 'Another UN disaster', *Salon.com*, 11 September 1999, www.salon.com/news/feature/1999/09/11/un/index. html.

107 See the comments of Tomas Goncalves in the ABC *Four Corners* transcript, 'The ties that bind', 14 February 2000, www.abc.net.au/4corners/stories/s99352.htm.

108 See Brereton's remarks in Commonwealth, *Hansard*, House of Representatives, 21 September 1999, p. 7635; Anthony Burke, 'Timor process deeply flawed', *Canberra Times*, 4 May 1999.

109 Don Greenlees, 'A full and free choice', *Australian*, 28 April 1999, p. 1; Paul Kelly, 'Indonesian friendship put to the test', *Australian*, 28 April 1999; see Howard's remarks in Commonwealth, *Hansard*, House of Representatives, 21 September 1999, p. 7619 and the comments of Ali Alatas and Dewi Fortuna Anwar in ABC *Four Corners* transcript, 'The ties that bind', 14 February 2000, www.abc.net.au/4corners/stories/s99352.htm.

110 John Lyons, 'The secret Timor dossier', *Bulletin*, 12 October 1999, pp. 24–9; Marian Wilkinson, 'Why we kept Timor secrets from the US', *Sydney Morning Herald*, 13 August 1999, p. 1; Paul Daley, 'Timor's pain, Australia's shame', *Age*, 11 September 1999, p. 1.

111 United Nations High Commission on Human Rights, Situation of Human Rights in East Timor: Note By the Secretary General, 54th Session, Agenda Item 116(c), A/54/660, 10 December 1999, paras 17–37; Mark Dodd, 'Suai massacre militia "will be punished"', *Sydney Morning Herald*, 7 August 2000. A definitive account of the

violence and those responsible for it is Hamish McDonald et al., *Masters of Terror: Indonesia's Military and Violence in East Timor in 1999*, Canberra Papers on Strategy and Defence No. 145 (Canberra: Strategic and Defence Studies Centre, ANU, 2002).

112 Elizabeth Becker, 'General speaks a language that Wiranto understands', *Sydney Morning Herald*, 15 September 1999, p. 1.

113 S. Lewis and B. Pearson, 'About 7000 troops ready to go', *Australian Financial Review*, 16 September 1999, p. 7.

114 See the parliamentary debates: Commonwealth, *Hansard*, House of Representatives, 21 September 1999, pp. 7617–59; Commonwealth, *Hansard*, Senate, 21 September 1999, pp. 8427–72; and media coverage including Brian Toohey, 'The public v the policy makers', *Australian Financial Review*, 11–12 September 1999, p. 24; Paul Kelly, 'Shattered myths', *Weekend Australian*, 11–12 September 1999, p. 25; Tony Wright, 'We're suckers to standover men', *Age*, 10 September 1999; John Schauble, 'How Indonesia betrayed its friends', *Age*, 10 September 1999; Geoffrey Barker, 'A tougher but more honest time ahead', *Australian Financial Review*, 22 September 1999; Greg Sheridan, 'A holocaust of Canberra's making', *Australian*, 16 September 1999.

115 Editorial, 'A rude awakening: We're on our own', *Age*, 11 September 1999; Geoffrey Barker, 'Anatomy of a crisis: Australia's futile call to arms', *Australian Financial Review*, 11–12 September 1999, p. 22.

116 Editorial, 'Timor tragedy shows where we stand', *Australian*, 11–12 September 1999, p. 24.

117 Les A. Murray, 'A Brief History', *Subhuman Redneck Poems* (Potts Point, NSW: Duffy & Snellgrove, 1996), p. 11.

118 John Howard, 'Address to the Nation', 19 September 1999.

119 Commonwealth, *Hansard*, House of Representatives, 21 September 1999, p. 7620.

120 Human Rights and Equal Opportunity Commission, *Bringing Them Home: Report of the National Inquiry into the Separation of Aboriginal and Torres Strait Islander Children from Their Families*, 1997; David Day, *Claiming a Continent: A History of Australia* (Sydney: Angus & Robertson, 1996), p. 266.

121 Michelle Grattan and Debra Jopson, 'Black fury explodes over stolen children', and Debra Jopson, 'Aboriginal disgust at denial of history', *Sydney Morning Herald*, 3 April 2000, p. 1; Robert Manne, 'The removalists', *Age*, 10 April 2000.

122 John Howard, Press Conference, Parliament House, 14 October 1998, p. 4.

123 Geoffrey Blainey, 'Drawing up a balance sheet of our history', *Quadrant*, July–August 1993, p. 12.
124 Blainey, 'Drawing up a balance sheet of our history', p. 15.

6   The wages of terror 2001–07

1 *ABC News Online* forum, 'Asylum seekers: The Pacific solution', www2b.abc.net.au/news/forum/forum30/default.htm.
2 This term, coined by the scholar Ole Wæver, refers to a case in which a routine policy problem is elevated into an existential threat to survival, the 'special nature' of which 'justifies the use of extraordinary measures to handle [it] . . . traditionally, by saying "security", a state representative declares an emergency condition, thus claiming a right to use whatever means are necessary to block a threatening development'. Ole Wæver, Jaap de Wilde and Barry Buzan, *Security: A New Framework for Analysis* (Boulder, Colo.: Lynne Rienner, 1998), p. 21.
3 Preceding days had been dominated by ALP revelations of a scandal involving attempts by Liberal Party branches to commit tax fraud in regards to GST revenues and expenses from fund raising. These attempts had been known to senior government ministers and Liberal Party officials.
4 Quoted on the *Sunday* programme, Nine Television Network Australia, 2 September 2001.
5 Michelle Grattan, Hamish McDonald and Andrew Clennell, 'Howard's *Tampa*-led recovery', *Sydney Morning Herald*, 4 September 2001, p. 1.
6 *Defence 2000: Our Future Defence Force* (Canberra: Department of Defence, 2000), p. vii.
7 United Nations Development Programme, *Human Development Report, 1994* (New York: Oxford University Press, 1995); Anthony Burke, 'Caught between national and human security: Knowledge and power in post-crisis Asia', *Pacifica Review*, Vol. 13, No. 3, October 2001, pp. 215–39.
8 Peter Chalk, *Non-Military Security and Global Order* (Basingstoke: Macmillan, 2000), p. 155.
9 Alan Dupont, *East Asia Imperilled: Transnational Threats to Security* (Cambridge: Cambridge University Press, 2001), p. 136.
10 Alan Dupont, 'Transnational security', in Robert Ayson and Desmond Ball (eds), *Strategy and Security in the Asia-Pacific* (Crows Nest, NSW: Allen & Unwin, 2006), p. 114.
11 Paul Sheehan, 'Migrant failure stories inspired passions over the *Tampa*', *Sydney Morning Herald*, 5 September 2001.

12 Ghassan Hage, *White Nation: Fantasies of White Supremacy in a Multicultural Society* (Sydney: Pluto Press, 1998).

13 www.defence.gov.au/oprelex2/index.cfm. See also Ruth Balint, '*Mare nullius* and the making of a White Ocean Policy', in Suvendrini Perera (ed.), *Our Patch: Enacting Australian Sovereignty Post-2001* (Perth: Network Books, 2007), pp. 87–104.

14 Thomas C. Schelling, *Arms and Influence* (New Haven, Conn., and London: Yale University Press, 1966).

15 Peter Mares, *Borderline: Australia's Treatment of Refugees and Asylum Seekers* (Sydney: UNSW Press, 2001), pp. 13–17; Joseph Pugliese, 'Penal asylum: Refugees, ethics, hospitality', *Borderlands e-journal*, Vol. 1, No. 1, 2002.

16 Debbie Whitmont and Peter McEvoy, 'The inside story', ABC *Four Corners*, transcript, 13 August 2001, www.abc.net.au/4corners/stories/s344246.htm; Robert Manne, 'Parents face Sophie's choice at Villawood', *Sydney Morning Herald*, 13 August 2001.

17 Whitmont and McEvoy, 'The inside story'.

18 Whitmont and McEvoy, 'The inside story'.

19 Whitmont and McEvoy, 'The inside story'. Peter Mares points out that a policy of deterrence contravenes the 1985 UNHCR guidelines on the detention of asylum seekers. Mares, *Borderline*, p. 79.

20 Anthony Burke and Matt McDonald (eds), *Critical Security in the Asia-Pacific* (Manchester University Press, 2007), Chapter 7, pp. 126–35.

21 'Human Rights Watch says *Tampa* crisis shows lack of humanity', *ABC News Online*, 31 August 2001; 'European Parliament condemns handling of *Tampa* crisis', *ABC News Online*, 7 September 2001; Buchizya Mseteka, 'Robinson rebukes Australian handling of asylum seekers', 2 September 2001, http://sg.news.yahoo. com/010902/3/1dzys.html.

22 Mares, *Borderline*, p. 185.

23 Border Protection Bill 2001. The Parliamentary *Bills Digest* suggested that the proposed sections 7 and 8 and subsection 4(2) of the Bill – which provide that decisions made under the Act 'are not reviewable in *any* Australian court', that 'proceedings may not be commenced in *any* court to prevent a ship being removed', and that 'civil or criminal proceedings in relation to any resulting enforcement action may not be brought *per se*' – would raise constitutional issues. 'It is undeniable', said the *Digest*, 'that a person with sufficient standing could bring a challenge under the constitutionally entrenched judicial review jurisdiction of the High Court.' Nathan Hancock, *Border Protection Bill 2001: Bills Digest No. 41 2001–02* (Canberra: Parliamentary Research Service, 2001), p. 12.

24 *ABC News Online*, 'Legal battle over asylum seekers nears end', 18 September 2001; Border Protection (Validation and Enforcement Powers) Bill 2001; Migration Amendment (Excision from Migration Zone) Bill 2001; Migration Legislation Amendment Bill No. 6 2001.

25 See Peter Mares, *Borderline*, pp. 95–113, and Frank Brennan, *Tampering with Asylum: A Universal Humanitarian Problem* (St Lucia: University of Queensland Press, 2003), p. 151. The Bill that would remove all avenues of judicial review of visa decisions by the Federal Court was the Migration Legislation Amendment (Judicial Review) Bill 1998.

26 Associate Professor Mary Crock, 'Memorandum on proposed changes to the Migration Act', Submission No. 6 to the Senate Legal and Constitutional Affairs Committee inquiry into the Migration Amendment (Designated Unauthorised Arrivals) Bill 2006.

27 Moira Coombs, 'Excisions from the Migration Zone – Policy and practice', *Research Note* No. 42, 1 March 2004 (Canberra: Australian Parliamentary Library).

28 Department of Immigration and Citzenship Fact Sheet no. 81: Australia's Excised Offshore Places. See also Savitri Taylor, 'The Designated Unauthorised Arrivals Bill and beyond', *Migration Action*, Vol. XXVIII, No. 1, 2006, p. 3.

29 Migration Amendment (Designated Unauthorised Arrivals) Bill 2006. Taylor, 'The Designated Unauthorised Arrivals Bill and beyond', p. 4.

30 Crock, 'Memorandum on Proposed Changes to the Migration Act'. See also the report of the Senate Legal and Constitutional Affairs Committee inquiry into the Provisions of the Migration Amendment (Designated Unauthorised Arrivals) Bill 2006 (Canberra: Senate, June 2006), pp. 23–4.

31 Cited in Savitri Taylor, 'Playing out the asylum seeker end game: Forced removal, voluntary repatriation and everything in between', *Migration Action*, Vol. XXVII, No. 2, 2005, pp. 6–15. See also Robert Manne and David Corlett, 'Sending them home: Refugees and the new politics of indifference', *Quarterly Essay*, Issue 13, 2004.

32 Taylor, 'Playing out the asylum seeker end game', p. 6.

33 David Corlett, *Following Them Home: The Fate of the Returned Asylum Seekers* (Melbourne: Black Inc., 2005), p. 192.

34 Senate Legal and Constitutional Affairs Committee inquiry into the Provisions of the Migration Amendment (Designated Unauthorised Arrivals) Bill 2006, Recommendation 1, p. ix.

35 Mick Palmer, 'Inquiry into the Circumstances of the Immigration Detention of Ms Cornelia Rau', July 2005.

36 AAP, 'I was never mentally ill, says Rau', *Sydney Morning Herald*, 23 May 2005.

37 AAP, 'Rau family sent faeces-smeared hate mail', *Sydney Morning Herald*, 18 October 2005.

38 Covering Statement by the Commonwealth Ombudsman to the Minister for Immigration and Multicultural And Indigenous Affairs Concerning Reports Under S 486 of the *Migration Act 1958*, 12 October 2005.

39 A commentary on the findings in the first 20 reports is Adele Horin, 'Brutal mix: Ruthlessness and carelessness', *Sydney Morning Herald*, 9 December 2006.

40 Statements of the Ombudsman's findings, completed reports and ministerial responses are available at: www.comb.gov.au/commonwealth/publish.nsf/Content/publications_immigrationreports.

41 Reports for Tabling in Parliament by the Commonwealth and Immigration Ombudsman under S486 of the Migration Act 1958, Personal Identifiers 102/06 and 107/06.

42 Palmer, 'Inquiry into the Circumstances of the Immigration Detention of Ms Cornelia Rau', Finding No. 9, p. ix.

43 Wæver et al., *Security: A New Framework*, p. 21.

44 Carl Schmitt, *Political Theology: Four Chapters on the Concept of Sovereignty*, trans. George Schwab (Cambridge, Mass. and London: MIT Press, 1985), pp. 5–6; Giorgio Agamben, *State of Exception*, trans. Kevin Attell (Chicago and London: University of Chicago Press, 2005).

45 Giorgio Agamben, *Homo Sacer: Sovereign Power and Bare Life* (Stanford: Stanford University Press, 1998).

46 Suvendrini Perera, 'What is a camp?', *Borderlands e-journal*, Vol. 1, No. 1, 2002, pt 12, www.borderlandsejournal.adelaide.edu.au.

47 Perera, 'What is a camp?', abstract.

48 Tony Wright, 'Our long path to war', *Bulletin*, 8 April 2003, p. 30.

49 See Matt McDonald, 'Be Alarmed? Australia's anti-terrorism kit and the politics of security', *Global Change, Peace and Security*, Vol. 17, No. 2, June 2005.

50 Tony Wright, 'Our long path to war, pp. 29–37.

51 Robert Garran, *True Believer: John Howard, George Bush and the American Alliance* (Sydney: Allen & Unwin, 2004), pp. 152–65.

52 Sally Neighbour, *In the Shadow of Swords: On the Trail of Terrorism from Afghanistan to Australia* (Sydney: HarperCollins, 2004), pp. 287, 273.

53 Bruce Lawrence (ed.), *Messages to the World: The Statements of Osama bin Laden* (London and New York: Verso, 2005), p. 175.

54 Louise Richardson, *What Terrorists Want: Understanding the Terrorist Threat* (London: John Murray, 2006), p. 10.

55 William Maley, 'Military intervention in the Middle East', in Fethi Mansouri (ed.), *Australia and the Middle East: A Front-Line Relationship* (London and New York: IB Tauris, 2006), p. 142.

56 For a more developed version of this argument see Anthony Burke, 'Cause and effect in the war on terror', in Roland Bleiker, Alex Bellamy, Richard Devetak and Sara Davies (eds), *Security and the War on Terror* (London and New York: Routledge, 2007).

57 Bruce Lawrence (ed.), *Messages to the World*, pp. 175, 238.

58 *National Strategy for Combating Terrorism* (Washington DC: White House, 2003), pp. 23–4.

59 *Transnational Terrorism: The Threat to Australia* (Canberra: Department of Foreign Affairs and Trade, 2004), pp. 76–7.

60 Nicholas Wheeler, 'Dying for "Enduring Freedom": Accepting responsibility for civilian casualties in the war against terrorism', *International Relations*, Vol. 16, No. 2, 2002; Anthony Burke, 'Just war or ethical peace? Morality and strategic violence after 9/11', chapter 6 of *Beyond Security, Ethics and Violence* (London and New York: Routledge, 2007); Carlotta Gall and David E. Sanger, 'Civilian deaths undermine war on Taliban', *New York Times*, 9 May 2007.

61 Gall and Sanger, 'Civilian deaths undermine war on Taliban'.

62 Burke, 'Just war or ethical peace?', pp. 156–8; Paul McGeough, 'Inside the Taliban's heart of darkness', *Sydney Morning Herald*, 22 May 2007.

63 William Maley and Daoud Yaqub, 'A long hot summer: Crisis and opportunity in Afghanistan', Policy Brief, March 2007 (Sydney: Lowy Institute for International Policy); Nick Grono and Joanna Nathan, 'Afghanistan: Keep up the war on terror at its source', *Australian*, 8 August 2006; 'Countering Afghanistan's insurgency: No quick fixes', ICG Asia Report No. 123, 2 November 2006 (Brussels: International Crisis Group).

64 Anthony Cordesman, 'Qana and the lessons of modern war', CSIS *Commentary*, 31 July 2006 (Washington DC: Center for Strategic and International Studies).

65 Paul Kelly, 'Stay the course in Afghanistan', *Australian*, 11 April 2007.

66 'UN marks soaring Iraq death toll', *BBC News Online*, 16 January 2007. http://news.bbc.co.uk/2/hi/middle_east/6266393.stm

67 Patrick Cockburn, 'Terrified US soldiers are still killing civilians with impunity, while the dead go uncounted', *Independent*, 24 April 2005.

68 UNHCR, 'Iraq Conference: UNHCR says conference agrees on urgent need to help the 4 million Iraqi displaced', www.unhcr.org/news/NEWS/462621bb4.html.

69 See James Cotton, 'Foreign policy and the management of intelligence', in James Cotton and John Ravenhill (eds), *Trading on Alliance Security: Australia in World Affairs 2001–2005* (Melbourne: Oxford University Press, 2007), pp. 329–51; Joint Committee on ASIO, ASIS and DSD, *Intelligence on Iraq's Weapons of Mass Destruction* (Canberra: Parliament of Australia, 2003), pp. 31–5.

70 David Wroe, 'Iraq was motive for bombing: Suspect', *Age*, 2 August 2005.

71 Cotton, 'Foreign policy and the management of intelligence', p. 340.

72 ABC *7:30 Report* transcript, 'Howard says Israel must defend its "right to exist"', 25 July 2006, www.abc.net.au/7.30/content/2006/s1696790.htm; *BBC News Online*, 'Al-Qaeda to avenge Israel deeds', 27 July 2006.

73 Anthony Bergin, 'The time to prepare for a terrorist attack is now', *Sydney Morning Herald*, 24 May 2007.

74 *Transnational Terrorism: The Threat to Australia* (Canberra: Department of Foreign Affairs and Trade, 2004), pp. 77–8.

75 See essays by George Williams and Katrina Lee Koo in *Borderlands*, Vol. 4, No. 1, 2005.

76 See Burke, 'Australia paranoid', in Burke and McDonald, *Critical Security in the Asia-Pacific*, p. 122; Suvendrini Perera, 'Race terror, Sydney 2005', *Borderlands*, Vol. 5, No. 1, 2006, www.borderlandsejournal.adelaide.edu.au/issues/vol5no1.html.

77 Brett Bowden, 'In the name of progress and peace: The standard of civilisation and the universalising project', *Alternatives: Global, Local, Political*, Vol. 29, No. 1, 2004; Anthony Burke, 'Security, politics and us: Sovereignty, violence and power after 9/11', in Suvendrini Perera (ed.), *Our Patch: Enacting Australian Sovereignty Post-2001* (Perth: API Network Books, 2007), pp. 197–218.

78 Kevin Rudd, 'Smart power', *Diplomat*, February–March 2007, p. 21.

79 Rudd, 'Smart power', pp. 21–22.

80 Tom Allard, 'Going to war secured US alliance, says Downer', *Sydney Morning Herald*, 3 March 2004; Rudd, 'Smart power', pp. 21–2; Gary Brown, 'Portrait of a loyal ally', *Diplomat*, October–November 2004, p. 22; Mark Beeson, 'Australia's relationship with the United States: The case for greater independence', *Australian Journal of Political Science*, Vol. 38, No. 3, November 2003, pp. 387–405; Jim George, 'Will the chickenhawks come home to roost?', *Australian Journal of International Affairs*, Vol. 57, No. 2, July 2003, pp. 235–42.

81 Rudd, 'Smart power', p. 22.

82 Rudd, 'Smart power', p. 22.

83 See Roland Bleiker, *Divided Korea: Towards a Culture of Reconciliation* (Minneapolis: Minnesota University Press, 2005).

84 Michael Abramowitz, 'Bush stands firm on policies', *Washington Post*, 12 October 2006, p. AO1.

85 Seymour Hersh, 'The Iran plans', *New Yorker*, 17 April 2006, www.newyorker.com/fact/content/articles/060417fa_fact.

86 Cynthia Banham, 'Nuclear ban divides US and Downer', *Sydney Morning Herald*, 13 April 2005.

87 *Australia's National Security: A Defence Update 2003* (Canberra: Department of Defence), p. 16.

88 Peter Robson, 'Labor changes its refugee policy, slightly', *Green Left Weekly*, 4 May 2007.

89 Mark Forbes, 'Yudhoyono ready to snub meeting with Howard after Papua row', *Sydney Morning Herald*, 24 June 2006.

90 Article 2(3) of *Agreement Between the Republic of Indonesia and Australia on the Framework for Security Cooperation*, www.dfat.gov.au/geo/indonesia/ind-aus-sec06.html.

91 Hugh White, 'Our duty to West Papua', *Age*, 11 April 2006.

Conclusion: A cosmopolitan future

1 Carmen Lawrence, *Fear and Politics* (Melbourne: Scribe, 2006), p. 127.

2 Matt McDonald, 'Constructing insecurity: Australian security discourse and policy post-2001', *International Relations*, Vol. 19, No. 3, 2005, p. 313.

3 Judith Brett, 'Relaxed and comfortable: The Liberal Party's Australia', *Quarterly Essay*, Issue 19, 2005, p. 11.

4 Brett, 'Relaxed and comfortable', p. 39.

5 Brett, 'Relaxed and comfortable', p. 40.

6 David Burchell, 'Correspondence: Latham's world', in Raimond Gaita, 'Breach of trust', *Quarterly Essay*, Issue 16, 2004, p. 79

7 Brett, 'Relaxed and comfortable', p. 40.

8 Jonathan King, 'At the beach', *Weekend Australian*, 8–9 September 2001, p. 3; 'Blast for Reith on terrorism', *Age*, 15 September 2001; John Howard, interview with Phillip Clarke, Radio 2GB, 31 October 2001, www. pm.gov.au/media/Interview/2001/interview1430.cfm.

9 Charter of the United Nations, Preamble.

10 United Nations, General Assembly, 'World Summit Outcome', 15 September 2005, Doc. A/60/L.1.

11 The UN High Commissioner for Refugees states that the 'population of concern' to it was approximately 21 million by the end of 2005. *Statistical Yearbook 2005: Trends in Displacement, Protection and Solutions* (Geneva: UNHCR, April 2007), p. 9.

12 *Climate Change 2007: Impacts, Adaptation and Vulnerability*, Working Group II Contribution to the Intergovernmental Panel on Climate Change Fourth Assessment Report Summary for Policymakers, April 2007, www.ipcc.ch/SPM13apr07.pdf.

13 Gareth Evans and Bruce Grant, *Australia's Foreign Relations in the World of the 1990s* (Melbourne University Press, 1995), p. 42.

14 McKenzie Wark, 'Preface', to Anthony Burke, *In Fear of Security: Australia's Invasion Anxiety* (Annandale, NSW: Pluto Press Australia, 2001), pp. xvii, xx.

15 Hannah Arendt, *The Origins of Totalitarianism* (London and New York: Harcourt, 1976), pp. vii, ix.

16 Arendt, *The Origins of Totalitarianism*, p. 478.

17 John F. Kennedy, Commencement Address at the American University, Washington DC, 10 June 1963.

18 Sean Hand (ed.), *The Levinas Reader* (Oxford: Blackwell, 1999), p. 83.

Index